SHOWDOWN

SHOWDOWN

WHY CHINA WANTS WAR
WITH THE UNITED STATES

JED BABBIN AND **EDWARD TIMPERLAKE**

Since 1947
REGNERY
PUBLISHING, INC.
An Eagle Publishing Company • Washington, DC

Library of Congress Cataloging-in-Publication Data

Babbin, Jed L.
  Showdown : why China wants war with the United States / Jed Babbin and Ed Timperlake.
      p. cm.
  Includes bibliographical references and index.
  ISBN 1-59698-005-2
  1. United States—Foreign relations—China. 2. China—Foreign relations—United States. I. Timperlake, Edward. II. Title.
  E183.8.C5B215 2006
  327.73051009'051—dc22

                              2006006519

The views expressed in this book are solely those of the authors and do not reflect official opinions or policies of the United States government.

Published in the United States by
Regnery Publishing, Inc.
One Massachusetts Avenue, NW
Washington, DC 20001

www.regnery.com

Distributed to the trade by
National Book Network
Lanham, MD 20706

Manufactured in the United States of America

10 9 8 7 6 5 4 3 2 1

Books are available in quantity for promotional or premium use. Write to Director of Special Sales, Regnery Publishing, Inc., One Massachusetts Avenue NW, Washington, DC 20001, for information on discounts and terms or call (202) 216-0600.

We dedicate this book to those who died in Tiananmen Square on June 4, 1989. In the hope that their sacrifice was not in vain, we have written this book to illuminate the challenge to freedom that the Pacific Cold War, and the Beijing regime, pose for us and our children.

CONTENTS

CHAPTER ONE: The Next War 1

CHAPTER TWO: The War of National Unity. 25

CHAPTER THREE: The Second Korean War. 43

CHAPTER FOUR: The First Oil War 57

CHAPTER FIVE: The Sino-Japanese War. 75

CHAPTER SIX: World War Oil 99

CHAPTER SEVEN: The Assassin's Mace War 121

CHAPTER EIGHT: China, the EUnuchs, and Arms 141

CHAPTER NINE: Containment, Engagement, or Deterrence:
            Working to Prevent a Sino-American War. 147

GLOSSARY. 157

APPENDIX 161

ACKNOWLEDGMENTS 209

NOTES 211

INDEX. 217

CHAPTER ONE

THE NEXT WAR

China? There lies a sleeping giant. Let him sleep! For when he wakes, he will move the world.

NAPOLEON BONAPARTE

IT TOOK HALF A CENTURY FOR THE UNITED STATES to win the first—the European—Cold War. That it did so without having to resort to open warfare with the Soviet Union is a tribute to the fact that neither of the superpowers was compelled by ideology or politics to make that cold war a hot one. The fact that both nations emerged as superpowers at roughly the same time—with the horrors of World War II fresh in their minds—imposed a historic equilibrium that was later reinforced by the threat of mutually assured destruction. China, an emerging superpower, is not governed by that equilibrium. It is now engaged in a second cold war, the Pacific Cold War, with the United States. This war might last as long as the European Cold War—and it is much more likely to turn into a hot one.

Our adversary, China, is either an emerging capitalist colossus with peaceful intentions or the most powerful and dangerous enemy we have faced since the collapse of the Soviet Union. China exhibits two faces to the world. One can be seen in Major General Zhu Chenghu, a dean at China's National Defense University. In July 2005, General Chenghu, speaking in the context of a conflict over Taiwan, said that if America interfered militarily in any conflict between Beijing and Taiwan, China would make a nuclear first strike on America. He also declared that China would be prepared to absorb the destruction of most of its cities in a nuclear exchange that would wipe out hundreds of American cities.[1] At the opposite pole are the endless professions of peaceful intent that come from China's leaders, including its president, Hu Jintao.

With nations, as with people, actions are the best barometers of future behavior, and China's actions demonstrate hostility toward the United States. The Pacific Cold War is being fought from the oil fields of the Middle East, Africa, South America, and the Far East—where China's presence is growing—to the seas around Taiwan, in diplomatic battles at the United Nations, and in a public propaganda war. China faces no military threats, yet is engaged in a military buildup that is larger and more intense than anything the world has seen since Nazi Germany's mad dash for arms in the 1930s. It implies a similar momentum toward war. China's cold war against America will almost certainly become a shooting war within the next ten years.

China pursues war without provocation. America has welcomed China as a trading partner, but we can't close our eyes to the military threat it poses. It is a threat we must deter if we can and defeat on the battlefield if we must.

What might a war with China look like? That's what this book is about. Using a series of scenarios, told much like short stories in Chapters Two through Seven, we hope to illustrate how wars with China might break out and be fought based on China's history, capabilities, and intentions. The crises we portray might happen singly or together, next year or five years from now. But they will, we believe, come to pass—not because they are inevitable, but because China's chosen route to power leads inexorably to them. If we can explain in vivid terms how war is likely to occur, perhaps America and its allies can find ways to avoid it through diplomacy, containment, and deterrence.

If war does become reality, it will be because China has chosen, clearly and decisively, to make war on America, its allies, and its interests. It will not be an accident, the result of an economic clash or a misunderstanding—and our diplomatic efforts need to bear that in mind. We believe that China has already decided in favor of war. The challenge for American diplomacy is to reverse that choice, to convince China that a war against America, its allies, or its interests will not be won quickly or decisively by China.

Whatever the precipitating event that triggers war—be it China's aggression against Taiwan, North Korean proliferation of nuclear weapons, or any one of a host of other possibilities—this war will not wait until the global war against Islamic terrorism is over, until America's economy is protected from the use of oil as a weapon, or until we decide our own political future in a presidential election. This war will begin when China decides the time for it has come. And unless we are very lucky, very smart, and very resolute in our preparations, it will be as massive in loss of life and economic damage to America and the world as either of the two world wars of the last century.

AMERICA'S NEW PARTNER?

The Communist Chinese have gauged well how to liberalize the Chinese economy while maintaining Communist control of the government. To quote the *Tiananmen Papers*: "So long as the[se] demands for acknowledging the Party's mistakes during Tiananmen continue to be rejected, the Chinese regime is not the liberalizing, corporatist, consultative or 'soft authoritarian' system that many in the West make it out to be.... It has learned that many areas of freedom are unthreatening to the monopoly of political power. But the Party also believes it has learned from Tiananmen that democratization is not an irresistible force."

The *New York Times* and most of the mainstream media, however, continue to believe that China is liberalizing and intent on improving its ties with the United States. A November 2005 *New York Times* headline characterized China and America as "Partners, if Not Friends." That would be news to totalitarian Beijing.

The British magazine the *Economist* reported, on November 19, 2005, that Hu Jintao, China's president, "has a favorite phrase these days: 'harmonious world,' where countries of different outlooks live together in peace." But the government-controlled Chinese media "have made it clear that [Hu's] harmonious world is part-rebuff to American 'hegemonism'. . . . The implication is that China, as an emerging power at odds with American ideology, would be a beneficiary of a world order in which American power is constrained."[2]

Meanwhile, China is facing enormous challenges at home. These challenges are the flip side of its phenomenal economic growth, which began when it started liberalizing its economy in 1978. And there is no question about how China responds to unrest and instability: China is a police state; it is the world leader in executions; it is the world's most successful blocker of the Internet; and its leader, Hu Jintao, came up through the Communist Party ranks and cut his teeth on suppressing Tibet (and supported the Tiananmen Square massacre).[3]

Nationalism is rapidly replacing Mao's Little Red Book as the popular ideology of the Chinese, and the Beijing regime is inflaming it as a way to enhance the Communist Party's power and prestige. Nationalism easily leads to war, especially when it is linked to material need—in China's case, a need for oil.

China is the world's second-largest consumer and third-largest importer of oil. (It imports about 40 percent of its fossil fuels.)[4] As the 2005 Defense Department report on China says:

> This dependence on overseas resources and energy supplies, especially oil and natural gas, is playing a role in shaping China's strategy and policy. Such concerns factor heavily in Beijing's relations

with Angola, Central Asia, Indonesia, the Middle East (including Iran), Russia, Sudan, and Venezuela—to pursue long-term supply agreements—as well as its relations with countries that sit astride key geostrategic chokepoints—to secure passage. Beijing's belief that it requires such special relationships in order to assure its energy access could shape its defense strategy and force planning in the future. Indicators of such a shift would include increased investment in a blue-water capable fleet and, potentially, a more activist military presence abroad.[5]

THE *PRAVDA* ABOUT THE BEIJING REGIME[6]

Today's China is not the China of classical history. It retains many of ancient China's characteristics: inventiveness, insular nationalism, and enormous strength. But, unlike the China of the past three thousand years, Hu Jintao's Communist China is a very modern despotism. Because its government rules by force and not by the consent of the governed, China shares a principal characteristic of every modern dictatorship: it is unstable. It is unstable at the top because it is ruled by a small group that believes its grip on power is always tenuous, regardless of how weak its internal enemies may be or how little threatens them from abroad. It is unstable at the bottom because glimpses of freedom reaching even the remotest villagers sow discontent with the Beijing regime's oppressions. The People's Republic of China (PRC) is only slightly smaller geographically than the United States but has more than four times America's population. Since October 1949, it has been a Communist totalitarian state. And since about 1978, it has been working hard to do what the former Soviet Union couldn't: make its economy grow (for the benefit of the military) without increasing democracy. China has learned how a totalitarian state can survive—even thrive—in the modern world. Two principal events—the Cultural Revolution of 1966–76 and the Tiananmen Square massacre of 1989—have shaped the Beijing regime's understanding of politics. In the mid-1960s, fearing a "capitalist" reformation, Mao launched the Cultural Revolution. Its "Socialist Education Movement" forced intellectuals and scholars to perform manual labor on farms and in factories.[7] By 1966, Mao's socialist offensive turned violent, with party purges and a student army (the Red Guard) that was Maoist the way Hitler's Brownshirts were fascist. But, unlike the Brownshirts, the Red Guard numbered in the millions. They sought to enforce Mao's will by intimidation and violence. By 1967, several leaders thought to be disloyal to Mao—including such future regime leaders as Deng Xiaoping—had been purged from public life.[8] When Mao died in 1976, so did the Cultural Revolution. But its effect lingers. Deng Xiaoping, having been "rehabilitated," was—with Mao's approval—brought back to public life and reinstated as vice premier in April 1973. Deng had evidently learned the lesson Mao's Cultural Revolution taught: while economic success is essential to national power, the freedom that comes with capitalism cannot be tolerated.

China's gross domestic product has quadrupled in the last twenty-seven years, but at an enormous environmental cost. China uses coal to produce electricity, so much of its urban environments suffer from high levels of pollution. According to the CIA, China has lost one-fifth of its arable land since 1949 and suffers water shortages, water pollution from dumping untreated wastes, and deforestation.[9]

China's leaders, reverting to Communist formula, have slowed the pace of economic reform over the last two years. Facing continued crises in labor, agriculture, and heavy industries, the government of Hu Jintao has stopped privatizing industries and has imposed new controls on foreign investment in the retail markets. In addition, Hu Jintao and Premier Wen Jiabao have, according to the Heritage Foundation's *2004 Index of Economic Freedom*, "ordered the government to bail out state-owned banks burdened with cumbersome non-performing loans."[10] Unemployment in China is steady at almost 10 percent.

Just as before Mao's Cultural Revolution, China's experiments with economic freedom have led to political unrest and increasing demands for personal freedom. China blocks freedom of speech on the Internet, but the profusion of cell phones has enabled the Chinese people—even villagers in remote areas—to communicate relatively freely with one another and to learn about protests against the Beijing regime.

The Chinese Communists do not intend to go the way of the Soviet Union. By early 1989, the Soviet regime was crumbling, and the Berlin Wall came crashing down. As the Beijing Politburo watched its Soviet counterpart begin to topple, it faced an internal crisis of its own. The Tiananmen Square massacre of June 4, 1989, was the culmination of weeks of student demonstrations. The demonstrations began as a tribute to reformer Hu Yaobang, who had died on April 15. Hu had been a protégé of Deng Xiaoping and had risen to power before being "purged" in 1987. His crime was his sympathy for pro-democracy student protests.[11] When he died, thousands of students gathered in Tiananmen Square and tried to send representatives to meet with the regime in the Great Hall of the People. They were turned away, but the crowds grew and international news coverage generated a crisis that the Beijing regime believed was a threat to its existence.

As the crowds in the square grew, Li Peng signed an order declaring martial law, citing "an outbreak of grave turmoil in Beijing [that] has disrupted social stability, normal life and public order" on May 20.[12] The regime reached a state of near panic when the demonstrators erected their own Statue of Liberty (which they called "Goddess of Liberty"—later renamed "Goddess of Democracy").[13] Party apparatchiks in the State Security Ministry, in a report to the Party Central Committee on June 1, blamed American interference in China's affairs, singling out the Voice of America radio.[14] Demonstrations near Tiananmen Square led to clashes with police. On June 2, China's leaders decided to clear the square by force. Troops, having been heavily indoctrinated for two weeks to prepare them to kill the students, were ordered in,[15] and on June 4 they attacked, killing more than two thousand students and wounding thousands more.[16]

The day after the massacre, Deng Xiaoping said of the demonstrators, "Even if they're functioning out of ignorance, they are still participating and must be suppressed. In China, even one million people can be considered a small sum."[17] Deng is dead, but his legacy is not. Both his immediate successor, Jiang Zemin, and the current president, Hu Jintao, were rising in the Party hierarchy at the time. Neither was of sufficient rank to play a role in ordering the Tiananmen Square massacre,[18] but there is no reason to believe that China's current rulers will react differently than Deng did.

This is especially true of Hu Jintao. Hu is another protégé of Deng Xiaoping. At the time of the Tiananmen Square massacre, Hu Jintao was the Chinese Party secretary—effectively the colonial ruler—of Tibet. He may not have been responsible for the Tiananmen Square massacre, but he was one of the three provincial leaders who announced support for the "Party Center"—for Deng—immediately after the massacre.[19]

In Tibet, Hu acted brutally in putting down demonstrations. On February 20, 1989, he ordered 1,700 armed police into the Tibetan capital of Lhasa. On March 5, the police opened fire on civilian rioters, killing at least forty. Martial law was declared and China's armed forces kept the area quiet through the summer of 1989.[20]

The lessons Beijing learned in Tiananmen Square and Tibet were the same as those taught by Mao in the Cultural Revolution and in *Quotations from Chairman Mao*, the famous Little Red Book the Red Guards carried as their totem: democracy is not an irresistible force, and power grows from the barrel of a gun. But China's leaders are worried about the increasing level of unrest in their country.

In July 2005, Public Security Minister Zhou Yongkang said that the number of "mass incidents"—protests and even riots—was rising fast across China.[21] As the *Washington Post* reported, "In 2004, Zhou said, 3.76 million of China's 1.3 billion people took part in 74,000 such protests, which he said represented a dramatic increase."[22] The Communist regime fears that these protests could threaten its existence.

The regime has other problems as well. The *Financial Times* reported in September 2005, citing an Organisation for Economic Co-operation and Development (OECD) study, that corruption in China is so severe and widespread that it threatens the country's economic development and "is becoming a major source of social discontent and poses a threat to the legitimacy of the country's leaders."[23]

According to some experts in the United States government, China's protests are more than local flare-ups. The "cell phone revolution" has meant that more and more protests are organized across geographic borders. Recent protests about water pollution and the SARS virus were organized by village elders in different provinces. The question for the Beijing regime is whether such protests are a greater threat than were the protests at Tiananmen Square.

Many China policy experts believe the threat to the Beijing regime is substantial, but the Communist Party is so well entrenched, and its power to crush protests so well organized and brutal, that a national revolution has to be considered extremely unlikely. Beijing's strategy for defusing protests includes "protest villages" outside the center city where protesters can present their petitions to the government, coupled with prison camps for recalcitrant political activists. Beijing outlawed torture in 1996 but, according to a December 2005 report by Manfred Nowak, the United Nations' special "rapporteur" on torture, Beijing's use of it is still "widespread" in Chinese detention centers.[24] Nowak's report cited the use of "electric shock batons, cigarette burns and submersion in pits of water or sewage." He also raised the problem of psychological torture, "which he said was designed to alter the personality of detainees."[25]

Still, there is one growing social problem—a demographic imbalance—that could explode the regime's grip on power. The Chinese call it *guang gun*, "bare branches." We know it as China's one-child policy, a law that limits every couple to one child. Because Chinese society strongly favors male children, China now has about twenty-three million more young men than young women.[26] That's a tiny fraction of China's population now, but the number will grow, and with it the possibility of severe social dislocation. China is taking a great many of its poor, unmarried young men into its People's Liberation Army and People's Armed Police[27] and it is all too easy to imagine the government diverting their passions to war.

Academics and foreign policy analysts increasingly describe China as a "peer competitor" of America. By that they mean that China's economic power—reflected in its huge trade imbalance with America, its appetite for oil, and its challenge to us on many economic fronts—makes China our near equal. That may be true economically, but the "peer competitor" label implies both peaceful intent and alignment with Western values. More accurately, China is a "peer antagonist."

For all the hopeful rhetoric in diplomatic and media circles, China is a totalitarian state, governed by a man *Parade* magazine included in its list of the world's ten worst dictators in 2005: Hu Jintao.[28] *Parade*'s one-paragraph summary of China is a model of clarity and realism:

> Despite China's economic liberalization, President Hu Jintao's government remains one of the most repressive. Some 250,000 Chinese are serving sentences in "re-education and labor camps." China executes more people than all other nations combined, often for nonviolent crimes. The death penalty can be given for burglary, embezzlement, counterfeiting, bribery or killing a panda. Hu's government controls all media and Internet use. Defense lawyers who argue too vigorously for clients' rights may be disbarred or imprisoned. And if minorities (such as Tibetans) speak out for autonomy, they're labeled "terrorists," imprisoned and tortured.[29]

So long as the Beijing regime is in power, China can never be anything other than America's adversary.

As such, China will try to increase the number of America's enemies and decrease the number of America's friends. China is doing this with special aggressiveness in Latin America (including oil-rich Venezuela and, more recently, Bolivia) and in Africa. But the policy is also obvious in China's continued friendliness with such state sponsors of terrorism as Cuba, Iran, North Korea (a Chinese client state), Sudan, and Syria.[30]

In Africa, China has become increasingly involved in Angola, which pumps almost a million barrels of oil a day for export. In 2005, the

Angolan oil minister bragged that his nation would soon have three million Chinese workers helping build the economy. In Zimbabwe, China funnels financial and technical aid to Robert Mugabe's kleptocracy and sells the government weapons. In Sudan, China works to achieve friendly relations with yet another source of Islamic terrorism.

China also indulges an enormous appetite for modern military weapon systems. It spends billions a year on the most modern aircraft, missiles, submarines, and electronics that it can obtain. And what China can't buy, it steals through its enormous espionage campaign against the United States.

In 1999, a U.S. House of Representatives select committee, chaired by Republican Chris Cox of California, issued a report[31] on the widespread—and highly successful—Chinese espionage campaign directed at America's defense systems. It found that the Chinese had stolen the designs for at least seven of our most advanced nuclear weapons (including the so-called neutron bomb), as well as designs for combat aircraft, satellites, anti-satellite weapons, and high-powered computers used in the design and development of virtually all advanced weapons. These stolen technologies are now the foci of China's military buildup. And the espionage continues.

On November 5, 2005, the *Washington Times* reported the arrest of four accused Beijing spies in what will likely prove to be "among the most damaging spy cases since [1985]." According to the *Times* report, this spy ring is believed to have operated

> since 1990 and has funneled technology and military secrets to China in the form of documents and computer disks...[containing] sensitive data on Aegis battle management systems that are the core of U.S. Navy destroyers and cruisers. China covertly obtained the Aegis technology and earlier this year deployed its first Aegis warship, code-named Magic Shield.... The Chinese also obtained sensitive data on U.S. submarines, including classified details related to the new Virginia-class attack submarines. Officials

said based on a preliminary assessment, China now will be able
to track U.S. submarines, a compromise that potentially could be
devastating if the United States enters a conflict with China in
defending Taiwan.[32]

China's appetite—and the billions of dollars it represents to the arms
merchants of Old Europe—resulted, in 2005, in the harshest diplomatic
exchanges between America and Europe in decades. All that thwarts
China's ability to buy high-tech arms from Europe is America. Europe is
quite willing to lift the West's post–Tiananmen Square arms embargo
against China. But the United States has, so far, successfully blocked such
proposals.

China, however, is still in the market—and Israel is China's second
choice for high-tech weapons and electronic systems. The result has
been enormous friction between the United States and Israel. American
diplomats and defense officials have intervened forcefully to prevent
Israel from selling China advanced radar systems. Israel has since
promised to discontinue all sales of advanced weapons to China that
America doesn't approve, but America's trust in the Israeli–American
relationship remains damaged. Europe and Israel seem eager to turn a
blind eye to the reasons for China's military buildup. But we cannot.

China, like the old Soviet Union, develops many of its weapon systems under a blanket of secrecy that we frequently fail to penetrate. In
recent years, it has rolled out "several new weapon systems whose
development was not previously known in the West."[33]

China diverges from the Soviet model in one very important and dangerous way. Joseph Stalin is reputed to have said, "Quantity has a quality all its own." China's post-revolution army of the 1950s followed
Stalin's advice. But since the 1980s—and with increasing speed—China's
military has been trading size for modernity and lethality. The Soviets
tried to do the same but failed because they could not afford the
expense. China, with its burgeoning export of low-cost products to
America and Western Europe, can.

Since 1985, China has reduced the size of its military forces, mainly its army, from about 4.2 million men to the present strength of about 2.3 million active-duty troops. China has learned—from watching the American military—the importance of high-tech weapons, network-centric warfare, and "jointness."

"Jointness"—an awkward word even by U.S. government standards—really means focusing on cooperation and interoperability between services. The Chinese substituted the word "reorganization" for "jointness," but the idea is the same. In 1999, two active-duty Chinese colonels, Qiao Liang and Wang Xiangsui, wrote, in light of America's "jointness" reforms, "Any country which hopes to win a war in the twenty-first century must inevitably face the option of either 'reorganizing' or being defeated. There is no other way."[34]

By 2003, America had taken the concept of "jointness" to another level: what military professionals now call "network-centric warfare," often shortened to net-centric warfare. In net-centric warfare, everyone from the soldier in the remotest corner of the battlefield to the Joint Chiefs of Staff in the Pentagon is linked, in real time, by a network of computers and communication interfaces that multiply military effectiveness. It's best explained by the example of one of its parts: the "JSTARS" aircraft. Calling it a "spy plane," as one commentator did, is like calling an Olympic decathlete a "runner."

JSTARS—the Joint Surveillance Target Attack Radar System aircraft (a much-modified Boeing 707)—combines many sensors, including radars, computers, and communications, to provide a true "battle management system." Combatant commanders use it to identify and track friendly and enemy forces on the ground, on the water, and in the air. It gives them a real-time three-dimensional picture of what used to be called the "battlefield" and is now more aptly called the "battlespace." Net-centric warfare boils down to information sharing. As practiced by the American military, it means that communication, decision making, and shared awareness of the military situation among troops and commanders result in better and quicker collaboration in accomplishing the mission.

The Chinese are studying net-centric warfare as assiduously as Americans are evolving and practicing it.

In an assessment of Operation Iraqi Freedom, the campaign that ousted Saddam Hussein's regime, the PLA deputy chief of general staff, General Xiong Guangkai, made several observations, among them:

- "U.S. armed forces are ever smaller in number but ever more highly trained, are of a lighter type, and have an ever higher mobility."
- "U.S. troops used as many as ninety military satellites, which provided continuous intelligence information and played a most important role in directing the war, especially in launching accurate attacks."
- "The U.S. and British allied forces gave full expression to the joint warfare theory [and] had all their arms and services...coordinate their actions in all directions and at all times to achieve rapid dominance on the battlefield, and their actions included air strikes, ground attacks, sea-based missile launches, satellites and information warfare."[35]

In the 1990s, Chinese military doctrine focused on fighting "local wars under high-tech conditions." In 2004, having digested the lessons of Iraq, a Chinese Defense White Paper described Chinese military doctrine in terms only a bureaucrat could love: "local wars under the condition of informationalization."[36] It is clear that the "condition of informationalization" is China's catchphrase for net-centric and high-tech warfare.[37]

In a 2005 press conference, before he became chairman of the Joint Chiefs of Staff, Marine general Peter Pace said, "You judge military threat in two ways: one, capacity, and two, intent....There are lots of countries in the world that have the capacity to wage war. Very few have the intent to do so. And, clearly, we have a complex but good relationship with China. So there's absolutely no reason for us to believe there's any intent on their part."[38]

But Pace, speaking diplomatically, could hardly have said otherwise. If he had, his statement would have been tantamount to predicting a Sino-American war. Pentagon leaders are very uncomfortable with China's military buildup because in the context of China's wealth and might it is inconsistent with peaceful intent. As Pace's boss, Defense Secretary Donald Rumsfeld, said in a June 4, 2005, speech delivered in Singapore:

> A candid discussion of China, however, cannot neglect to mention areas of concern to the region. The U.S. Congress requires that the U.S. Department of Defense report annually on China's perceived military strategy and its military modernization. The department's 2005 report is scheduled to be released soon.
>
> Among other things, the report concludes that China's defense expenditures are much higher than Chinese officials have published. It is estimated that China's is the third-largest military budget in the world, and clearly the largest in Asia.
>
> China appears to be expanding its missile forces, allowing them to reach targets in many areas of the world, not just the Pacific region, while also expanding its missile capabilities within this region. China also is improving its ability to project power, and developing advanced systems of military technology.
>
> Since no nation threatens China, one must wonder: Why this growing investment? Why these continuing large and expanding arms purchases? Why these continuing robust deployments?[39]

The answers to Rumsfeld's questions reveal China's intent to use its rapidly growing capabilities. According to Chen Yonglin, a recent defector who worked at the Chinese foreign ministry, the Communist regime now speaks of creating a "Greater Neighboring Region,"[40] which sounds uncomfortably like Imperial Japan's "Greater East Asia Co-Prosperity Sphere." Japan conquered Korea, Taiwan, Indochina, the Philippines, Malaysia, Indonesia, and Manchuria as part of this "Greater East Asia

Co-Prosperity Sphere," and fought China, Britain, India, Australia, and the United States. Does China plan similar aggression? It plainly intends to swallow Taiwan, and it is ramping up nationalist hatred of Japan, not only for its brutal conduct in World War II, but also in diplomatic disputes over oil and gas rights in the South and East China seas. China ignores Japanese claims to gas reserves close to Japan's home islands and parades its military might with increasing frequency in those waters.[41]

WHAT CHINA IS SPENDING

Another way to measure China's intent is to look at its defense budgets. According to our best estimates, the PRC's defense budget in 2005 was about $90 billion, and in 2006 will be about $100 billion. That equaled, in 2005, 7.5 percent of China's $1.2 trillion gross domestic product, more than double the percentage America spends on defense. At that spending level, China has the third-largest military budget in the world, behind only the United States and Russia.[42] And that is lowballing Chinese expenditures, because a dollar buys more in China than it does in the United States. Even allowing that half of China's military expenditures might be spent abroad, we can reasonably assume that in terms of what economists call "purchasing power parity," the Chinese military budget for 2005 is closer to $150 billion. And what is China buying? The answer is telling: a mix of weapons, a major portion of which cannot be labeled defensive. They fall into five major categories.

SPACE AND COUNTER-SPACE

Deploying anti-satellite weapons is one of China's highest military priorities. Why? Because satellites are the foundation of America's battle-space superiority. They enable commanders to communicate with ground, sea, and air forces, and for those forces to talk to each other. They give "smart bombs" the precise navigational and positioning information that makes them smart. They tell soldiers and airmen where they are and give rapid and accurate reconnaissance of both friend and foe.

American military leaders don't take these things for granted. In fact, losing our satellites to enemy action is one of their gravest concerns.

There are hundreds upon hundreds of satellites in orbit, so the first step, if you want an anti-satellite capability, is to develop a targeting mechanism. To that end, China is building a satellite tracking and identification network. It already has the ability, as do America and Russia, to destroy enemy satellites by launching a nuclear weapon and detonating it near the target. But that is a confessedly crude system, and China, unlike America, isn't stopping there.

China is developing and may have already tested ground-based lasers to "blind" or even destroy satellites instantly.[43] In addition, China is developing small, lightweight "microsatellites" that can be prepared and launched quickly. Though the microsatellites launched so far are not believed to have offensive capability, others could be armed with a variety of anti-satellite weapons. Moreover, these non-offensive microsatellites could replace Chinese or Russian satellites accidentally destroyed in a nuclear space strike against U.S. satellites. There is no reason for China to develop anti-satellite weapons except to attack. China knows our satellites are large and expensive. They cannot be readily stockpiled.

COMPUTER NETWORK OPERATIONS

In their 1999 book, *Unrestricted Warfare*, Qiao Liang and Wang Xiang-sui set forth in considerable detail how a war might be won without a shot being fired:

> [I]f the attacking side secretly musters large amounts of capital without the enemy nation being aware...and launches a sneak attack against its financial markets, then after causing a financial crisis, buries a computer virus and hacker detachment in the opponent's computer system in advance, while at the same time carrying out a network attack against the enemy so that the civilian electricity network, traffic dispatching network, telephone communications network and

mass media network are completely paralyzed, this will cause the
enemy nation to fall into social panic, street riots and a political crisis. There is finally the forceful bearing down by the army, and military means are utilized in gradual stages until the enemy is forced
to sign a dishonorable peace treaty.[44]

Though derided by some analysts as a theoretical exercise, Qiao and
Wang's book appears to be a blueprint for China's current development
of precisely this kind of warfare in the years since the book was published. According to the Defense Department's 2005 report:

China's computer network operations (CNO) include computer network attack, computer network defense, and computer network
exploitation. The PLA sees CNO as critical to seize the initiative and
"electromagnetic dominance" early in a conflict, and as a force multiplier. Although there is no evidence of a formal Chinese CNO doctrine, Chinese theorists have coined the term "Integrated Network
Electronic Warfare" to describe the Chinese approach. This concept
outlines the integrated use of electronic warfare, CNO, and limited
kinetic strikes against key C4 nodes to disrupt the enemy's battlefield network information systems. The PLA has likely established
information warfare units to develop viruses to attack enemy computer systems and networks, and tactics to protect friendly computer systems and networks. The PLA has increased the role of CNO
in its military exercises. Although initial training efforts focused on
increasing the PLA's proficiency in defensive measures, recent exercises have incorporated offensive operations, primarily as first
strikes against enemy networks.[45]

There are many reasons for nations dependent on technology (as America is and China aspires to be) to build defenses for their computer networks against adversaries' attacks. But China isn't choosing defensive
measures—it's choosing offensive ones.

CHINA'S NEW NAVY

The Defense Department believes that China presently has only a limited ability to "project conventional military power beyond its periphery."[46] That is changing as China acquires ships, missiles, submarines, and aircraft that can project its power across the oceans.

With about three thousand miles of coastline, China needs a navy that can do two things: protect the sea lanes it depends on for oil and other imports, and protect its coast from smugglers or other unauthorized landings. The navy China is buying and building has little to do with these defense interests.

By early 2005, the Chinese navy had sixty-four major surface combatants, about fifty-five attack submarines, more than forty medium and heavy amphibious lift ships, and about fifty coastal patrol missile boats.[47] This force is not an "area denial" force such as would protect the Strait of Malacca, the eight hundred miles of ocean between Indonesia and the Malaya Peninsula (passing across Singapore) through which about 65 percent of China's oil imports travel. Rather, many, if not most, of those ships are designed for warfare against other navies.

- In 1996, China bought two Sovremenny-class guided missile destroyers from Russia. Each of the first two was bought at a price of $400 million.[48] Another two are being built now at a reported price of $1 billion.[49] They are the largest and most powerful warships ever operated by the Chinese navy. Sovremenny destroyers are designed to kill ships at long range with supersonic cruise missiles and to defend surface ships from both submarine and air attack. Russia designed the Sovremenny to destroy American aircraft carriers that operate within its range.
- By 2010, the PLA navy may have a fleet of fifty nuclear and non-nuclear submarines, equal in number to the entire U.S. submarine fleet. Among them will be new Type 093 nuclear attack submarines armed with land attack cruise missiles and Type 094 ballistic missile nuclear submarines (both capable of operating in U.S.

coastal waters); eight new Russian-built Kilo-class diesel-electric submarines at a reported price of $1.6 billion; and as many as twenty new Chinese-built boats of similar type.

- Four types of surface combatants with reduced radar signatures qualify as "stealth" ships; there are numerous other ships, some of which also have stealthy designs, to carry troops and heavy vehicles, including tanks.[50]

Such a robust shipbuilding program costs tens of billions of dollars.

CHINA'S AIR AND MISSILE FORCES

China now has at least seven hundred combat aircraft within non-refuel range of Taiwan. Among them, in great numbers, are highly advanced aircraft such as the Russian-built Sukhoi SU-30MKK fighter-bomber and SU-30MKK2 maritime strike aircraft. China also has other highly capable and advanced aircraft, such as the SU-27.[51]

How good are these aircraft? In early 2004, the U.S. Air Force engaged in a very large air combat war game against the Indian air force. USAF pilots were flying our primary air defense fighter, the F-15. Indian pilots were engaging them with SU-30s, French-built Mirage 2000s, and old Russian MiG-21s. Though the results of the exercise are still classified, it is clear that the U.S. fighters were defeated in a great many engagements by the Indians piloting the Russian-built SU-30s.[52]

The Chinese air force might have three hundred SU-27s, including the F-11, a Chinese-built version, as well as seventy-six SU-30MKKs. The Chinese naval air force has about forty-eight SU-30MKK2s. These aircraft can play offensive and defensive roles. China is also apparently pursuing aircraft that are purely offensive.

Readers of Tom Clancy's novels know about the TU-22M Backfire bomber. It is the Russian equivalent of the B-1 Lancer that the U.S. Air Force has been using to great advantage in Afghanistan. Like the B-1, the Backfire is a supersonic, long-range, nuclear-capable bomber that is designed primarily to perform strategic missions. Russia is marketing the improved TU-22M-3 version to China. It has a range of about four thousand miles.[53] Details of China's plans to purchase the Backfire are vague, but the profound impact of its doing so is not. Were China to acquire even a few of these aircraft, Japan, South Korea, Taiwan, and even much of India would be within range. Aircraft such as the Backfire are different from missiles in that their use is imaginable in many short-of-Armageddon scenarios. Because the possibility of their use in an attack is all too real, they are even more menacing than Chinese ICBMs that are, right now, pointed at Taiwan or America.

One advantage American air forces usually have is the airborne warning and control system (AWACS) aircraft. (NATO AWACS aircraft were among the first in America's skies after the September 11, 2001, terrorist attacks, directing the "combat air patrols" over New York and Washington, D.C.). China, using a Russian A-50 aircraft and Israeli Phalcon phased-array radar, was building its own AWACS aircraft until intense American pressure forced the Israelis to terminate the Phalcon radar sale. Since then, the Chinese have substituted less capable radars.

The difference between a local power that cannot project its influence and a regional or global power can be found in one simple, mundane aircraft: the air refueling tanker. In the words of former USAF chief of staff General John Jumper, "We are a global air and space power because of these tankers."[54] Jumper explained, "The first thing that happens in any contingency is that you put the tanker bridge up there. We deploy tankers to places such as Spain, Hawaii, Guam, and their sole purpose is to get large numbers of transport aircraft halfway around the world without stopping." No tankers, no superpower.[55]

China understands that all too well. It has already converted a number of its H-6 bombers to serve as air refueling tankers and, according to one respected source, is about to purchase six Russian Il-78 tankers that could enable Chinese aircraft to strike targets more than 1,500 miles from the Chinese coast, including the U.S. airbase on Guam.[56] Forward-basing of these tankers, in places ranging from South Pacific islands to the Middle East or even Venezuela, could extend that range.

China calls its strategic missile forces the "Second Artillery." It has about seven hundred short-range ballistic missiles deployed within range of Taiwan and is increasing that number by about a hundred missiles every year.[57] Its ICBM force is being modernized with a road-mobile missile, the DF-31 (including an extended-range version), and the JL-2 submarine-launched ballistic missile.

China's aim for regional hegemony is again demonstrated by its planning to adapt ballistic missiles for "sea-denial" missions, meaning to deny entry into those areas by hostile naval forces.[58] China is arming its other forces—air, land, and sea forces—with land attack cruise missiles.

CHINA'S GROUND FORCES

Even with its continued reduction in size, the People's Liberation Army numbers at least 2.3 million.[59] According to Defense Department analysts, the reduction in the PLA's size is accompanied by an improvement in its quality. China's revolution in military affairs is transforming its army into one capable of using all the advantages that joint operations and net-centric warfare afford. In its officer education system—establishing a corps of professional noncommissioned officers and using a system much like the U.S. Reserve Officers' Training Corps (ROTC) to train future officers during a civilian college education—China is reforming its ground, naval, and air forces to match its changes in operational doctrine.[60] As it is reduced in size, China's military manpower is being increased in its ability to conduct net-centric warfare, to maneuver, and to conduct operations outside China's mainland.

One hallmark of the transformation of the PLA is the Chinese effort to create a large force of unmanned aerial vehicles (UAVs). It is reportedly converting old fighter aircraft to perform this mission, and in 2003 and 2004 acquired Israeli Harpy UAVs to assist in air defense of ground units. In 2004, the PLA began converting older army formations, including "motorized rifle" and armored infantry brigades, to mechanized infantry.[61]

More important, at least with respect to Taiwan, is the formation of the first and second airborne armies and China's investment to equip them with light armored vehicles that can be airdropped onto a battlefield.[62] It is also developing, and probably mass-producing, advanced troop and vehicle landing craft, including the stealthy ones previously described.

For a week in August 2005, Chinese and Russian military units conducted a joint exercise called "Peace Mission 2005" around the northern Russian port of Vladivostok and the Chinese Shandong Peninsula. Almost ten thousand troops—part of a force that included bomber and fighter aircraft, destroyers, frigates, submarines, and AWACS-like aircraft—first blockaded and then sent amphibious tanks ashore in a mock invasion.[63] The purpose of the exercise was, according to the Chinese official news service, Xinhua, to "help strengthen the capability of the two armed forces in jointly striking international terrorism, extremism and separatism."[64] "Separatism" is Beijing's word for the Taiwanese independence movement.

The modernization of the Chinese ground forces, transforming them from a set-piece massed battle force to the lighter, quicker forces America can deploy, will take several more years. When completed, they will be able to threaten not only Taiwan, but every nation on China's periphery—and in a way meant to prevent successful American intervention.

THE VERDICT: CHINA MEANS WAR

None of China's neighbors are arming at this frantic pace. None are threatening China with attack. We have to conclude that China's military buildup is focused on meeting and defeating American forces in any engagement over Taiwan, the Koreas, or the Pacific Rim. China is investing heavily in expensive anti-satellite weapons, cyber-warfare capability, and other high-tech armaments and would not be doing so unless its strategy were to make war—with America as its chosen adversary.

China has awakened. As Napoleon prophesied, it is about to move the world. The most likely flashpoint is Taiwan.

The chapters that follow are war game *tour d'horizon* as seen through the eyes of a group of fictionalized players, among them a Navy SEAL,[65]

his Air Force older brother, several presidents of the United States, and
the president of China. These chapters read like the fiction they are, but
each of them—one at a time, or many in combination—could easily
become fact. Though some of the characters carry over from one situation to the next, the scenarios that follow are not in chronological order
because they are discrete possibilities for the future, not an escalating
series of crises.

CHAPTER TWO

THE WAR OF NATIONAL UNITY

The State Council and the Central Military Commission shall "decide on and execute" non-peaceful means "to protect China's sovereignty and territorial integrity" if "secessionist forces ... cause the fact of Taiwan's secession from China," if "major incidents entailing Taiwan's secession" occur, or if "possibilities for peaceful reunification" are exhausted.

ARTICLE 8 OF THE "ANTI-SECESSION LAW" ENACTED BY THE
BEIJING NATIONAL PEOPLE'S CONGRESS, MARCH 14, 2005

Beijing, China
Tuesday, 11 March 2008
1100 Hours Local

Hu Jintao far preferred to bury his face in his papers than speak with the tiresome members of the Central Military Commission (CMC). But as president of China and head of the Politburo, Hu had transformed the CMC, which he also led, into the government's most important political-military council. An outsider could easily confuse it with America's Joint Chiefs—which it wasn't modeled after—or its National Security Council, which it also resembles, but only superficially. The heads of the People's Liberation Army, Navy, and Air Force were all there, as were several

Politburo members and their staffs. Hu preferred to rule by pretext of consensus, but the decisions had already been made. One after another, the generals made their statements, debated their plans as they had debated for months, came to the conclusions they had already reached, and fell silent, waiting for Hu to speak.

"We are agreed, comrades. There is little to be said and much to do. The election in Taiwan is only nine days away. How soon can we begin?"

"We begin tonight, comrade." The commander of the People's Liberation Army spoke in his trademark curt, clipped voice. "And the operation will dominate the news in Washington and London tomorrow night. We have coordinated everything. And the Second Artillery Forces are moving their mobile launchers to the proper positions now."

The People's Liberation Navy commander stood. "The new Russian aircraft carrier *Boris Gudunov* has already joined up with our destroyers and submarines. It will maneuver with us throughout, unless the Americans intervene."

"And the American navy?" asked Hu.

"They are doing what they always do before an election on Taiwan. They are sending a token force to demonstrate north of Taiwan."

The White House
10 March
2200 Hours

The national security adviser's ears were still ringing from the president's blast. "For gawdsake, Eric," the president had said. "Tell the damned Taiwans that they have all the backing from us they're gonna get right now." The president was too preoccupied with the presidential primaries to worry much about the usual saber-rattling from Beijing. He couldn't run again, but he still had to hopscotch the country making speeches and being the main attraction at party fund-raisers. Though he had said repeatedly that America would use military force to defend Taiwan, he had little patience with the Taiwanese, who seemed willing to fight to the last drop of American—not Taiwanese—blood. In any event, the USS *John C. Stennis* and her small task group had been sent to make a show of America's intent to defend Taiwan. The president and Eric Stahl, his new national security adviser, weren't inclined to do more. Stahl pressed the speed dial on his secure cell phone. The call was routed through the White House's secure cell network. The outgoing president of Taiwan, Chen Shui-bian, answered on the first ring.

"My honored friend," Stahl began, "I hope you are well today."

"I am indeed, my most honored friend," President Chen answered, upping the ante on political flattery. "I am most pleased to hear from you."

"I do not bear the answer you wished for. As I told you two days ago, the president is still of the opinion that we are doing what we must, and need do no more."

"But how can that be? Beijing's navy is surrounding us, its missiles are at this moment being deployed against us, and your own reconnaissance satellites tell us that Russian ships are near. Does it not shock you that the Beijing navy is embarking troops on landing craft? Surely, this is more than just a show of force. That fool Yuanqing and his 'secret plan' for independence! Our polling numbers tomorrow will show he has a narrow lead. If he is likely to be our next president, how can Beijing fail to stop our election?"

Xi Yuanqing, the Democratic Progressive Party candidate, had been a political unknown only a year ago. Now he was dominating the campaign against a milquetoast competitor in a race that would be over in little more than a week.

"My honored friend, the president says we will not defend a nation that refuses to defend itself. He offered to sell you missile defense batteries, aircraft, and submarines seven years ago. And what has happened? Your parliament has refused to appropriate the monies to buy them. Fifty times they have turned aside the legislation necessary to buy the arms. Now the president is unwilling to do more. Surely you understand. And Beijing is only months away from hosting its first international Olympic Games. They will not risk that by taking military action against you."

Eric Stahl listened to Chen complain for another minute, then politely terminated the call. He pressed another button on the speed dial. It wasn't late by government standards, and the chairman of the Joint Chiefs, he knew, was available whenever he was needed by his superiors or subordinates. The old Marine had an uncanny ability to be awake instantly, even if roused in the hours before dawn. *God bless the jarheads*, Stahl thought as the call went through.

Beijing
11 March
1930 Hours Local

"President Hu, I wish to report our progress."

Hu was, as usual, working into the night. He lifted his eyes to see the PLA commander in chief. "Yes?"

"May I turn on your television?"

Hu reached for the remote control. The set was tuned to al Jazeera. Breathless reporters followed each other, surveying scenes of devastation.

The general smiled. "Our special operations teams have performed admirably. Bombs have gone off in ten places in Taipei and at least two in each of the six other cities we planned to disrupt. The wife of the independence candidate was killed, and the assassin escaped, leaving his weapon and the small notebook." Hu had personally approved the notebook's contents. Written in sloppy Arabic, it portrayed its owner as a suicidal jihadist.

Hu smiled thinly. "You may continue, comrade. The special session of the National People's Congress will convene very early. I will rehearse my speech before then. Will you join me for breakfast in my quarters at six?"

The White House
Office of the National Security Adviser
12 March
0610 Hours

Eric Stahl and his staff had been there for hours. They had talked to the Taiwanese president, briefed the president in the Oval Office, and were working to get information from the CIA, which so far could tell them only that the English translations on al Jazeera, the all-bad-news-all-the-time channel, were accurate. "Marvelous," Stahl said aloud, "freakin' marvelous." The small group assembled around his circular conference table waited in silence. "What the heck is up, General?"

The chairman of the Joint Chiefs added what he could. "As far as we can tell, the bombings haven't done much damage. There are a few hundred casualties. But the Taiwanese have gone into panic mode. There are protests against the independence party that have turned into riots, and the whole Taiwanese military is mobilizing. As the president ordered, the *Stennis* strike group is about to enter the Taiwan Strait. They should be off Taipei in about another five hours."

"So who's behind the attacks? Al Qaeda can't be that strong in Taiwan."

"Sir, we have no intel on them being there at all."

"So what else can you tell me?"

"I can tell you, sir, that as the president instructed, we have pulled our military exchange people out of Beijing and are sending them to Japan."

"Didn't you say a bunch of Green Team guys were in that delegation?" The Green Team is the most versatile and secret group among the SEALs. Very few people knew they existed, far less what they were doing at any given moment.

"Yessir, we had a platoon of them talking to Chicom special ops people."

"How hard would it be to divert them to Taiwan, General?"

Over the East China Sea
Fifteen Minutes Later

The loud throb of a C-130's engines can feel like a whole-body massage if you have your earplugs in. Navy commander Cully O'Bannon stirred briefly when he felt the aircraft bank sharply. It seemed like only seconds later when he woke, a firm grip shaking his shoulder with a rough approximation of gentleness.

"Whuzzup, frog?" O'Bannon woke to a coffee cup held under his nose. He pried out his earplugs and grasped the steaming cup.

"Orders, boss." Master Chief Romeo Wilson's fire-hydrant silhouette was unmistakable even in the darkened cabin. As the longest-serving SEAL on active duty, he was known as the Bullfrog. Call him "chief," call him "frog," or almost anything else, but don't call the black gentleman "nigger," as the small gang of soccer hooligans had in a pub in Britain the previous November. O'Bannon smiled at the memory of the fight: how they'd cleaned the hooligans' clocks, jumped into their rental car, and roared clear of the parking lot before the town constables arrived. Their hosts at the nearby Special Air Service school swore that the SEALs had been at the base all night. The bandaged knife wound to Cully's hand was explained, with solemn apologies, as a training accident. Captain Rajiv Singh, the chief unarmed combat instructor at the school, volunteered that it was his fault. He always seemed to have a knife in his hand and sometimes people got stuck. The constables didn't know that Singh had never, ever wounded anyone with a knife—by accident, anyhow.

"What's goin' on?"

"Big trouble in Little China, boss. We're diverting to Taiwan."

"Like I said, what's goin' on?"

"Dunno yet. The cockpit crew is decoding a long transmission. Seems like a lot of bombings and assassinations happened over the past few hours and riots broke out all over the island. Whole place is upside down. We gotta take a look-see around Taipei and Tai'chung."

"How long till we land?"

"About two hours." O'Bannon looked around the cabin, grateful that his men weren't displaying themselves in more than the usual dishevelment. He had to shout to make himself heard above the engine noise. "Okay. Get some shut-eye, chief. I'll wake everybody up in an hour." Wilson didn't go to sleep. As O'Bannon knew he would, the chief went about inventorying all their equipment. Green Team units never went anywhere without all the stuff they needed to do covert recon. Or to kill people and break things.

White House Situation Room
14 March
0820 Hours

"France and Russia are supporting China's proposal for a peacekeeping force to enter Taiwan. The Security Council is taking it up today," said Eric Stahl.

"Typical." The president sighed.

The Air Force chief of staff, General Duke Patterson, said, "We could always fire a Tomahawk missile into the secretary-general's office." No one laughed.

"Don't even joke about that, General." The president looked tired and sounded worse. His scowl turned into a thin smile. "Only I get to make jokes like that one, Duke. Okay?"

Patterson smiled back. "Yessir. But if you want to make a joke, I'll fly the aircraft that delivers it."

The president frowned again. "So what do we do after we veto it in the UN?"

Eric Stahl looked at the secretary of defense. "Henry, what's your take on Hu Jintao's speeches?"

Defense Secretary Henry McPherson stood up. He didn't like sitting— too passive for his temperament and too tension-inducing for his lower back. "Hu's speeches are a pretty clear indication that they're about to invoke their anti-secession law of March 2005.[1] It authorizes the use of military force if Taiwan tries to secede or if 'major incidents entailing secession' should occur.[2] Hu's claiming Chinese citizens are endangered by the riots. But I think they'll wait to see if the UN gives China authority to intervene."

The chairman of the Joint Chiefs chimed in. "We have *Stennis* on station, and both *Nimitz* and *Kitty Hawk* en route with their battle groups. The Green Team platoon is dispersed in Taipei and Tai'chung, and we have five sat recon birds over-flying the area." The door opened and a young-looking colonel ran in. The chairman looked at the note handed to him. "Sir, I think we'd better open the video-link."

The picture came from the USS *John C. Stennis*, her skipper on the video-link. "Sir, we detected a missile salvo from the mainland, headed over Taiwan, about six minutes ago. Our Aegis destroyers tracked them. We thought it was a demonstration." The captain swallowed visibly. "Then one of the missiles started falling short. We fired two Standard missiles to intercept it in accordance with the ROE. They missed. We tracked the bird all the way down. It hit smack in the center of Taipei."

Beijing
14 March
2130 Hours Local

Seated in the grand conference room of the State Council, Hu Jintao addressed the television cameras. He disliked teleprompters, but the occasion required them.

"Every Chinese citizen has watched in horror as the forces of secession have let blood in the province of Taiwan. Now, to the shock of the world, a foreign power has caused one of our missiles, fired in a peaceful test, to fall on our people in Taipei. We have seen the pictures of bloodshed everywhere. This imperialistic act cannot be tolerated any longer. Because the American imperialists have intervened in a Chinese internal matter, we tell them now, withdraw. If you do not leave our territorial waters, you will be attacked.

"The American imperialists have blocked the legitimate action of the United Nations Security Council that was acting, in the interest of human rights, to condemn their intervention and authorize an international peacekeeping force to enter Taiwan. But the UN General Assembly today will condemn America for its designs on the Chinese citizens of Taiwan.

"When we see our countrymen dying in droves, slaughtered by a foreign power and unable to resist, we must act. The State Council has voted unanimously to invoke the powers granted us under Chinese law. In accordance with the anti-secession law of 2005, enacted by the unanimous vote of the National People's Congress, we declare that an outbreak of grave turmoil in Taiwan has disrupted social stability, normal life, and public order. The People's Liberation Army will now act to restore stability, life, and public order in the province of Taiwan. And all those who attempt to interfere shall be regarded as having declared war on the People's Republic of China."

White House Situation Room
14 March
1120 Hours

The National Security Council had met for two hours.

Several Democratic senators, including the Democratic front-runner in the primaries, had demanded that the Navy task force be withdrawn from the Taiwan Strait. The question was what to do. The secretary of state and the head of the CIA thought the president would not be harmed politically by pulling back the task force and argued that it might be prudent. The secretary of defense disagreed; he believed the al Qaeda connection made it a new front in the War on Terror.

Stahl looked around. "Where the hell's the JCS chairman?"

As if he had read Stahl's mind, the Marine general marched into the room and said, "May I interrupt? I've just had a conversation directly with a SEAL platoon commander who is doing covert recon for us in Taipei. About an hour ago, two of his men showed up with a prisoner."

The secretary of state started to speak, but he cut her off. "I know, ma'am, but please hear me out. Our guys are sometimes more lucky than smart, and this is probably one of those times. Two of the Green Team guys, they're all in civilian clothes, followed one of the al Jazeera reporters filming the riots. The reporter went into a hotel room and had a loud, emotional conversation with someone inside. Our guys listened, and fortunately, though neither of them speak Arabic, the people inside were speaking Chinese. One of the SEALs is fluent in the dialect used by the PLA. When the reporter left, our guys, ah, entered the room and found two guys with satellite phones, computers, and a whole layout of Taipei. They, ah, captured one of them and brought him back to their hidey-hole. We are going to extract him, and two of the SEALs with him, in about an hour."

"So what does that mean other than your men are acting illegally, General? Did they kill the other man?" The secretary of state wasn't feigning anger. She was livid.

"Ma'am, I won't admit our guys are doing anything wrong. And in this case, we've uncovered the facts, plain and simple, that prove Beijing has its special forces operating in Taiwan and that they are responsible for the bombings, assassinations, and riots."

Stahl held up his hand to stop the discussion. "Okay, I'm going back upstairs. I'm sure the president is going to want to hear the rest of this himself."

New York City
New York Times Publisher's Conference Room
17 March
2245 Hours

It was one of the nights they loved and hated. The politics were wonderful but the mess they made of the next day's paper was horrendous.

In between the Democratic front-runner's speech, which called for complete American withdrawal from the Taiwan Strait, and the president's speech, Beijing had declared it was invoking the anti-secession law. The statement, broadcast worldwide on al Jazeera and Telesur, the Venezuelan channel that reached all of South America, said that Beijing had "received many calls for help from Chinese citizens on the island of Taiwan and they would be answered." Beijing also demanded that the UN Security Council disregard American veto threats and act immediately on its resolution condemning American intervention and declaring it illegal under international law.

The president's speech was awkward and uncertain, obviously written long before both the speeches that preceded his. In it, the president tried to reassure everyone that the world was not falling into war and pleaded with the Beijing regime to meet with him personally in Singapore in two days. He reiterated that American forces would defend themselves and the "democratic elections" two days hence in Taiwan. He said he had just ended a conference call with both Taiwanese presidential candidates, each of whom was horrified at the terrorism Taiwan had suffered. They assured him that the Taiwanese would not be cowed by the terrorists of Beijing.

"We're about sixty minutes past deadline already," said the publisher of the *New York Times* to his assembled editors and reporters. "I want the headline to be something like, 'President pushes the world to war,' and we have to pick up on this idea that he's out of control, acting against international law, and probably violating the War Powers Act." Before any of the editors present said a word, the Washington editor spoke through the conference phone.

"We have to go much further than that," she said. "This guy is totally out of his mind. We're intervening in Chinese internal politics. Taiwan isn't able to hold their election with any confidence of getting a fair result. We need to take a very clear position: Taiwan isn't our concern, and the UN can't be ignored. I suggest"—and here she paused dramatically—"that we ought to listen to my Washington sources. They tell me they're going to introduce a resolution of impeachment against the president in the morning. We might not want to anticipate them altogether, but why can't we ask Congress to prevent this madman from starting World War Three?"

The publisher looked around the room and heard no dissent. "Okay, so that's it then." He pushed the button on the conference phone, ending the call. The editors and reporters scurried out to rewrite the front page and the lead editorial.

White House Situation Room
18 March
1530 Hours

The president stared at the videoconference screen. The joint task force commander aboard the USS *Nimitz* had his game face on. "It's not all bad news, Mr. President. Before the Chinese missile strike hit Guam, the B-2s and B-52s, as well as our tanker aircraft, were already in the air. We've taken a lot of casualties, and the aircraft won't be able to recover to Guam, but we can still strike back."

An hour before, Chinese missiles had struck at every airbase on Taiwan and every ship in the USS *Stennis* strike group. *Stennis*, badly damaged, was still making enough headway to limp out of the Taiwan Strait. One Aegis destroyer was sunk, as was a supply ship that accompanied *Stennis*. Beijing had dropped paratroopers into Taiwan and launched a fleet of landing aircraft. The few Taiwanese forces left after the missile strike were fighting the paratroopers.

"So what are our options, Admiral?" the president asked.

"We have a few, sir. We can withdraw, which I don't recommend. We can use the air assets already flying to take out the Chinese invasion force. And we have some other assets that can protect the bombers in the air and—even more important—our satellites. The Chinese have that station on Tarawa Island that may go active any minute. We're pretty sure their directed-energy weapons can blind any satellite they can track."

"Yeah, so? What can we do to stop them?"

"We still have a few tricks up our sleeve, sir. Like that special weapon to destroy all the electronics in the area. It's on one of the B-2s in the air, headed to Tarawa right now."

"I don't want an all-out war with China."

"Sir, I don't want a nuclear exchange with them either. But they have already sunk two of our ships and heavily damaged another. And they bombed the hell out of Andersen Air Force Base on Guam. They've probably killed thousands of Americans and they're fighting all-out just short of the nuclear threshold. How can we not do the same?"

The president sat silent for several minutes. Letting out a long sigh, he said, "Okay, so we have to do it. We hit their invasion force with everything we have. But nothing—and I mean nothing, Admiral—on the Chinese mainland gets hit."

"But sir, if we don't take out their command and control, this thing can go on indefinitely. And if we don't hit Tarawa, we can lose a really big chunk of our own."

"You heard me, Admiral. Nothing on the Chinese mainland gets hit unless you talk to me first. Last time I heard, Tarawa Island wasn't part of mainland China."

Above the East China Sea and the Western Pacific Ocean
Near One Degree North Latitude
19 March
0400 Hours Local

Of the four B-2s that had gotten out of Guam before the Chinese missiles struck, three were headed toward the Chinese invasion fleet in the East China Sea. As they cruised along at about fifty-five thousand feet (roughly a mile higher than the unclassified ceiling), the pilots were thinking the flight was an easy one compared to the thirty-six-hour round trips they'd flown during the 2001 Afghanistan fight and the 2003 Iraq campaign. Going from Guam to the seas off China was almost a milk run. And at fifty-five thousand feet, the B-2s didn't guzzle gas. They were as comfortable as they could be. And there were enough bottles of water and protein bars for them to get along for a day, maybe two. Hot coffee was limited to three thermos bottles, and they rationed it as if it were Napoleon brandy.

Three of the planes had made harrowing takeoffs. The new non-nuclear weapons they carried weighed in at twenty-one thousand pounds, and they weren't alone in the bomb bay. The B-2 normally flew like a bulky glider, its stealthy, batwing design giving it enormous lift but making it difficult to maneuver. With full loads of fuel and weapons, they needed every foot of runway Andersen Air Force Base had. And "had"—past tense—was the right word, thanks to the Chinese missile attack. There was still no plan on where they'd go after hitting the Chinese invasion fleet. It could be a helluva long ride back to their usual home, Whiteman Air Force Base in Missouri.

The fourth B-2 had more than its usual two crewmen on board. The third wasn't used to combat flying. Lieutenant Colonel Matt O'Bannon sat comfortably in the pilot's seat and glanced back toward his passenger, Colonel Luddy Brown.

"Hey, Luddy, you okay? You look a little green."

"I'm fine, Matt. Just thinking about another test I'd like to run on the weapon."

"Jerry, recheck Luddy's computer again. I don't want any emissions." A minute passed.

"Still okay, boss."

"Okay, Luddy. Run your tests."

Colonel Ludwig Brown was a scientist, not a warrior. When Brown took his Ph.D. at the Massachusetts Institute of Technology, people were still singing a 1960s tribute to his famous relative: "Once the rockets go up, who cares where they come down? That's not my department, said Werner von Braun." He'd never asked why his family name had been anglicized after World War II. Even if rocket science might run in the family, that was no reason for overconfidence. He had to make sure his special weapon worked. If it did, a huge electromagnetic pulse would burn out every printed circuit on the island. But Brown's thoughts weren't only on the weapon. He couldn't forget that his entire science crew at Andersen, men he'd eaten dinner with last night, were probably dead. He might soon be as well. He wished he could call his wife, but that was impossible. He turned back to the laptop computer he had linked to the special weapon in the bomb bay.

O'Bannon, meanwhile, mused about their target, Tarawa. His grandfather, a World War II mud Marine who had taken a company ashore on Tarawa, had told him stories about Marines wading through two hundred yards of chest-deep water into machine-gun fire to reach the beach. As important as Tarawa had been then, it was even more so now. The Beijing satellite "tracking station" there had been emitting strange pulses of energy, and two navigation satellites had stopped working. If the Chinese were about to take out America's space technology, the attack would probably come from directed-energy weapons on Tarawa. If it succeeded, every U.S. aircraft and ship would be sent back to the 1960s. *Luddy's weapon had better work,* he thought, *or we're all going to be flying deaf and almost blind.*

White House Situation Room
18 March
2335 Hours

"So what's the final word?" asked the president.

"Well, before the big boom," said General Duke Patterson, "Beijing destroyed almost all of Taiwan's air force, as well as its navy. Their paratroopers fell just short of taking the capital. The Taiwanese army managed to save two companies of attack helicopters for a counter-strike. And they recaptured two operational runways so that what was left of Taiwan's air force, two squadrons of F-16s, could make two long sorties against Beijing fighters and troop-carrying aircraft, before they ran out of missiles and ammunition. And then our B-2s arrived."

"We didn't lose any of them?"

"No. We blindsided Beijing with them. They dropped their weapons on the invasion fleet and disappeared before the weapons detonated. They're fused to explode at low altitude, these twenty-one thousand MOABs—I'm sorry, sir, massive overhead blast bombs—and they destroyed everything within a mile's radius. On the surface of the Taiwan Strait, the invasion fleet is now only scattered shards of metal and bodies. A few landing craft have plowed on, but we're talking about hundreds of Communist troops, not hundreds of thousands. USS *Nimitz* and USS *Kitty Hawk* are in the Strait now, our submarines cleared a path for them. Maybe I better turn it over to the admiral."

The president nodded.

The chief of naval operations nodded in return. "Sir, the subs weren't supposed to leave their carrier-guarding stations. But they're skippered by men who believe it's better to ask forgiveness than permission, thank God. Our subs sank virtually everything in their path, including two Sovremenny destroyers, about twelve Chinese subs, and dozens of other Chinese ships."

"And what about Tarawa?"

General Patterson answered, "Our bomb worked. It created a huge electromagnetic pulse over the island that fried the printed circuits of every computer on the island, as well as every other electronic device that wasn't buried deep underground. The island's fiber-optic communication lines aren't affected, but they've got nothing to use them with. The radios and telephones are all fried, and we expect a few brains are too, as if they'd had an electronic lobotomy."

Beijing
Central Military Council
19 March
1200 Hours Local

Hu Jintao looked around the room, wondering which of his colleagues would succeed him. The reports of the devastated invasion fleet were beyond his imagination. He knew now there would be no bullying the American president, no bluffing with a nuclear threat, and no way to save face beyond achieving some sort of cease-fire.

The PLA commander spoke first. "We cannot accept anything other than the complete governing power over Taiwan."

"And just how do you intend to achieve that, comrade?"

"It is simple. I cannot believe you have not thought of it."

With that slap, Hu knew who would replace him.

The general continued, "We offer a cease-fire and say we will rebuild what has been destroyed in Taiwan. We will need to send tens of thousands of men and machines, as well as capital, to do that, and when Taiwan is rebuilt, it will be our people who control the government, the schools, and the industry."

"If it is so simple, comrade, how can you be sure the Americans will stand for it?"

"Because, comrade, they cannot do otherwise. They will never fight again for Taiwan, and Taiwan will never again be able to fight for itself."

White House Situation Room
19 March
0930 Hours

"So you're telling me that we're not winning, but neither are the Chinese? I was nearly impeached yesterday," said the president. "I'm a pariah on every news channel and on the front page of every newspaper in the country. And you're telling me that we're not gonna win this thing?" The president wasn't the only person in the room who looked haggard. Of the entire National Security Council, the only one who seemed fresh was the chairman of the Joint Chiefs. He had a larger supply of clean clothes in his Pentagon office than anyone knew about except his wife.

"Yes, sir, that's about it. We don't have the muscle to drive the Chicoms out of Taiwan, but they don't have the muscle to stay. The Taiwanese are fighting back with what they have, but they don't have enough left to win decisively."

"So what the hell are we going to do? You realize the Chicoms are threatening a nuclear strike against us, Japan, and anyone else they can hit? And you're telling me we have about five thousand dead Americans and we're not gonna win this thing?"

"Yes, sir. But if I may, the Chicoms are bluffing. They don't want a nuclear exchange any more than we do. And the Russians are bluffing too. They don't want a war with us, so all this talk about intervening is just that. You remember their carrier?"

"Yeah, the *Boris* something or other."

"Sir, please remember it took off at high speed just before this all broke out."

"Okay," said the president. "So what's the answer to this?"

The secretary of state said, "Mr. President, we've talked to the Chinese and the Russians and worked out an agreement for a proposed cease-fire. The Chinese will withdraw all troops from Taiwan except for their mortuary details and doctors. They've also volunteered to help rebuild Taiwan if they can put up a candidate in the next presidential election, which won't be held for a year. I don't like it, but the Taiwanese president does. He thinks Beijing is finished in Taiwan, and Taiwan's only problem is rebuilding. I told him we'll help."

The president shook his head. "I don't like it either. But if you're telling me it's the best we can get without a bigger war..."

"I'm afraid it is, Mr. President."

"All right, tell the Chinese we will declare a joint cease-fire in thirty minutes. By then we can get word out to our forces. General, make that happen." The chairman of the Joint Chiefs motioned to an Army general behind him, who dashed out of the room, grasping his secure cell phone from his belt holster.

"The war," said the president, "is over."

CHAPTER THREE

THE SECOND KOREAN WAR

North Korea says it is withdrawing immediately from the Nuclear Non-Proliferation Treaty (NPT), which seeks to control the spread of nuclear technology. The official Korean Central News Agency said that, although Pyongyang was pulling out of the NPT, it had no intention of producing nuclear weapons.

BBC NEWS, JANUARY 10, 2003[1]

East China Sea
Aboard USS *Ohio*
Depth Approximately 550 Feet
Tuesday, 9 September 2008
0710 Hours Local

Navy commander Cully O'Bannon and two SEAL platoons had been living the high life aboard the USS *Ohio*. The *Ohio* was an old Trident nuclear submarine that had been converted into a SEAL delivery vehicle. It didn't have all the comforts of a *Nimitz*-class aircraft carrier, but it was close enough. It had a great galley, an exercise room, and space enough to cram in a few luxuries, like the two tiny but heavily armed "little bird" helicopters that were stored where the missile tubes used to be. And its small combat information center (CIC) had every secure communication device American ingenuity could invent.

When they told him his call was coming in, O'Bannon dashed half the length of the sub and swung through the narrow door of the CIC.

O'Bannon was ready for anything. He and Master Chief Romeo Wilson had made sure the whole platoon was as well. The briefing they'd received before leaving Pearl Harbor had been on how to handle crudely made North Korean nuclear weapons—the kind that leaked radiation and that Kim Jung Il was selling. Beyond that, the SEALs were in the dark.

"Are they ready, Master Chief?"

"He's hot to trot, Mr. O'Bannon. He should be on the line in just a few seconds."

The four-star Air Force general, commander of Pacific Command, appeared on the videophone screen.

Few people even tried to pronounce the PACOM commander's name. "Skrzypczak" had far too many consonants and too few vowels to tempt any but the bravest. To his face, everyone—including the president—just called him "General Skip." To others who knew him, and only behind his back, he was the Crafty Old Bastard—the COB.

"O'Bannon? Here are your orders. We have, or at least CIA and NRO are sure we have, two small ships coming out of Nampo right now. According to very specific information, one or the other is carrying nuclear warheads and missile parts for Iran. They'll likely make about fifteen to twenty knots, south and then southeast. The orders, which are on the secure link e-mail to you and the rest of the task force, require that they not be stopped in Chinese or North Korean waters. That means you have about another twenty-four hours before they pass near Cheju Island in the East China Sea. At that time, you are to board both ships, employing one platoon on each, search them, and determine if they are carrying those prohibited cargos. If they are, you will divert them to Cheju Island, accompanied by South Korean patrol boats, and we'll seize the contraband. Your boarding will be covered by an attack boat, two U.S. Aegis destroyers, and a squadron of F-16s operating out of Osan. These orders come from the president himself."

"Are the South Koreans cool with this, sir?"

"We think they are. You know they're not the pals they used to be, but the White House twisted the Korean president's arm and worked something out. This is a big deal for the president, and for us. We need to catch these guys dead-bang, exporting nukes. Then, maybe, we can disarm 'em without going to war."

"Sir, forgive me, but this one could be pretty messy if the ROKs leak the op."

"Yeah, I know. And Kim Jung Il ain't gonna be happy regardless. Do what you have to, Commander, but keep the lid on as best you can."

"Sir, one more question. Sorry, but why not track these guys into open water and take 'em there?"

"Because, Commander, that's all you need to know right now."

Pyongyang, North Korea
Presidential Palace
Office of the Dear Leader
9 September
1210 Hours Local

Kim Jong-nam walked confidently into his father's office. Four years ago, he'd been named his father's successor, and his power kept growing. But the younger Kim knew that if he challenged his father, he'd be dead. He would take power soon enough. His father was sixty-six years old, and his dissolute life was catching up with him. There was always a bottle of Napoleon brandy within reach, usually in the lap of a young Japanese girl. Kim arrived just in time to see the latest girl wriggling her skirt back in place. His father waved her out of the room.

"Father, I have the Chinese president on the phone. He says it is urgent."

Kim Jung Il grunted and picked up the receiver. "President Hu, it is a great honor, as always, to speak with you."

Hu Jintao knew Kim to be a volatile conversationalist. The fact that China held North Korea's lifeline of food and oil did not guarantee Kim's good behavior. "My dear friend, I have confirmed our cooperation in your shipping enterprise. But do you think it is wise to undertake such an operation simultaneously with your other venture?"

"I am convinced, President Hu, that there is no better time to impose our policy on Seoul. They will certainly agree. You need not worry about any war. This will all happen so swiftly. Remember the effect of what we did in Rangoon almost thirty years ago? The South Koreans nearly surrendered then."

"I do not remember it quite that way, my dear friend. You managed to assassinate almost half their cabinet, but the result was nearly war, not capitulation. Perhaps I was so low in rank then that I did not appreciate the success of what you did. I agree that you may do as you wish now, and you will have the support you requested."

Aboard USS *Ohio*
11 September
0003 Hours Local

Cully O'Bannon tried to push himself up in the hospital bunk, but his arms were as weak as his head was fuzzy. "You're gonna be okay, boss. Just lie still."

"What . . . what the hell, Chief?"

"You remember anything about how you got here, Commander?" The navy surgeon standing between him and Chief Wilson had a face that wouldn't come into focus.

"Yeah, I remember searching the ship. We found nothing and were starting to extract when somebody started shooting at us. The rope slipped out of my hands and I fell into the IBS. I obviously bashed my head and it's blank from there. What the hell happened? Where are the rest of our guys? Who's hurt? Did everybody make it?"

Wilson, sitting in a chair next to Cully and wearing some sort of hospital gown, sighed deeply. "We walked into a really cool ambush, boss. We were all back over the side when the shooting started and you hit your head on the Zodiac and fell into the water. There were a buncha guys shooting down on us from the deck. I scooped you out and we ran like hell back to the sub. I took a round in the hip that almost took out a kidney. Thank God we had the two little birds covering us. They strafed the hell out of both ships. But some of our guys weren't as lucky as you and me. Schaeffer, Colon, Bitterman, and Lewis are dead. Michaels is missing. He either drowned or was picked up by the Chinese."

"Chinese?"

"Yeah. Nobody spotted their subs until it was too late. The two NK ships may have signaled them when we were coming in, and they opened up as soon as we started to extract. There's a lot more. The COB said to have you call in as soon as you regained consciousness."

O'Bannon sat back in silence for a moment. He would make this call and then call his mentor, retired SEAL captain Stan Schaeffer, to tell him his son was dead.

PACOM Headquarters, Hawaii
10 September
1330 Hours Local

"Of course you were set up, O'Bannon. We all were. Just sit tight and you'll be back here in a few days. If there's any 'here' here by the time you arrive. Out." The COB didn't have time for longer conversations. He and his staff had a war on their hands, or at least they might have one, but no one really knew, least of all the White House and the State Department. He wanted to tell O'Bannon why the raid took place where it did, but that was between him, the Pentagon, and the White House. He'd warned them about operating in those waters, but they had overridden his cautions.

Two days before the raid, four critical reconnaissance satellites had simply ceased functioning. The COB didn't believe in coincidences, but the president chose to. The COB suspected—but could not confirm— that the Chinese had taken the satellites out with directed-energy weapons, long rumored to have been in development at the Chicoms' satellite tracking facility on Tarawa Island. Without those satellites to provide the U.S. early warning, the Chinese were able to sneak two flights of fighters and a surface ship into battle, sinking an Aegis destroyer. The U.S. forces recovered quickly and sank the Chicom surface ship, but the damage was done.

One of the North Korean freighters, caught between Chinese and American warships, had been sunk, and the other fled into a Chinese port. It wasn't long before the airwaves were full of hysterical announcements. China was condemning American aggression and praising the North Koreans' restraint—which wasn't much in evidence, because Kim Jung Il was demanding that South Korea throw all Americans off the Korean peninsula, threatening all-out war in defense of his shipping.

At first, the South Koreans tried to negotiate a compromise solution with the North, but after a sniper assassinated three South Korean cabinet members and a bomb planted by a fake road repair crew assassinated the South Korean president, what was left of the South Korean government was ready to surrender. North Korea demanded an answer from the South. The South pleaded for more time—demanding an apology from the United States and financial concessions if it were to allow American troops to remain.

Without satellites, the COB didn't know what else was coming. Observation posts in the Korean DMZ reported a massive North Korean mobilization. But all the intel analysts and State Department "experts" were saying it was just more saber-rattling. The COB didn't buy it—and it was time to do something about it. He called Major General Daniel Rubia using a secure ground line.

"Howzit hanging, Doc?"

"Lousy, sir. How's by you?" Rubia, a Ph.D. in mathematics from MIT, liked being called "Doc," and he liked to talk about his "kids," which were in medium or geosynchronous orbit miles above the Earth. The doc was daddy to all the CIA and Defense Department spy satellites. He couldn't talk about them to anyone outside the small circle of military personnel and civilians cleared at the highest level, so the COB's calls were always welcome. When the Chinese ASAT attack took some of them down, he was sad for the loss of his "kids," and then he got mad. He was pretty sure why the COB was calling.

"You still have that old Clint Eastwood CD?"

"Sure do, sir. Want me to send it to ya?"

"Go ahead. Make my day."

The Clint Eastwood CD wasn't a movie. It was the COB's code word for the three "Misty" spy satellites that were in medium Earth orbit. They were stealthy—with a radar cross section about the size of a bumblebee— and powerful. And aside from a few milliseconds of tests, they hadn't been turned on since entering orbit, so the enemy couldn't track them.

About 430 miles above Earth, the three satellites came awake, their circuitry humming to life, unheard in the vacuum of space.

PACOM Headquarters
14 September
0630 Hours Local

"Okay, gents, what's the story?" The COB was in his small underground conference room. He and his staff had been there for two hours, fielding reports and waiting for decisions to be made in Washington. The story wasn't good.

Seoul, South Korea, had been bombarded with North Korean missiles. Tens of thousands of civilians were dead, South Korea's roads were full of panicking civilians fleeing farther south, and the ROK army was, belatedly, on full alert. All across the DMZ, ROK units fanned out according to their well-rehearsed defensive plan. That plan called for an immediate retaliatory attack, but South Korea's interim president nixed that. He declared a cease-fire and begged China to negotiate a truce with North Korea.

The North Koreans breached the cease-fire before dawn. Tens of thousands of troops and thousands of tanks poured through the tunnels they had dug under the DMZ. Kim Jung Il demanded South Korea's unconditional surrender. Worse, he threatened to use nuclear weapons if Seoul didn't capitulate before sundown.

The COB looked around the table. The air boss spoke up first. "Sir, every U.S. aircraft at Osan AB is either in the air or will be in the next ten minutes. We're redeploying according to the scatter plan you approved last month. We have enough tankers in the air, but just barely. We have a couple coming from Iraq, but that's gonna leave us a little uncovered there. The problem is, we've diverted three to the Hammer force, and that's gonna leave some thirsty F-16s if we don't sort it out in the next fifteen minutes or so. I know we gotta make sure Hammer is okay, but I'm gonna lose a lot of fighters on the ground pretty soon. I've just gotten reports of at least three Chinese F-11 squadrons in the air around the DMZ. If they come in, we're in trouble."

The COB nodded to an Army two-star. "Sir, we have all our people deployed, and the Marines are falling back quickly toward Seoul. We've taken a lot of casualties in the past few hours, but unless the crazy sono-fabitch starts throwing nukes, we might make it. Our guys are retreating, running like hell, as you ordered."

"Good. And keep 'em running. I want at least three miles' separation between our guys and theirs. If the NKs go nuclear, that's another matter. But Hammer One is in the air, and will be over the battlefield any minute."

Near Sokch'o, South Korea
Aboard the B-2 bomber *Spirit of San Diego*
45,000 Feet
14 September
0632 Hours Local

"Feet dry, boss."

Matt O'Bannon nodded to his copilot, scanning the sky for fighters. Every passive sensor the B-2 had was tuned to maximum range. He knew he was invisible electronically, but the sunrise at his back wasn't welcome. The B-2, so big and slow, was a sitting duck for any fighters who got a visual. As they passed over the coastline, he risked a millisecond-long blink on his secure radio. In answer, the six other B-2s strung out behind him blinked back.

"Okay, everybody is where they're supposed to be. Time to target, I make it about twelve minutes."

"Same here, sir." The blaze of an afterburner lit the sky ahead, ten miles or more away.

"Is that what I think it is, boss?"

"Let's hope so." O'Bannon knew the fighters were now executing their part of the mission, sweeping a clear path to the target. The fighters needed to do the same on the way back or there would be a lot of expensive B-2 parts strewn across the Korean peninsula. They cruised for eight minutes until O'Bannon said, "Arm the weapons."

"Weapons armed."

"Here we go. IP."

Even at their altitude, from the IP—the initial point on the bomb run—he could tell the ground was clogged with men and tanks. It was full of blinking lights: acres of artillery firing at American troops miles away.

He sat back. Everything was automatic from here. The B-2's navigational computer read the bombing coordinates and verified its position with the satellites above. At one-minute intervals, the three twenty-one-thousand-pound MOABs dropped away. O'Bannon turned sharply and pushed the throttles to full military power. The other B-2s, strung out to the north and south, did the same.

There was a series of huge flashes and then everything went dark and still. The rising sun played over the newly crafted moonscape where tens of thousands of North Korean troops and square miles of tanks and artillery had been a moment before. Each one of the MOABs had destroyed everything within a mile or more of the fuel-air explosion it created.

Pyongyang
Presidential Palace
15 September
0430 Hours Local

"Father, wake up. President Hu demands to speak to you now." Kim Jong-nam wasn't sure he would survive the day; he was almost sure his father would not. He chased the European whore out of his father's bed, but he couldn't chase the drug-induced stupor out of the paternal skull. The son picked up the telephone again.

"I am most sorry, President Hu. My father continues to be indisposed. I will make sure he calls you the minute he is able."

"That is insufficient, my new friend." The words "new friend" sent a chill up the younger Kim's spine. "I must have action, and I will have it now. There is nothing to stop the American troops from coming across the demilitarized zone and capturing all of your country. Your father acted unwisely, counting too much on the weakness of the bandit regime in Seoul. His threat to use nuclear weapons against the Americans has propelled them to counter-attack. The American Marines are racing north almost unopposed."

"My father will soon rally our men and stop them, I assure you."

"That, too, is not enough. I am sending three Chinese armies to aid in your struggle and preserve the revolution. You—personally—will meet General Li and he will take command of your country's defense."

"But sir, I cannot do that. It is the prerogative of my father."

"Your father is on another drunken binge, is he not?"

"No, no, sir. He is just indisposed for the moment."

"And he will remain so. Forever. See to it, or I shall call your younger brother in ten minutes."

PACOM Headquarters
18 September
0410 Hours Local

The COB liked quiet time. He was always in the office well before his staff. His wife of thirty years was used to it by now. Living with a fighter pilot meant waking up alone.

The COB made his coffee and walked to the window, gazing out as he often did when lost in thought. The Chinese intervention made this an open war. The president promised he could have as many Marine and Army units as he needed. But it was an empty promise. The troops tied down in Iraq, Syria, Lebanon, and the Horn of Africa weren't going anywhere, and there wasn't time to move them by sea or even by air.

The Chinese meant to stop the American advance short of the North Korean capital, which meant fierce fighting, but at least their presence also meant the North Koreans wouldn't use nuclear weapons, though they threatened to do so every few hours. The COB had to assume that the Chinese, not the North Korean madmen, were in charge.

Skrzypczak weighed his choices. None of them were good. He had no reinforcements (even the Aussies were sitting this one out), and the Chinese had sent missile strikes against Taiwan and Japan (for harboring American "warmongers") and were mobilizing their naval forces, including landing craft, against Taiwan. The COB couldn't cover all these bases *and* fight a land war of attrition in Korea. He figured the war would be won or lost within the next five days, and there was only one way to win it.

It took three phone calls to the president and the Joint Chiefs. The president had to get past the "you're gonna do WHAT?" stage. But he eventually did, and the plan was approved. The COB called General Li— commander of the PLA forces in North Korea—and told him he was coming to the old DMZ to discuss a cease-fire, personally, and would be withdrawing the American navy from Korean waters. The Chinese general was sure it was a ruse until his intelligence officers reported American carriers pulling back from the waters near the Korean peninsula. Instead of rushing to reinforce Korea, the Americans appeared to be withdrawing every aircraft carrier battle group and every nuclear submarine at flank speed.

The president had said, "Put the genie back in the bottle, General." The COB was going to try. If it didn't work, at least he wouldn't live to see the disaster he had crafted.

Pearl Harbor, Hawaii
Military Hospital
16 October
0810 Hours Local

"Did we beat 'em, boss?" The naval aviator was lying in a hospital bed, bandaged from head to toe. According to his chart, he'd suffered burns over 60 percent of his body. He'd be heading to Texas on the next flight, to the best burn treatment unit in the world.

"I think we did, lieutenant. How are you doing?" The COB spent at least two hours a day talking to the wounded at the hospital.

"You sure sucker-punched those bastards, General. The guys were talking earlier. They said we surprised them all over the place: Taiwan, Africa, even the Middle East."

"Well, it worked pretty good, but only because guys like you put it on the line."

"But sir, you had 'em comin' and goin'. Nobody thought we'd have the balls to sink every Chicom ship in every harbor in the world. And that business of blocking their oil..."

"Well, it wasn't that complicated, lieutenant. I knew the only way to hurt the Chinese bad enough was to hit 'em in a way that would cut back their reach. Now that they've lost about 75 percent of their navy and damn near all their commercial ships, it'll be a while before they bother us again. And that oil blockade was the easiest of all. Had you ever heard of the Strait of Malacca before you went to drop sea mines all over it?"

The general thought for a minute he'd seen a small grin flash underneath the bandages.

"Well, son, you can call it victory. The North and South Koreans are in the same places they were two months ago. And the Chinese genie is back in the bottle. So you rest easy. I'll be back to wheel you onto that C-17 in a few minutes."

CHAPTER FOUR

THE FIRST OIL WAR

If there is any aggression, there will be no oil.

VENEZUELAN PRESIDENT HUGO CHAVEZ, MARCH 4, 2005[1]

Fidel is more than a friend. Fidel is like an older brother.

HUGO CHAVEZ, OCTOBER 17, 2005[2]

Caracas, Venezuela
Monday, 9 August 2010
1015 Hours Local

"Señor Presidente, Fidel is dead. And the counter-revolutionaries in Miami have already said they will return and take over Cuba."

Hugo Chavez shook his head sadly. "He was the greatest of men. His birthday was only a few days away." Then, suddenly, he snarled, "How can you even worry about the counter-revolutionaries? They will never be allowed to return. The Bay of Pigs taught them a lesson. And this new American president—she would never allow it to happen. The Fidelista revolution cannot be defeated by a few people in boats."

"But Señor Presidente, there are already demonstrations around Fidel's palace. The anti-Fidelistas are on television; the counter-revolutionaries

in Miami are planning to fly huge planeloads of people to Havana to cel-
ebrate and seize the government."

"They will be shot down."

"But what if the Fidelistas do not act?"

"Then we will act. We will get there before the imperialists can. We
will preserve the Cuban revolution. Call in the military staff immediately.
And get me General Xin."

Caracas
Twenty Minutes Later

Within a period of twenty minutes, President Chavez had gone from
sadness over the death of a friend to preparing eagerly for war in Cuba.
He had ordered the presidential photographer to attend him immediately and constantly. Venezuela's ambassador in Cuba told him the
island was in turmoil; he expected mass bloodshed, especially if the
Miami counter-revolutionaries tried to invade. Next on the line was
China's military attaché. General Xin's Spanish was both perfect and
accentless.

"It is sad tidings, Señor Presidente. The world has lost a great leader
and you have lost a great friend."

"It is true—and now I must act. We are a great nation, but we need
your help. You have many ships and aircraft in our port. I have decided
to move one thousand troops to Havana to help the Cuban people
restore order. The counter-revolutionaries from Miami will try to get
there first. We need your ships and aircraft to get our forces there
tonight."

"That may be difficult, Presidente. I will have to get approval from
my senior officers in Beijing, and they are, as you know, about twelve
hours ahead of us. It is the middle of the night there."

"Then wake them."

"I will do my best, Presidente."

Paradise Ranch, Nevada
10 August
0430 Hours

The secure cell phone by the side of the bed rang, eliciting a groan from its custodian, Lieutenant Colonel Matt O'Bannon. He rolled over to grab it.

He was in the middle of nowhere: the visiting officer's quarters in the Paradise Ranch section of Nellis Air Force Base, Nevada. Ben Rich—the 1980s head of the super-secret Lockheed Martin "Skunk Works"—had called it "Paradise Ranch" to lure young pilots there. It wasn't anybody's idea of paradise, just scrub desert and hills where wives and girlfriends couldn't visit. In his twenty years in the Air Force, O'Bannon—and his three (so far) unsuccessful marriages—had spent a lot of time here, because it was the secret test area for two of his favorite aircraft: the B-2 stealth bomber and the F-117A stealth fighter. The Hollywood types liked to call it Area 51, which wasn't quite right. Area 51 was next door, another part of Nellis where other classified stuff went on at all hours of the night.

"O'Bannon here."

"Up and at 'em, hotshot." The deputy commander of Air Combat Command was always annoyingly cheerful when he was delivering bad news. O'Bannon snapped awake.

"Whuzzup, boss?

"You won't freakin' believe it, but we—meaning you—have just been put on alert for a Cuba mission."

"Cuba? I thought our beloved president was restoring relations with the leftover commies. I was counting on getting a Cuban cigar again—legally."

"That was yesterday. Now is now. The Cubans are rioting, the Castroites are gunning people down, the Venezuelans are airlifting troops in there, the UN is in an uproar, and get this—it looks like the Chinese are providing airlift and sealift to get the Venezuelans into Cuba. They're denying it, of course, but the com traffic between Beijing and Caracas sure implies it. CIA and State have their heads up their asses as usual. We have some sat recon, but not much else. The U-2s are unable to get in past the Cubans' double-digit SAMs. The other B-2 squadrons are either deployed to Guam or Diego Garcia. You're the only one in easy flying distance. You want more good news?"

"No."

"Well, here it is anyhow. The Cuban exiles in Miami want to flood back into Cuba by charter plane and everything floatable. Florida's senators are raising holy hell that the president needs to do something."

O'Bannon's mind was racing. His squadron of B-2 bombers could be readied and in the air in less than three hours—maybe a lot less. "What're our orders, sir?"

"Roust your people ASAP. Get in the air and back to Whiteman immediately. I want you loaded and ready to launch by nightfall. Stand by for a deployment order. It could come at any time."

"What do you want us to load with, sir?"

"Everything you have except nukes and sea mines. Use the normal mix, but I want one aircraft loaded with the new MOAB. Fly that one yourself."

Caracas
10 August
1200 Hours Local

"But General Xin, the aircraft you lent us cannot be withdrawn."

"Señor Presidente, they already have been. I most humbly apologize, but my government has cautioned you again and again. The Americans have been very tolerant of our actions here. But we cannot antagonize them directly. Your forces have been delivered to Havana. We will not do more."

"Then what if I tell you that you cannot operate your ships in our harbor? That you cannot rely on us to reduce oil shipments to America and send them to you? What will you do then, eh?"

"Please, Señor Presidente. Calm down. You know how much Beijing has invested in your nation, and how much we value your personal trust and friendship. Especially the new ports you let us build for our oil tankers and submarines. We do not intend to let you down. But we are urging caution."

"Then let us be cautious together. The Cubans have asked for our help, and we have given it. I am flying to Havana today to meet with the revolutionary government. I will offer them advice and aid—and with China behind us we cannot fail."

"We have what you need, Señor Presidente. We have in Caracas one of our newest and best aircraft. It is an F-11 fighter, a two-seat version of the Russian SU-27 we have made in China. It is very fast and very capable. You may use it to fly to Cuba."

"You brought this new weapon here without my permission?"

"Consider it a gift, Señor Presidente."

Whiteman Air Force Base, Missouri
10 August
1230 Hours

"So what the hell are the Chicoms up to?" Matt O'Bannon hadn't had breakfast, and lunch was going to be a protein bar and coffee. No place to smoke here, but he had three Paul Garmirian Family Reserve cigars waiting in a Tupperware container in his flight bag.

"As usual, my guess is better than yours, Colonel." The ACC deputy had flown to Whiteman to oversee the mission planning. "It's pretty complicated. The Chicoms are trying to let Chavez play the big hero and keep him from doing something stupid at the same time. The UN Security Council meeting is right now, considering our resolution to condemn the Venezuelan intervention and demand their withdrawal. The president has her pantyhose in a knot, and our UN ambassador is getting the one-finger salute from the French and the Russians."

"So we stand down?"

"No such luck. The boss just told me that the Senate is preparing a war resolution and may vote on it this afternoon."

"So we go tonight?"

"That's not what I said, Colonel. I said we stand by." The secure phone on the table between them didn't ring. The red light on it blinked rapidly. "I'd answer that, Colonel. I think it's for you."

"O'Bannon here."

"Hi, sweetie." Navy commander Cully O'Bannon was the boss of a group formally—and secretly—known as "Green Team." When SEAL Team Six was disbanded under the Clinton administration, the members of the team had migrated to Dev Group and Green Team. They still called themselves "the Jedi," as they had when Team Six was operational.

"Okay, couch potato. Listen up. I only have about one minute." Cully was sitting beside a curtained window, looking out on a stretch of beach just north of downtown Havana, which he had first seen at about 0245 that morning when he and his men swam up to it and slipped into Cuba unseen. "I just heard from two of my guys who are in a building near the presidential palace. This joint ain't Mogadishu yet, but if it accelerates much, it'll be that way by dawn tomorrow. The streets are crowded with civilians and Cuban and Venezuelan troops. They are taking potshots at the crowd, which is getting bigger all the time. This thing could blow any minute. If we're gonna do anything, it'd better be soon or there will be thousands of civilian casualties."

Matt knew better than to ask his little brother what orders he had. "What's going on at the port?"

"Nothing much now, but every damned Cuban patrol boat went outta here like a bat outta hell about an hour ago. Near as I can tell they're headed into the path of anything coming by water from Miami. And there are a lot of Cuban fighter aircraft in the air, covering the same course over and over again. They're not too calm either. A couple of them popped mach over me. Almost spilled my coffee."

"You're just full of good news, swabbie. Check six and don't get killed. Mom will never forgive you if you do. Out here."

Caracas
11 August
1330 Hours Local

Hugo Chavez paced around his desk. His staff and General Xin were trying to calm him down.

"It is your fault, Xin. That toy fighter plane did me no good at all."

Xin smiled thinly. "Señor Presidente, it got you to Havana. It enabled you to embrace the Cuban people. And it got you back quickly. You could not have made the flight without the tanker aircraft we sent along."

"But did it stop the Americans? No. Did it prevent the American Congress from demanding war? No. Did it stop them from landing thousands of paratroops in the night? No. Did it prevent the American air force from shooting down most of the Cuban air force and ALL—I remind you, General—ALL of the precious Venezuelan fighter jets that we had sent to Cuba? No, it did not."

Xin continued to smile, though he was getting grief not only from this useful idiot but also from the Central Military Commission in Beijing. His orders were to keep Chavez from provoking a real war with America and to protect the Chinese buildup in Caracas and the former Panama Canal Zone. Chavez knew—at least knew part of—what the Chinese were doing there: that the new and secret submarine port was a strategic asset for China's submarine fleet, not just a station for training missions; that the Chinese weren't merely fraternal comrades, but had their own hidden interests; that the thousands of Chinese in Caracas and elsewhere weren't all civilian contractors. What he didn't know was that none of them were civilians, really. All the port workers, advisers, and construction people were PLA soldiers, including nuclear specialists who could service ballistic missile submarines. A new Chinese ballistic missile submarine was only a week away from passing through the Panama Canal and into Caracas harbor, as a test for the new American president.

"Señor Presidente, have I not offered you every support?"

"Yes, I suppose you have done your best. I will do mine, Xin, in two days, in New York."

Whiteman Air Force Base
14 August
0810 Hours

That secure cell phone was never more than an arm's length away, but it rang several times before Matt O'Bannon could grab it. "Sorry, boss. Just getting outta the shower."

The general was, again, intolerably cheery. "So you don't know the news?"

"No, sir, I guess not. I didn't drop the MOAB, so it's not that."

"It's a bigger mess than I'd have bet on. Not only did the UN refuse to condemn the Venezuelans and Chinese, but now we're the bad guys. The Security Council passed a resolution labeling us the aggressor—and can you believe we abstained in the vote? You see the latest on the casualties? At least five thousand civilians are dead in Havana, and God knows how many have been killed in the water. It's full of smashed boats, small planes, and bodies. The Cubans, of course, are denying they bombed and strafed anybody in small boats. And later today our UN ambassador will show the sat photos we have of Cuban aircraft and patrol boats murdering all those people.

"But nobody is interested in the facts. We've taken out the Venezuelan forces, blown down the Cuban air force, saved lives, and restored order, and we're being blamed for all the deaths."

"So what's our next move?"

"Nothing, yet, as least as far as you're concerned. Havana is pretty stable, and some of the old political prisoners, at least the ones we found alive, are trying to form a government now with locals and some of the guys from Miami. Stand down, but stand ready. I'll probably put you on a two-hour standby tomorrow. And don't get too far from that cell phone, Colonel."

Caracas
18 August
1500 Hours Local

Hugo Chavez was very pleased with himself. General Xin had finally come through with the contracts. He had it in writing. All the oil shipments to America were about to stop, suddenly. And the oil would go to China, at a higher price than America had been paying. He was going to take revenge on the Americans and do what he'd promised to do for years. Oil was a weapon, and for more than thirty years the Americans had known this and not done anything to protect themselves from it.

He smiled to himself and reached for the water carafe. It was the lime-flavored water he liked, specially prepared for him every day. He drank quarts of it. It was healthy and delicious. Almost as delicious as the conversation he had just finished with the last of the OAS members. They, too, had lined up to condemn American intervention in Cuba. The OAS action had gone almost unnoticed. It attracted no great publicity, but the momentum it caused—and the Chinese presence in the former Panama Canal Zone—provided the leverage he needed to get Mexico to join in his oil war.

Mexican president Vicente Fox was furious that the new American president had won her election by running to the right of the Republican candidate on illegal immigration. He was incensed that she had followed that up by actually completing a fence along the California–Mexico border. And he was livid that the United States had intervened in Cuba without consulting him.

Still, he had done nothing to help Chavez until the Chinese made Fox an offer he couldn't refuse: a ten-year guaranteed contract. China would agree to buy 90 percent of Mexico's oil exports at double the current price paid by the United States.

Chavez smiled and leaned back in his chair. With China's help, he had just achieved a Latin American oil boycott of the United States. He would announce the boycott tonight on his own show on Telesur. Thanks to Telesur's partnership with al Jazeera, his speech would reach the whole world. The Americans could read it in their newspapers. At least the *New York Times* would print part of it. The BBC would probably run the whole thing. And tomorrow at the United Nations, his ambassador would issue a formal invitation for other nations to join the boycott.

Langley Air Force Base, Virginia
Air Combat Command Headquarters
28 November
0710 Hours

Matt O'Bannon sat listening as the generals got off the line with the Joint Chiefs and were put through to Southern Command. SOCOM was in charge of running the war plan. It was to be the largest invasion since Iraq, and the mission's ACC units—everything from fighters to bombers to tankers and transport aircraft, even the civilian standby airlift force (CSAF)—were under the control of the SOCOM commander.

With oil at $275 a barrel, the American economy was choking. Chavez's boycott had cut off almost 25 percent of America's oil imports. Middle Eastern suppliers couldn't make up the shortfall. Winter was coming on, and the president couldn't face the prospect of old people dying in cold, dark houses.

The generals were sure their plan would work, but the White House hadn't made it easy. America had often been accused of going to war for oil, but it never had, unless you counted the 1991 Gulf War to free Kuwait. But the UN had authorized that war. This time, the president was alone. She had asked Congress to secretly pass a war resolution, but her request was leaked by a Hill staffer almost immediately. So the generals had had to act fast. Thanksgiving leave was cancelled, and Marines were loading up at Camp Lejeune, North Carolina.

Two whole teams of Navy SEALs—about four hundred men—and Army Special Forces units had already been deployed to Venezuela and were snooping around for real-time intelligence. Virtually every American reconnaissance satellite was focused on the area—and on China.

An unlucky squad of green beanies had been spotted and captured after a bloody gunfight on the outskirts of Caracas, and Venezuela's ambassador at the UN demanded that the American war machine be stopped. The media was in an uproar, the president was dithering, and China was issuing threats.

The ACC deputy commander wasn't cheery when he spoke. "So the Chinese have a small fleet in Caracas. We knew that. We know damned well they have a boomer there. They say they'll use all the forces they have to block an American invasion. Why isn't the president taking this seriously?"

The SOCOM commander breathed a long sigh. "Jimmy, don't ask me questions you know I can't answer. A ballistic missile sub operating off Caracas can stop us in our tracks if the Chinese threaten a missile launch against CONUS, but they're being cagey. They say they will bar any American action against Venezuela but they're both denying the boomer is there and saying they will use their other subs and surface ships to block us."

"Yessir, but we can deal with that sub one way or the other."

"Yes, we can. We have enough attack subs in the area to take out anything they have. But we'd have to get real lucky to catch the boomer. It's the best they have, and thanks to the Walker spy ring, this boomer—and most of their diesel-electrics—are just as quiet as ours. But we're tracking the boomer pretty well. She doesn't have the ELF system our boomers have, so she has to pop a communication buoy up every few hours to talk to Beijing, and sometimes the ship itself pops up to periscope depth or right to the surface, because their O2 system apparently isn't working up to snuff."

"So we'll nail her."

"If we have to. Now listen up. Here's how we're gonna play this."

50,000 Feet over the Golfo de Venezuela
1 December
0310 Hours Local

The autopilot kept them in a slow, lazy racetrack pattern. It was fifty miles around and back, at low speed with nothing to look at but black sky, electronic readouts, and the control panel gauges. Matt O'Bannon was bored stiff until some of his buttons started blinking orange. More fan mail from SOCOM?

Matt and his copilot had drilled for days, arming, checking, and rechecking the special weapon in the bomb bay. With it were fifty MK-62 sea mines. That was less than the full load, but the special weapon took up a lot of space. Other B-2s had sown sea mines all around the approaches to Caracas harbor, bottling up the Chinese subs and Venezuelan navy. Come sunup they were in for several nasty surprises, including the 82nd Airborne Division, which would be dropped inland, eastward of Caracas. The lead elements of the 2nd Marine Division would hit the beach directly north of where the Airborne was landing. The two would link up and drive westward through the Venezuelan capital.

Meanwhile, the president was doing her Hamlet imitation about whether to sink the Chinese boomer or leave it alone. Until she made up her mind, American units were under orders to attack only Venezuelan forces. Just how, precisely, they could keep from hitting the Chinese units close by wasn't explained by the White House. The president's mind kept changing. Matt and his copilot had gotten the "go" code three times in the past five hours, and had it cancelled just as often, usually within seconds of it being given. Now what?

"Okay, boss. SOCOM said go." Matt looked at the small computer screen and pressed the "verify" button. It blinked green, just as it had for his copilot.

"Whaddya wanna bet we get another cancellation?"

"Dunno. How about a bottle of Jack in the Black?"

"You're on. Okay, here we go. I say this time we get the recall before we hit thirty-five thousand feet." The B-2 began a shallow descent. The

Chinese boomer had apparently been bottled up by the sea mines. SOCOM said that it had floated a communications buoy and might be coming to the surface.

"Gimme the readouts as they appear."

The special weapon would detonate at about twenty thousand feet. It was a small, powered glider craft, much like a cruise missile but far larger. It would cruise at that altitude waiting for a coded signal from the B-2. If everything worked as planned, the boomer would be taken out for good.

Forty thousand feet, and no recall. Thirty-five thousand and no signal from home. "Boss, got flash traffic from SOCOM." Matt pulled back gently, stopping their descent.

"No, no, boss. It's not a recall. SOCOM says the boomer is on the surface. Better lucky than smart, huh?"

The big B-2 resumed its descent as the pilots went through their checklists for launch. Everything was green. "Weapon away. Let's get the hell outta here." He pulled back and pushed the throttles to full military power. The B-2 hummed and thrummed and ran away from its former cargo.

Seven minutes later, at precisely twenty thousand feet, the special weapon detonated. Not with the eruption of a nuclear explosion, but with a tremendous burst of electromagnetic energy that fried every printed circuit—every computer, radio, television, and combat system—within its ten-mile range. On the surface of the Golfo de Venezuela, the Chinese boomer captain felt his ship slow and then stop. The nuclear reactor did what its Russian designers had built it to do: it shut itself down, and with it went all power to the ship. Then the lights went out in nearby Maracaibo harbor.

Caracas
6 March 2011

"I have told them that I do not recognize the legitimacy of their court. They will try me tomorrow for what they laughingly call treason against my country and crimes against humanity. I will refute them with my thoughts, my truths, and my destiny. They will not be able to answer what I say. They will do their best, but I am a master of the media and they dare not shut the television cameras out of the courtroom. Among them will be my friends from Telesur. The BBC will be there. So will my friends at al Jazeera. And so I will secure my place in history. No matter that they order my execution. There will be not just my page, but my whole chapter in history. And I will write it today.

"I will compose my opening speech now, and though I may work through the night, I will write a masterpiece that will be the beginning and the end of this unjust trial. And so I begin.

"I, Hugo Chavez, the democratically elected president of Venezuela, need no lawyers. I need no one to say for me things I cannot say myself. I stand before this court not as a defendant, but as the democratically elected leader of this nation. I am a humble man, as I have always been. I am a servant of people who love me as they love their own fathers. In a way, I am their father. Like the great man, Simon Bolivar, after whose example I have modeled my life, I have been a father to a new nation, a new Venezuela, and a new revolution.

"I have developed the wealth and strength of this nation as the great Bolivar himself would have. I do not claim to have never made a mistake. Only a god would never err, and I am no god: I am a man. The men who have brought me here seek to shame me, to claim that I have led our beloved nation and our most precious asset, our people, to war and ruin. You who pretend to sit in judgment of me have no goal other than power. You want to stop our revolution and turn back the clock to the days when our proud nation was a mere colony of the European powers. But you cannot. The revolution, once begun, is irreversible. The people—the people of Venezuela and Cuba—will see to that.

"My great revolution in Venezuela has only just begun. Since I became president, our wealth and influence has grown to be so great, we are no longer a small nation, a weak nation. The great powers of the earth can no longer ignore us. My alliance with Fidel, my greatest friend, was not predicated on bribes. We sent oil to Cuba to help the Cuban economy prosper, and it did. Every nation in the Americas, even the

Yanquis, made no objection to the helping hand of friendship we extended to the Cuban people. The American president, in her inauguration speech, said that Cuba was no danger to America or the world, and that America would restore its economic relations with Cuba. Without our help, Cuba could not have lasted until that moment. Without our oil, it would have been impoverished beyond imagination by the decades-long American trade boycott, and its people would have continued to suffer.

"That friendship brought great benefits to our society. Cuban doctors came and helped make our national health system strong. Cuban military advisers came with them and helped train our million-man militias. When China and Russia offered their help as well, we welcomed them with open arms. The Russians sold us arms for cash, and we bought the rifles and artillery we needed to defend our borders against *Yanqui* imperialism. The Chinese were much more generous. They helped us expand our port at Caracas to handle even more oil tankers and other ships. All they wanted in return was oil, not cash, and it cost us nothing to begin to reduce the oil we sold to the Americans and to increase the shipments to China. China paid more than America, so it profited us to chasten the Americans.

"When the new American president complained about our reducing oil sales to them, I replied, 'How can I do otherwise? Where is the help you provide us? All we have from you is threats against me. When the television preacher said America should kill me, what did you do? Did you silence him? Did you send him to jail, as any civilized nation would have done? No, you let him continue to speak his vile threats and lies.' Against this logic, America had no answer. Our oil exports to China increased, and so did their help to us. When they asked to build a small private port for some of their ships, I immediately agreed. Who would not? And when that port grew, I let the Chinese use it as a port of call for training cruises, because their presence would help protect us against *Yanqui* invasion.

"And then the great tragedy struck. The greatest man I've ever known, the greatest man of the twentieth century, the man who had given me so much wise counsel, the man who helped shape our revolution, Fidel, died suddenly. The anguish of the Cuban people was heart-wrenching. If I can be faulted for anything, I can be faulted only for not anticipating the death of my friend.

"When the legitimate government of Cuba—people who had served Fidel so well, people I know and trust—asked us for help, to prevent the *Yanquis* from invading their country, how could I refuse? It was a great natural disaster, an earthquake that shook Cuba and left it vulnerable to American aggression. When I sent troops and aircraft into Cuba it was an act of mercy. Our brave soldiers helped the Cubans put down the small revolt outside Havana. Many of our men were killed. The situation was desperate. I did what any president would do. I sent reinforcements. But they were thrown back by the imperialist Americans.

"The speed of their attack showed it was planned long before Fidel died. In a matter of hours, their commandos and bombers had rendered our forces confused and battle-weary. When their 82nd Airborne Division arrived before dawn the next morning, our brave commander, General Monteverde, called me to say the situation was hopeless and that he was surrendering. America had proved itself an outlaw nation, but no one, not even I, could see how far they would go to thwart international law and how little respect they had for the community of nations.

"Within hours, our Chinese allies were pleading with me to help them broadcast to the world the truth of this atrocity and to call for justice. All of China was enraged. Their media sent us videos of huge Chinese protests against the Americans. There were millions of people in the streets, demanding that Beijing act to avenge American imperialism. I told Beijing they had to act—and they did. They protested to the Americans, and warned them against taking any action to punish Venezuela for its brave actions to help the Cuban people. The whole world condemned them. And I had to take revenge.

"Oil is our power. As the example of our OPEC friends proved, it immunized us from American action. Look at how many years they stood by while Saudi Arabia sponsored terrorism against them. There was no reason to think they would do otherwise with us. The mere threat of withholding oil, and actually stopping shipments to them for a time, would have to bring them to heel.

"For many years I had warned the Americans against interference in Venezuelan affairs. Long had they plotted invasions and covert actions against us. In answer to these threats I gave them fair warning that I could use oil as a weapon. And this, I decided, was the time to do it. I did not tell the Chinese. I knew they would try to dissuade me. But I acted peacefully and legally to strangle the American menace. Venezuela and all our region would finally be safe from *Yanqui* aggression.

"But then came the great invasion of our precious nation, the destruction of our navy, and even the attack on our Chinese allies off our shores. America will never again be trusted by any of its neighbors.

"You who sit in judgment of me cannot accuse me of treason to my country. I built the power of Venezuela to its most glorious height. China was our ally, and all but the *Yanquis* were our friends. You are the traitors. You who serve the *Yanquis* in this puppet government you call a democracy. I do not submit myself to your judgment. The people of Venezuela love me. And if you hang me, their revenge on you will sweeten the soil of my grave."

CHAPTER FIVE

THE SINO-JAPANESE WAR

> Japan will defend itself and respond to situations in areas surrounding
> Japan, including addressing new threats and diverse contingencies such
> as ballistic missile attacks, attacks by guerrilla and special forces, and
> invasion of remote islands.... U.S. and Japan operations in defense of
> Japan and responses to situations in areas surrounding Japan must be
> consistent so that appropriate responses will be ensured when a situation
> in areas surrounding Japan threatens to develop into an armed attack
> against Japan or when such a situation and an armed attack against
> Japan occur simultaneously.
>
> COMMUNIQUE OF SECURITY CONSULTATIVE COMMITTEE ON U.S.–JAPAN ALLIANCE, OCTOBER 29, 2005

The White House
20 January 2009
1635 Hours

"The *what* islands?" Standing in the Oval Office for the first time as president, the newly inaugurated commander in chief didn't bother to hide
her exasperation. Dorothy Clutterbuck[1] had managed to govern a liberal
state as a sort-of-moderate Democrat, raise considerably more than $200
million in campaign funds, and perform flawlessly in three nationally

televised debates against an unusually flustered opponent. Now the inaugural parades had barely ended, the parties were about to start, and the congratulatory call from the Japanese prime minister had turned awkward. As always, her press secretary was at her side.

The Japanese prime minister spoke with uncharacteristic emotion. "The Senkaku Islands, Madam President. They are near Okinawa off southern Japan. They have rich oil and gas fields. We consider them ours, but China and Taiwan dispute our ownership."

"Mr. Prime Minister, I thank you for bringing this to my attention, but is it really an urgent problem?"

"Yes, Madam President. They are small islands, easily taken, and Chinese and Russian naval forces are exercising close to the Senkakus. They have never done that at the same time before. We fear they have reached a diplomatic and military agreement and will seize them at any moment."

"Thank you, Mr. Prime Minister. I'll give this issue serious consideration and talk with you again in a few days. I appreciate your concern." The president hung up the phone and turned to her two intelligence chiefs—the CIA director and the director of national intelligence. They were temporary holdovers from the previous administration and would be dismissed in a matter of days.

"There's no way the Chinese will start shooting before tonight's inaugural balls," said the president. "In case you gentlemen didn't notice, this is a new administration—and we have no problems with China. I'm sure they'll act responsibly. And until then, I don't want to hear another word about this."

"Madam President," said the CIA chief. "On the contrary, China might see this as a moment of opportunity—a way to test your resolve. Remember the incident when the Chinese forced down the American reconnaissance plane soon after your predecessor was inaugurated?"

"Oh, please. I understand the Chinese and what they want. The previous administration didn't. It's all about triangulating. I danced around John McCain all day and half the night through the damned campaign. We can do the same with the Japs and the Chinese. If you don't think so, just watch me." The president abruptly terminated the meeting. She barked at a Navy lieutenant in dress uniform standing in a corridor. "Hey, you. Go find my hairdresser."

Beijing
Central Military Commission
1 June
1945 Hours Local

The military leaders sat stolidly, shuffling through their papers and reading or scribbling notes. They waited for President Hu Jintao, the man who had launched a Second Great Leap Forward. Hu had chosen not to fight the cultural shift among China's young people. They were dropping Mao's Little Red Book in favor of cell phones and the Internet. Hu had chosen to capture this momentum and turn it to his own purpose, which was to rouse in young Chinese a new sense of fervent nationalism.

Hu took his seat at the head of the conference table and arranged his papers for several minutes before looking up.

"Comrades, we have made much progress in the last two months. Comrade Li, please give us your latest report." The slim man, the second most senior member of the Politburo behind Hu, smiled broadly.

"Comrade President, members of the Central Military Commission, over the past few days the last of the counter-revolutionary leaders in the northern provinces have been captured and executed, and with them all of their families and friends. There will be no more demonstrations against the Party in Shenyang or anywhere else.

"And we have other successes to report. The people are now well aware of how the Peripheral Nations threaten our safety. They resent Malaysian and Indonesian piracy. And they hate Singapore for not ending piracy in the Strait of Malacca, a failure that threatens oil shipments to our country."

Hu interrupted. "Comrade, that is all very good, but it is also entirely beside the point. The problem we face is the Party's lack of credibility.

Unemployment is high and there is—despite what you say, comrade—there is still the misperception that our Party is corrupt. There are still riots and protests, and I tire of crushing them. We can use the people's energy to much better effect. We need to reunite the people around a goal."

The PLA commander stirred. "Comrade President, the Chinese people have always been a proud race. The Party and the people are united to restore China as the hegemon. Unemployment and poverty are nothing to that, to bending the Peripheral Nations to our will."

"Comrade General, you must be mad," blurted another Politburo member. "You are talking about war—endless wars—all over the region."

"No, comrade, I am not. I am saying that if we topple one domino the others will fall of their own accord."

Hu Jintao interrupted. "The point is sound. A lesson, applied to one of the Peripheral Nations with sufficient brutality, may encourage the rest to cooperate—granting us free access to natural resources, physical possession of ports and airfields, and other concessions. But which nation?"

"There are so many that we could easily defeat, Comrade President."

"Yes, yes, yes. But which of them, strong or weak, has the most symbolic value?"

"Japan," said the commanding general of the PLA. "But they are a long distance from our shores, Comrade Hu. To invade—"

"To invade, my dear general, is neither necessary nor advisable. We can conquer from afar. And even if we do not conquer, imagine how our people will react if the Japanese emperor were forced to apologize and then sign a declaration of guilt on one of our ships in Tokyo Bay? Come back to me in three days, comrades, with a detailed plan to humiliate and subjugate Japan."

White House Cabinet Room
25 June
1100 Hours

Damn, thought the old Marine. *I'm the only one in the whole freakin' room who isn't a lawyer.* The chairman of the Joint Chiefs knew this would be a long meeting, but even he couldn't anticipate the fact that after more than two hours, the national security agenda—a whole raft of crises and crises-to-be—would be skipped over. The president obviously wanted to wrap up the meeting, but there were several voices insisting on topics that just had to be discussed. The new secretary of defense sat quietly in his new seat. In previous administrations, the SecDef had sat next to the president. In this one, he'd been moved two seats down in favor of the attorney general and the secretary of Health and Human Services.

"Madam President, may I raise something before we adjourn?"

"Sure, General. You know I always have time for you." Her smile could have frozen the bearings of a tank engine.

"Ma'am, the People's Republic of China"—the president disdained any use of the term "Chinese Communists"—"is a growing danger—"

The secretary of state cut him off.

"Oh, please, General. The PRC is still basking in the goodwill of last year's Olympic Games."

"Yes, sir, but they hosted those games at a huge cost. That's part of their problem. The Olympics pushed China's infrastructure to the breaking point. To deliver electricity, gas, and gasoline to the Olympic venues, the Chinese have starved their populace of energy, and the people feel poorer and more oppressed than before. The Beijing regime knows it has to displace that anger and frustration, and their military modernization plan has given the PRC the means, motive, and opportunity to do it by acting aggressively in Asia."

"Please, General." The president sighed. "We have nothing to fear from the PRC."

"Ma'am, that request from the ASEAN nations[2] for a military exchange mission is still hanging out there. I think we should grant their request—as a gesture that we recognize the Chinese threat and will not abandon our friends in Asia."

President Clutterbuck glared at him over her half-glasses. "China is also our friend in Asia, General. You might have forgotten that China is a major trading partner, a rapidly developing country, and a favorite

destination for American investment. No, General, I am going to deny
that request. There is no need to provoke China. Is that understood?"

"But, ma'am—"

"Not a chance, General. We will cancel the mission."

Beijing
Central Military Commission
1 July
0930 Hours Local

"But what of Japan, comrade?" Hu tilted his head slightly. "Have we
found the Japanese spies yet?"

"No, Comrade President. But we have several of whom we are sus-
picious. There is a group of agriculturalists in Nanchang and a group of
computer scientists working in Guangzhou. Each of them could easily
fall under suspicion of subversive activities. The agriculturalists can be
stirring up counter-revolutionary sentiment among the farmers, and—I
think this may be worse—the computer scientists may be trying to sabotage our national security systems. They could even be in league with
the separationists in Taiwan."

Hu looked around the room. "What is your consensus, comrades?
Shall it be the agriculturalists or the computer scientists?"

One PLA general stirred. "Comrade President, should we not wait to
see what the Japanese prime minister does next week before we make
this choice? He is scheduled to visit the Yakusuni Shrine again. At that
point, we may make a better decision."

"Good. It is settled. We will issue a diplomatic demand that the Japanese prime minister not visit the shrine. We will make it clear that if he does
so, it will be an insult to the Chinese people, and we will say that we cannot guarantee how the people of China will regard this warlike act. And
we will meet again on this subject when the visit is accomplished. Now,
gentlemen, I shall resume the burdens of the paperwork you immerse me
in." Hu stood abruptly, gathered his papers, and walked out.

The White House
Oval Office
6 July
0745 Hours

"Well, good morning, Mr. Prime Minister. And how are you this bright cheery morning? I am sad that you could not join us for our Fourth of July celebration. The fireworks were awesome."

"Ah, I am well, Madam President. But it is a cold, clear evening here. I, too, am sorry I could not attend your celebration, but there is much anxiety in Japan. I wished to speak with you about the Chinese again."

"Well, they're pretty quiet these days. What's the trouble?"

"Madam President, you know our Lantern Festival is about to begin. We call it *obon*, and in these days we honor our ancestors. It is my intention, at the emperor's request, to visit the Yakusuni Shrine again. Every time we do this, the Chinese protest. And this time, the emperor himself will visit the shrine as well."

"So why do it, then? Aren't World War Two war criminals buried there?"

There was a pause before the prime minister said, "Thank you, Madam President, for your concern. We will go nevertheless. The Chinese cannot forbid us to visit a shrine that honors the two and a half million Japanese who died in the war."

"But why provoke them? Why not just skip it for once? And why on earth would the emperor go himself?"

"Madam President, I cannot question the emperor. I shall go because our people demand it. What will you do if they fire missiles over Japan as they have in the past?"

"We will do what we always do: we will protest in the strongest possible terms. But, Mr. Prime Minister, there is no reason to provoke them."

"Please, Madam President. Our *Diet* has asked me to encourage you to sell us more aircraft and strengthen the missile defense batteries President Bush placed here. This is a time of great concern. The Chinese are again threatening our islands. Our people are worried about Chinese aggression. I believe we are sitting on a powder keg."

"Then don't light the match, Mr. Prime Minister."

Yokota Air Base, Japan
Headquarters, 5th Air Force
8 July
0445 Hours Local

"Well, that was about a five on the puckerometer." Lieutenant Colonel Matt O'Bannon let the heavy binoculars rest against his chest. He'd crept out of bed an hour ago, leaving his wife asleep. His squadron deputy stood with him in the parking lot behind their hangar.

"C'mon, boss. Don't wimp out. That's only a two or three, max. And I counted ten. How many'd you get?"

"Nine or ten, Jerry."

The Chinese missiles had passed over Japan in the clear night sky, lit by the bright moon. The Japanese had received a warning that the missiles would be launched at about that time, and when they were, they made quite a show in the sky.

"So what does it mean?"

"Probably not much. They've done this before, but the Japs are always antsy about it. Can't blame 'em. Let's get inside and see what's in the morning traffic." The two walked into the squadron building next to the hangar and sat down at one of the encrypted computers.

"Oh, this is just great, Jerry. The Chinese navy and the Russians are announcing exercises. Guess where."

"Tokyo Bay?"

"Not quite, but close enough. They're doing live-fire drills just southwest of Okinawa. Remember that little string of islands the Japs were telling us about last week?"

"The Sokikus or something like that?"

"Yeah. The Senkakus. That's only one target. Looks like the Chinese are going to go active on the Spratly Islands too. Guess they think now's the time to take the oil fields there."

Beijing
Central Military Commission
8 July
2140 Hours Local

"We have the spies in custody. We are interrogating them now, and we should expect the first confessions tomorrow morning."

Hu Jintao looked pleased. "Do not be in too much of a hurry on the confessions, comrade. Time is our friend for managing the media coverage of the trials. No, the question is: shall we begin the bloodless part of this war?" He looked at an unfamiliar man sitting at the table. He was an admiral of the PLA navy and the commander of Beijing's biggest secret: the cyber-warfare center buried deep in a remote area of Guangdong province, many miles away. He looked uncomfortable sitting among his nation's leaders. "Tell us, Admiral, is everything ready?"

"Yes, Comrade President. We can begin at any time. As you have ordered, we shall first disrupt the Japanese stock exchange. Their computers will be disabled by our viruses. We will send a shock wave through their economy and then through the Western financial world. Hours after they absorb that blow, their entire military communications network will dissolve. Last, and we will reserve this for your special order, their electric power grid can be knocked out. The Japanese nation will cease to function. They will be alone and in the dark."

"Alone?"

"Our anti-satellite weapons will destroy the American and European communication and navigation satellites as soon as you order it. When neither the Americans nor the Europeans can lend theirs to the Japanese, Japan will be defenseless."

"Comrades, it is well that we can do this. We do not intend to conquer Japan by invasion. But if they—or any other nations in our new
Peripheral Zone—resist, it will be only for a moment, and only in a futile
gesture.

"The Americans will dither for many days before they react. This is
something they will not resist in the end. Especially when I tell the
American president we can destroy America's communications and
power grid as well. Return to your headquarters, Admiral, and make
your preparations."

The White House
Oval Office
10 July
0755 Hours

"Wow. Is it really that well orchestrated?"

The president's daily intelligence briefing—the first thing most presidents do after breakfast—was stuck on China. There were crises brew-
ing all over the Middle East and even in Europe, with young Muslims
rioting in France and Spain, but China was the sole topic of conversation. The CIA director leaned forward.

"Yes, it is, Madam President. Every major Chinese city is in an uproar.
There were at least twenty million demonstrators out in the streets yesterday. Even a lot of smaller towns and villages were the scenes of anti-
Japanese demonstrations, some turning violent. The PLA has organized
these demonstrations, but even they seem to have underestimated the
anti-Japanese sentiment.

"The Chinese are demanding that Japan withdraw from the Senkaku
Islands. The Chinese call them the Diaoyu Islands. They're uninhabited,
but the seabed around them probably sits on top of one of the richest
undrilled oil and gas fields in the world. On top of that, Hu Jintao himself was on television demanding the Japs apologize for everything from
the Rape of Nanking to the Kennedy assassination. It's just nuts."

"So where are they going on this?" asked the president.

The CIA chief said, "We know they're aiming to seize Japan's oil and gas claims—"

The national intelligence director cut in. "We don't know any such damned thing. We can see how they can—"

"That's absurd. We know the Chinese are threatening missile strikes on Japan and the Japanese are about to wet their pants—"

"Oh, please, the Japanese are fine. They've mobilized their navy and air forces—"

"Which don't amount to speed bumps for the Chinese—"

The president raised her hand, and both men were silenced. "Okay, what you're telling me is that we don't know jack about what the Chinese are gonna do. Right? And we don't have a dog in this fight about those crappy little islands, right? So what we're gonna do is watch and wait, right?"

A low voice rumbled from the back of the room. "Ma'am, if I may?" All eyes turned to the deputy national security adviser. Even in civilian clothes, the active-duty Marine three-star always managed to grab attention with his deep western drawl. His voice commanded respect and attention, even from those who disliked him, which was pretty much everyone in the room. Especially the president.

"Go ahead, General Hunter."

"Ma'am, I think we'd do well to get ourselves in a position to know more about what the Chinese are doing, and we have to get some of our people into some odd places to do it. We can track the Senkakus with satellite ops because there's nothing on 'em yet, but other places, like the Spratlys, the Chinese have been building something for two years."

"Now that's the first sensible thing I've heard this morning. Get the secretary of defense on the phone for me."

"Ma'am, he's waiting in the Roosevelt Room with the rest of the cabinet."

"Oh, right. Of course. Let's go."

Spratly Islands, between the Indian and Pacific Oceans near Taiwan
Mischief Reef
24 July
0340 Hours Local

"Damn it, come in." Navy SEAL commander Cully O'Bannon was losing patience with a couple of his people. Two members of Golf platoon of the Green Team were fifteen minutes overdue for the rendezvous, and with any other two SEALs, that could only mean trouble. With these two, it could be anything. Down on one knee on the edge of the beach, he pushed the TALK button on the scrambled radio again. "Heckle and Jeckle, where the hell are you?"

"Right behind you, sir." Two black and green faces emerged from the brush. Heckle and Jeckle—Gunners' Mate Master Chief Al Parker and his hyperactive sidekick, Senior Chief Dale Quincannon—were where they were supposed to be, smiling as usual. The former, the SEALs' martial arts expert, had the build of a linebacker. The latter, their chief scout-sniper instructor, was a smaller version of his pal. Cully could barely make them out, dressed in their ghillie suits, even in the still-bright moonlight. Inseparable and totally (well, almost totally) reliable, the two were the worst practical jokers in the Navy. Training with them was a hilarious misery. "You two are gonna be the death of me yet. What's the scoop on the big buildings?"

Parker spoke. "Well, boss, surprise, surprise: the CIA got it wrong. The Chicoms aren't building a resort hotel for fishermen. Looks to us like a big barracks, some sort of headquarters building, a training area for PT, and a helluva collection of elint gear and anti-aircraft weapons. We saw three batteries of double-digit SAMs and five or six light armored vehicles."

"Okay, get ready to extract. The sub will be here in about twenty minutes, so we need to be in the water in five. I'll report this in right now." Cully turned to the satellite radio set up behind him. "No contact, right? You got in and out, clean?"

"Well, uh, almost." Quincannon ducked back into the heavy brush and came back carrying a Chinese officer slung over his shoulder. The man was so bound and gagged in black duct tape that he looked like a mummy. "This guy was awake enough to look when we came up to one of the SAM batteries. We thought we'd be better off bringing him along than leaving a body for someone to find." Quincannon affected a sad puppy-dog face. "Can't we take him home with us, boss?"

"That's the worst idea I've heard since the last time you had one. Okay, where's the doc?" O'Bannon looked at the prisoner. His eyes betrayed only fear, not any understanding of what was being said. The platoon medic knelt next to Cully.

"Doc, you have those syringes of Versed?"

"Sure do, boss."

"Well, check this guy out. If he's okay, give him a dose and a half. He'll wake up in a coupla hours wondering how the hell he got here." Versed, Cully knew, wasn't just a tranquilizer. A large dose induced short-term memory loss. The man would be fuzzy-headed for about two hours and would never be quite sure about his memories of that night. And, for the second time that year, Cully wouldn't have to court-martial Heckle and Jeckle.

The White House
Oval Office
26 July
0755 Hours

"Mr. Prime Minister, you have put me in a very awkward position with the Chinese. Why did you so unnecessarily provoke them?"

"It was not a provocation at all, far less an unnecessary one, Madam President. It was my duty to visit the shrine and lay the chrysanthemum blossom by the memorial. The Chinese reaction is an outrage and an insult to my nation. This idea of putting Japanese citizens on public trial for spying is an insult to every Japanese, living and dead."

"Please, Mr. Prime Minister. Everyone knows that nations spy on each other. Why not try to defuse this crisis by simply admitting it and arranging an apology and getting them released?

"But they were not spies, Madam President."

"Why are they putting them on trial then?"

"Madam President, these men are computer scientists and technicians. Why would they be spying on China? There is nothing the Chinese have that we want."

"I spoke to Hu Jintao yesterday. He assured me that these men would get a fair trial. He was very worried, though, about how worked up his people are about Japanese aggression. And that visit you made to the Yakusuni Shrine really got them going. Why on earth did you lay a knife blade beside the flower you placed at the foot of the shrine? Hu Jintao said that was an act of war."

"It was a traditional tribute to our war dead. I hope you can understand. There is nationalism here, as well as in China. The knife blade is a sign of strength, not warlike intent. It is the historical companion to the chrysanthemum. We are a Buddhist nation, and the Shinto religion is stronger now than at any time since World War Two.

"Madam President, we cannot let the Chinese casually threaten us. Our people do not like the idea of war, but the Chinese are now powerful enough to invade Japan, and they could use nuclear weapons. That is why we must obtain a ballistic missile defense immediately. China has nothing to fear from us. And it is outrageous for them to dictate how we remember our dead. It is even more serious when they deny that we have legitimate economic claims and interests in Asia. We cannot allow our economy and trade to be held hostage by a foreign power."

"Well, Mr. Prime Minister, maybe they don't see it that way."

"Madam President, you know Japan is a peaceful nation. We have learned every lesson that World War Two taught us. But we must look to our defenses. The *Diet* has doubled our defense budget to meet the Chinese threat. We have arranged to purchase a number of F-15 and F-16 aircraft from Israel and three submarines from Australia. Both need your permission to sell them to us. Can we be sure you will consent?"

"Yes, of course. But Patriot anti-missile batteries and Aegis anti-missile destroyers are another thing entirely."

"Please, Madam President, we have had Chinese missiles fired over us three times in the past year. I beg you to reconsider selling us an adequate missile defense, and doing so now."

"I can discuss that with our congressional leaders, Mr. Prime Minister, but I'll promise nothing. I've been told it would take us years to build the destroyers and that we have very few anti-missile batteries ourselves."

Beijing
Central Military Commission
29 July
2130 Hours Local

The Politburo member in charge of the Japanese spy case was bubbling, "Comrade President, the proceedings today were a success."

"It was only a small step," Hu Jintao replied, putting his smirky subordinate in his place. "We will not know how well you have done until we hear from the Western media, especially the *New York Times*." Hu turned to a PLA admiral. "I expect that within a day of the end of the trial, you will be able to act?"

"Yes, Comrade President. We can destroy the Japanese air traffic control system, stock market, and government computer systems at your order."

"I think, comrade, we have erred somewhat in our planning. To make the point of humiliating Japan, we need to do more than break computers. We need to spill blood. Not a lot, but enough."

"How much is enough, Comrade President?"

"We shall know when we have done it. For now, Admiral, I want you to seize the Diaoyu Islands. Establish a base there and begin building oil platforms around those islands."

The Politburo prosecutor asked, "And how shall the trial end, Comrade President?"

"It will end in convictions. We will spare one Japanese and return him to Japan. A death sentence will be pronounced for the rest. The Japanese prime minister must be punished too." Hu turned to another Politburo member. "Can we increase our shipments to Comrade Kim Jung Il?"

"By at least 10 percent, Comrade President."

"Good. Tell Comrade Kim we shall do so, and in return he will condemn Japan's continued aggression against his nation. He will put all of his forces on alert and move them closer to the border of South Korea."

The White House
2 August
0940 Hours

The National Security Council members sat silently, listening to one side of the conversation. "Mr. Prime Minister, we cannot do more than we have. Our protest has been lodged with the Beijing ambassador. I am meeting him later today."

The Japanese prime minister calmed himself before speaking. "Madam President, executions of Japanese citizens are about to occur. You must do more than just protest."

"Like what, Mr. Prime Minister? Your navy is provoking the Chinese at this very moment. I know you have claimed the Senkaku Islands for decades, but this naval maneuver you are conducting is just another provocation. And what's more, do you have any idea how this is destabilizing the whole region? North Korea is mobilizing its troops and missile forces. Are you mad? Your needless provocations have created an international crisis."

"I know very well the effect of this crisis, Madam President. I have spoken with the president of Taiwan. He too is worried about Chinese aggression. He is worried about Chinese retaliation even if we—not they—defend the islands."

"Well, I know all about Taiwan, Mr. Prime Minister. They are desperate to stay out of any war, and you should be as well. I will confide in you. The North Korean ambassador has given us an advance copy of a speech Kim Jung Il will deliver later today. He threatens to attack your country if you act provocatively in the East China Sea, and calls on us to restrain you. The man is erratic. He could launch nuclear missiles at Japan. So I repeat, are you mad?"

"Madam President, Japan knows the danger of nuclear weapons better than any nation. You forget, I was born near Nagasaki. But the Chinese are about to kill innocent Japanese, and are about to invade our territory. Will America just stand by and let them do this?"

"Mr. Prime Minister, we are not about to go to war over a couple of uninhabited islands and Chinese spy trials. That is an internal matter between Japan and China." Clutterbuck hung up the phone. After a glaring pause, she said, "Well, ladies and gentlemen, how do we defuse this damn crisis? The UN Security Council, I suppose?"

The secretary of state said, "Madam President, we must do exactly that. Perhaps we can mediate a settlement."

"But Madam President," said the defense secretary, "we have a security treaty with Japan. If the Chinese seize the Senkakus, that could trigger our obligations under it. And there's something else: we still occupy parts of the Ryukyu Islands—and the Senkakus are part of them. Any attack there would literally be an attack on us."

"Which is why we should withdraw from the Ryukyu Islands. We are not—and I repeat *not*—going to war over a couple of crappy little islands, no matter how much oil is under them. This meeting is adjourned."

The president turned to her press secretary. "Gina, I want polling data on this—and I want it now."

The White House
Oval Office
3 August
1755 Hours

Chinese cruise missiles were striking Japan, and Chinese and Japanese naval forces were fighting near the Senkaku Islands.

President Clutterbuck was sympathetic, understanding, and immovable. "Mr. Prime Minister, I know it must be a severe blow to you, but there are very few casualties."

"Madam President, the cruise missiles hitting our homeland are carefully aimed. The Yakusuni Shrine is completely destroyed. There was a very large worship service there. Hundreds of civilians are dead. Our navy has suffered enormous losses. Are you going to help defend Japan or is America's treaty with us worthless?"

"Mr. Prime Minister, I am well aware of our obligations to your country. But now, this whole incident is your fault, isn't it? Didn't I tell you not to visit the shrine and provoke the Chinese? The Chinese have warned us that they will not tolerate our intervention, and I'll be damned, Mr. Prime Minister, if I'm going to let you bully me into a war with China."

"Madam President, this *is* a war. The Chinese are attacking us at this very moment, and not just with bullets and bombs. We have suffered a massive cyber-attack. Our air traffic control system, our stock exchange, and many of our other electronic systems have been sabotaged. Our economy could collapse—and militarily we will be helpless to repel any Chinese attack if they do the same to our defense systems. They demand our surrender. This *is* a war, I tell you."

"Mr. Prime Minister, we are doing what we can in the United Nations. We must all rely on the UN."

Beijing
Central Military Commission
10 August
2010 Hours Local

"So, Comrade President, it appears the Japanese are still not willing to surrender. We have brought their economy to a halt, and their government has fallen. But they are still willing to fight."

Hu Jintao frowned. "And what are the Americans waiting for? The Japanese invoked the security treaty weeks ago, and they have done nothing but talk."

The PLA admiral held out his open hands. "Comrade President, that is a mystery, yet it is only what you predicted. But when we attack Okinawa, they will suffer great losses."

"Wait, comrade. Is it entirely wise? Why not wait? Now that Comrade Kim has invaded South Korea, the Americans have a war of their own. We do not need to kill the Americans on Okinawa. The Japanese cannot recover from the damage we have inflicted."

"No, they cannot, but the Japanese are a stubborn people, Comrade President."

"What reports do we have from Korea?"

"The fighting is intense there. And the Americans are moving reinforcements from their homeland."

"So you think now is the time to attack—while they are distracted?"

"Yes, Comrade President."

"Then you must attack as planned. But be sure of what you do. The Americans have substantial forces in Japan and they must be dealt a decisive blow or even this president will have to act."

Yokota Air Base
11 August
0410 Hours Local

"Get the hell outta here, right frigging now." Matt O'Bannon stood by the big door of his squadron's hangar as his crews dashed out to their aircraft. He pushed the last man through and ran a half step behind him, turning to his own aircraft. In less than three minutes, his B-2 was racing down the taxiway, following the other three stealth bombers onto the runway and then into the sky to join up with their covering force of F-15s.

As the big bomber climbed through ten thousand feet, he keyed the intercom. "Jerry, signal Colonel Atkins and see if everyone is cleared."

His copilot, sitting on the other side of the cockpit, communicated with the mission commander by blinker light. The commander's fighter was tight alongside. "Yup, everybody is up and out. On course and schedule, boss. The fighters are clearing away, leaving us with a clean RCS. Just another calm morning at the office."

"Yeah, Jerry. Calm as the loony bin before the Prozac gets handed out. Thank God the COB gave us the go when he did." Somehow, the COB knew the other side's moves before they did. Looking at the satellite photos of all the action at sea and the approaching Chinese armada, he'd had a hunch and ordered the emergency evacuation.

O'Bannon's copilot sat forward, ticking off items on his checklist. "So, boss, what the hell, over? We have the entire 5th Air Force blasting off and—uh, oh—hold on. Flash traffic coming in. The Chicoms have launched a crapload of cruise missiles, and they're headed right for Okinawa. More coming in. And there's a pile of Chicom fighters and bombers headed there at this minute." They both looked sharply up as several squadrons of F-15s and F-16s flashed overhead. The big bomber rocked and shook from the sonic booms they left in their wake.

"Sir, more from PACOM. COB wants to know our combat status. I just told him we have a standard load of Tomahawks, and nothing else. We're good for several hours before we have to tank."

"Okay, so what's our orders?" Anticipating what he would hear, O'Bannon began a slow turn, the other three B-2s following. Okinawa had thousands of Marines who were probably going to die in a few minutes. Maybe the Tomahawks could do some good against the Chinese ships approaching Japan. Maybe they could save some of those Marines.

White House Cabinet Room
23 September
1120 Hours

"Madam President? Please?"

The president hadn't recovered from the shock of the first attacks. Thank heaven she could take credit for getting the Air Force off the ground in Japan and into the fight. Japanese and American forces had lost a lot of aircraft, but the Chinese invasion of Okinawa was turned back.

She read hourly polls now. Her job approval rating plummeted as the casualty lists grew at a horrifying pace. Generals were impatient, demanding decisions. She suspected her vice president was leaking to the press to cover his own ass. There were critics everywhere, even though she had only tried to keep the peace.

A telephone call from the NORAD commander interrupted her stream of thoughts. "Madam President? I have to confirm to you and the secretary of defense that a nuclear weapon has just detonated in Osaka, Japan. We tracked the launch from North Korea. There's no doubt where it came from. We estimate the size of the explosion as ten megatons. It's vaporized the whole city, ma'am."

"Oh my God, how could they do this?" She hung up the phone and simply screamed—until she noticed a tall man sliding into the Oval Office.

"Madam President?"

"What the hell do you want, General? Do you realize the North Koreans have just nuked Osaka?"

The tall man was the deputy national security adviser. An active-duty Marine, he was wearing his uniform, and she noticed, for the first time, the rows of ribbons that started at his breast pocket and climbed nearly to his shoulder. In his soft western drawl, he said, "That's what I'm here about, ma'am."

"The Japanese are going to surrender tomorrow. You know that?"

"No, ma'am, I didn't know that, but I don't think we're done. Everybody is here, ma'am. The Joint Chiefs, the SecDef, State, everybody on the National Security Council. I know you admire FDR, ma'am. Whaddya think he'd do in this situation? How about I get you a cup of coffee, and let's walk across the hall together."

The president dragged herself up from the big chair. "Okay, Jim. You're on."

Challenger Deep, Western Pacific Ocean
Aboard USS *Alabama*, SSBN 731
Depth 1,100 Feet
24 September
0110 Hours Local

The poker game was winding down, and there was nothing left to do but sleep. Cully folded his cards and stood up to stretch. Then the battle stations alarm went off. "All hands, general quarters. Battle stations, missiles. All hands, rig for launch."

Heckle and Jeckle looked at Cully. Quincannon said, "What the hell, boss?"

"Dunno. I'm going up to CIC. You guys get the platoon squared away, everything secured." He darted out of the room as he felt the submarine rise steeply. In the combat center, the sub's captain had the most intense frown Cully had ever seen.

"Curious, Mr. O'Bannon? Well, stand the hell back and watch the show."

"What's up, sir?"

"Oh, not much. Just that the North Koreans nuked Japan yesterday, and we're gonna return the favor."

Cully watched, awestruck for the first time in his adult life. The crew went through their drill with a lot of "I can't believe this is happening" glances among them. The Trident D-5 ballistic missile had been in the U.S. arsenal for decades. Its huge booster could shoot the six nuclear weapons it carried over four thousand miles. This would be the first time a Trident was fired in anger.

"Depth 500, slow rise. XO, reconfirm orders."

"Sir, reconfirming again. One D-5 to be launched immediately. Targets are: one, Yongbyon, coordinates entered and confirmed. Airburst at ten thousand feet. Two, Pyongyang, coordinates entered and confirmed. Airburst at ten thousand feet. Four other warheads set on safe and will not detonate on impact."

"All right, XO. Proceed."

A minute later, Cully felt the rumble as the missile left its tube.

Above the Indian Ocean
40,000 Feet
30 September
0515 Hours Local

They'd been flying for four hours in silence, thinking how small their two-ship formation must look. It was all that was left of two squadrons. Six of them—twelve men and almost one-third of the B-2s in the Air Force—had been lost. Two were salvageable, damaged in runway accidents on Guam and back in the States. The others were just gone. "About another two hours to Diego, boss."

Matt O'Bannon checked his copilot's calculation. "Yup, about two-ten, Jerry. Hope you're gonna like our new home."

"Oh, yeah. It's gonna be great. Five thousand miles from the nearest decent bar, crappy Internet service, and an O-club that only serves frozen food. I can hardly friggin' wait."

"Yeah, I know. I wonder how our new president is gonna do in the peace talks."

"Who knows? Has to be better than Clutterbuck did during the war. I was kinda surprised when she quit, but the new guy sounds okay."

"Well, last I got before takeoff was that the cease-fire was holding. The North Koreans are gone, though. Just gone. Maybe the Chinese will take them over."

"Yeah, that seems pretty likely. They can put some puppet in charge there, and now that the Japanese surrendered those islands, maybe they can get along with China for a while. But what can they do? One of their biggest cities was vaporized, we've had to abandon all our bases in

Japan, and they don't need to take out the Koreans since we did it for them."

"Maybe, but I'm betting more is gonna happen there."

"Like what?"

"Like the Japanese are not going to do what they did after World War Two. They're not going to disarm and trust us to defend them—now that we didn't do it when it counted. Look at their history, Jerry. I'm betting the Japs are going to rearm big time."

"You mean nukes?"

"And then some, Jerry. They're as mad at us as they are at the Chinese. Who do you think they're gonna be mad at ten years from now? The Chinese—who started a war with them—or us, the guys who didn't prevent Osaka from getting nuked? They're going to have those nukes pointed both ways."

"Huh. Guess we're lucky to be able to land in Diego."

"Yeah. I think the Chinese can do whatever they damned well please in the whole western Pacific now. And we ain't gonna be welcome there for a long time."

"Ain't our fault."

"Fault doesn't matter—winning and losing does. We lost everything we had in Japan. We only have a token force left in South Korea, and we'll have to yank that out in a year or so. China rules the region now, and there's nothing to stand in their way."

CHAPTER SIX

WORLD WAR OIL

An unprecedented need for resources is now driving China's foreign policy. A booming domestic economy, rapid urbanization, increased export processing, and the Chinese people's voracious appetite for cars are increasing the country's demand for oil and natural gas, industrial and construction materials, foreign capital and technology. Twenty years ago, China was East Asia's largest oil exporter. Now it is the world's second-largest importer; last year, it alone accounted for 31 percent of global growth in oil demand.... Although China's new energy demands need not be a source of serious conflict with the West in the long term, at the moment, Beijing and Washington feel especially uneasy about the situation. While China struggles to manage its growing pains, the United States, as the world's hegemon, must somehow make room for the rising giant; otherwise, war will become a serious possibility.

DAVID ZWEIG AND BI JIANHAI, "CHINA'S GLOBAL HUNT FOR ENERGY"[1]

Beijing
Central Military Commission
27 March 2013
1110 Hours Local

Hu Jintao was tired of pointless arguments. "General, you have failed us again. All I hear from you is that there are riots spreading in Guangdong, in Jiangxi, and in Hunan. You come here day upon day, week upon week, and tell me the riots are spreading. Why have you not stopped them?" The PLA general in charge of internal security looked down at his shoes.

"President Hu, we have done much, but the news spreads faster than we can take action to stop it. No matter where a disturbance occurs, word gets out over the cellular telephones. And the Internet is spreading word from city to city, and village to village."

"Did I not tell you to do what was done in Tibet? Did I not tell you to put these disturbances down, no matter how you may need to? It is of no concern to us if you have to kill one thousand people or one million. I want these riots stopped now. Do you understand? And if you need to jam all the cellular telephones and block all the Internet connections in a whole province for a month to do it, you must do so. Do I need to tell you anything else?"

"No, sir."

"Now, let us talk about oil. We have shortages all across our land. Industrial production is falling, and this unrest is part of the result. We will solve this by executing the agreement we made with Venezuela to end oil shipments to America. But that will take time. I have also asked our friends in Sudan and Nigeria to do the same, but they are more reluctant." Hu looked at a member of the Politburo seated to his left. "What other options do you see?"

"I think, Comrade President, that we can do more with the Saudis. They are amenable to increasing production, but that will take years, and they demand billions of dollars from us to help finance the expansion. Iran is also very amenable to helping us. But until their new port facility opens, they too are unable to increase production. I have talked to President Ahmadinejad, and he is seeking other ways to help us. But that, too, will take time."

Hu looked pleased. "We have time, comrades. Let us use it wisely. And put those disturbances down, General. I do not wish to hear more about them."

Tehran Airport, Iran
2 April
1200 Hours Local

"It is well, my friend, that we understand each other so completely. And I thank you for your openness and your agreement on our plans." With that, Hugo Chavez pushed himself out the door of the limousine and trotted up the stairs of the waiting Airbus A-320 for the trip home to Caracas. At the top of the stairs, he turned and waved to the slim face of Mahmoud Ahmadinejad, who smiled back from inside the car. Ahmadinejad ordered the car back to Tehran.

"What do you think, Ahmed?" the Iranian president asked the man beside him.

"Sir, I think the man is an idiot. He believes we have an understanding that will allow him to have a small nuclear arsenal within a year. He believes we will protect him with our nuclear weapons until he can protect himself. And he believes he is controlling our relationship with Beijing. A more complete fool I cannot imagine."

"But he is a useful fool, Ahmed. Didn't Lenin say those capitalists who praised him were useful idiots? Chavez is the same. His arrogance blinds him. Now I will talk with Hu Jintao. Call him on the secure cell phone. When the French sold us that system, I was skeptical that it even worked."

"But surely they sold it to us to make us think it was secure when it was not?"

"It was not. But the Chinese engineers made it Paris-proof for us. And I am sure that they made it so that Beijing can eavesdrop. And that is why I use it only to call my dear friend, Mr. Hu."

"Is he just another useful fool?"

"No. Hu Jintao is a valuable ally."

"But the Chinese are not even People of the Book."

"He will never walk the path of the Prophet, Ahmed, but we can benefit much from this alliance if we remain wary. Get him for me. It is only late afternoon in Beijing. He will still be in his office."

Nellis Air Force Base, Nevada
Paradise Ranch
7 July
0700 Hours

"You gotta be freakin' kidding me! *Sir*." Colonel Matt O'Bannon was speaking through clenched teeth. "This is the fourth reduction in flying hours in as many months. My guys are getting pretty rusty, and I'm not gonna be able to keep them sharp unless they get some stick and throttle time soon. You know how pilots are."

"Cool your jets, O'Bannon." The deputy commander of Air Combat Command sounded so cheery, it was simply nauseating. "SWMBO says we all have to reduce our fuel consumption to help with the oil crisis." SWMBO—She Who Must Be Obeyed—was the military's not-so-loving code word for the second-term president. There were more derisive terms used around the officers' club bars, and still worse ones used among the senior sergeants. Unfortunately, they were all accurate. This was the president who had ordered American troops home from Iraq, and then refused to send them back in as the nascent democracy began to fall apart. The whole Middle East was in flames. What had been Iraq was now three smoldering mini-states. Turkey had invaded northern Iraq after the Kurdish north (which extended itself into eastern Turkey) declared its independence. The small Sunni principality in the middle had asked Saudi Arabia for help, but got Syrian troops instead. And the Israelis were getting more nervous by the day.

"You know the situation just as well as I do. We've had to cut into the strategic petroleum reserve and her poll numbers are falling almost as fast as the level of oil in the SPR. We just got the word from Caspar the Unfriendly Ghost. We cut flying hours or the airlines do. Until someone cuts the cojones off Hugo Chavez and gets the Venezuelan oil back, we're all screwed." Caspar Blenheim, the secretary of defense, rarely appeared outside his Pentagon office. He preferred brief phone calls with the brass—calls that almost invariably reversed his decisions of the day before and kept the Pentagon in perpetual turmoil. After he missed three consecutive sessions with the Joint Chiefs, the nickname "Caspar the Unfriendly Ghost" gained wide currency.

"I do have some good news. You may not get a lot of jet fuel, but there's some I cut loose just for your new command."

"What new command, sir?"

"Yeah, well, as of about an hour ago, you're commander of the 495th Combined Air Wing. And don't look for it on any organization charts, or anywhere else, 'cause it ain't there. And 'combined' in this case means that you get only stealth aircraft: B-2s, F-117s, and F-22s. You have more hours flying stealth than anyone in the Air Force, and that's why you're the guy for this job. You've been flying with the Raptors and the Nighthawks for quite a while. As of now, Matt, you and all your boys are back in the black. Everything you do is classified, and you report directly to me when you're not assigned to a combatant command. Get checked out in F-22s and Nighthawks ASAP."

"But how can I get checked out in everything if we don't have gas to fly?"

"Look, colonel. This oil shortage is making the 1973 oil crisis look tame. Now—and you're not supposed to know any of this—the Saudis have cut us back too. The whole damned country is gonna be slowed down, and the strategic petroleum reserve is gonna be out of oil in about another four or five weeks. This is going critical. And your job is to get the new force online and ready with or without gas. I'm gonna squeeze every drop I can get for your unit, but burn it wisely, O'Bannon. Get that force online, and do it in the next two weeks."

"Sir, how much more are we gonna have to do with so much less?"

"I don't know, O'Bannon. You and I both know damned well that we can only do less with less. Now the Chiefs have to convince the president. Be on the horn in the secure conference room in thirty minutes. We have too much crap goin' on right now. And I'm damned well not gonna be caught without options if the whole thing comes apart."

Beijing
Presidential Offices
23 September
1700 Hours Local

Hu Jintao was getting used to the mild manner of the former terrorist. Mahmoud Ahmadinejad had been one of the hostage-takers in the assault on the American embassy in Tehran in 1979. Physically small, Ahmadinejad overcompensated for his stature with a burning messianic fervor. The man had not mellowed, but he had learned. If nothing else, the Iranian leader was a quick study.

"It is a pleasure to greet you on the eve of Ramadan, my dear friend. I will soon go back to prayers, but I wished to speak with you about the old fool Abdullah. He calls himself the keeper of the two Holy Mosques, but he does not keep them safe from infidels. Europeans and Americans are still in every place in Saudi Arabia but Mecca and Medina themselves. And now, with your people there, my leaders are growing restive."

"You cannot assure them with our secret agreements? We have combined to reduce the flow of oil to America and their economy is starving. They are down to less than five million barrels a day. Their people are growing uneasy, their economy is falling apart, and their president— for all her bluster—has come to Abdullah, hat in hand, to beg." Hu Jintao sounded pleased.

"But your people are not of the Faith, my friend. You have ten thousand engineers and laborers now in the Saudi port cities. They replace some of the Europeans and Americans. We trade one set of infidels for another."

"But you should remind your people of our guarantees. We will, once the Americans starve, proclaim every Islamic nation our friend, under the protection of our nuclear forces. We share your desire to restore the caliphate in all the holy lands. And if you wish to move into Europe, what is it to us? All we ask is that we buy your oil in as great a quantity as you can sell it. Our thirst for it grows every day."

"It is a quandary we face. You wish to buy our oil, and we wish to sell it to you. But we cannot allow the defacing of our most holy lands by the presence of any infidels. And how can you buy it when so much of your money comes from the Americans? If their economy collapses, so does yours."

"Do not think that, my friend. We have built our economy more wisely than you know. We do not depend on the Americans to buy our products. There are so many nations that buy from us, we can well afford a diminution of American trade."

"I believe you, my friend. But some do not. And their haste to free the most holy sites in Islam from the infidels and those who befriend them grows greater by the day."

"Please do what you can, my dear friend. It would not benefit either of us for them to be too impatient."

Outside Riyadh, Saudi Arabia
2 November
0710 Hours Local

"Your men are gifted teachers, Captain," said the Saudi colonel, smiling broadly. Changing the barrel of a .50-caliber machine gun had taken his men almost half an hour. The task wasn't complicated, but if the threaded barrel wasn't spaced precisely to the breach, the gun either wouldn't fire or would blow up in the face of the man firing it. The U.S. Navy SEALs had shown the Saudis how to do it as they did, in less than a minute.

Navy captain Cully O'Bannon watched his SEAL platoon training the Saudi anti-terrorist forces. The Arabs seemed eager to learn, but none of the SEALs thought they would be worth much in a fight. The young Saudis always seemed more eager to get off the training range and back to relaxing in air-conditioned comfort.

"Yeah, too bad we can't do more. But orders are we're packing up."

"I understand. Your nation's financial crisis makes it necessary."

O'Bannon shrugged. "I've never had much money, Colonel, so the stock market crash didn't hurt me, but it obviously hurt a lot of other people. And with the oil crisis, the economy's on the fritz."

"I'm sure, Captain O'Bannon, that when your president arrives tomorrow, King Abdullah will do everything he can to help."

Ten Miles off Ras Tannurah, Saudi Arabia
Aboard USS *Harry S. Truman*, CVN 75
12 November
0110 Hours Local

The captain of the *Truman* turned to his XO. "Okay, Jimmy. You have the con. Those SEALs should be coming aboard any minute. We gotta get outta Dodge and back to Italy for a couple days of shore leave, and that can't happen soon enough to suit me. Let the admiral know when we're hightailing it."

"Yessir," replied the XO. The captain turned and began half-sliding and half-bouncing down the steep stairs to his cabin. He was only two decks down when he heard the alarms ringing through the ship. "General quarters. All hands, man your battle stations. Condition One." He flew back up to the bridge.

"What the hell, Jimmy?"

"Skipper, we have the two SEAL helos coming in, but radar picked up two small craft approaching at high speed. They don't answer our hails."

"Okay, make flank speed and weapons free on the Sea Whiz." The "Sea Whiz"—really "CIWS," the close-in weapons system—was a 20 mm Gatling gun that shot a stream of radar-guided lead at its target. "And wave off the helos, unless they're bingo fuel."

Three miles away, Cully O'Bannon looked out the side of the Super Stallion heavy helo. He saw one of the suspected terrorist boats battering through the waves and alerted the pilot. Cully waved at Master Chief Romeo Wilson and Lieutenant Vinny Chung to lean over and listen up.

"That M-19 on the sidemount. Find some ammo for it, and you get on it, Vinny. Get helmets and headsets, both of you."

It looked like a big machine gun, but the M-19 could fire 40 mm grenades over a thousand meters. Wilson threw a belt of ammunition onto it, and Chung stood by the weapon, one hand on the left grip and one on the charging handle. A few years older than the usual junior grade lieutenant, Vinny Chung was not the typical anything. He was a Chinese-Italian-American, with a master's degree in electrical engineering and fluency in three languages, albeit with a Bronx accent. The guy was not only smart, he had the fastest hands Cully had ever seen, and was—by a hair—the best shot in the platoon with heavy weapons. Cully spoke a few sentences into his headset and heard an almost-shouted reply.

"Okay, we're going in hot to take a look-see at those two boats. Stay ready. If they are what I think they are, we're gonna take 'em out." The platoon was on its feet, quickly getting into combat gear. Body armor and helmets came first, then web gear and weapons. Chung pulled back the charging handle, feeding a grenade into the firing chamber.

The helo picked up speed and dropped almost to the wave tops. It overtook the two boats and passed directly over one, shining a huge spotlight down on it. A machine gun opened fire, missing the helo. The pilot banked steeply away and came back in, lights off, fast and steady for the gun run.

"Dammit, hose 'em, Vinny!" Chung looked down the barrel as his thumbs came down on the butterfly triggers. The gun thumped out a long burst of ten grenades at the boat, now about five hundred yards away. Chung walked the stream up the boat's centerline, about three grenades detonating on its deck. There was a secondary explosion, and the boat—or what was left of it—sank in seconds.

"Get that other bastard." The second boat kept coming, closing to within a thousand yards of the *Truman*. "Cease fire, cease fire, break right high." As O'Bannon bellowed the order, the helo climbed sharply and banked right. As they turned, it looked as if the *Truman* had turned a huge spotlight on the speeding boat. It was the muzzle flash of one of the CIWS guns. In less than a second, the stream of lead found its target and the second boat blew up just as the first had.

"Let's get aboard and find out what the hell is goin' on."

Ten minutes later, O'Bannon and Chung were in the combat information center of the big ship. The *Truman*'s skipper was not a happy camper.

"Okay, so those buttheads were trying to do a *Cole* on us." The terrorist attack on the USS *Cole* was one of the reasons the *Truman*—and every other ship in the Navy—wasn't letting any strange boats within striking distance. "And there's a crapload of other news, all of it bad."

The admiral commanding the carrier battle group walked over from the communications console. "Okay, guys. We don't know much, but it seems like there was a series of terrorist attacks on the port facilities. It looks pretty bad. And there's a huge amount of chatter between Riyadh and Washington. Looks like there were coordinated attacks all around the Saudi capital. That's all I know, except that we are gonna hold here for a day or two until we get orders. We may have to go in and help the Saudis put some stuff back together. Meanwhile, O'Bannon, I want one of your platoons readied for a helo insertion to do some recon around the port." He turned to the skipper. "Keep your birds on the deck, Captain, except for a recon bird that I'll fly myself. We need to get over there quickly to see what we can see. Get permission from the Saudis, and get that aircraft ready on plus-five. No need for any escort fighters. At least not yet."

Beijing
Presidential Offices
12 November
2340 Hours Local

Ahmadinejad didn't like the Chinese leader's tone. He shot back, "The old fakir is dead, that much I can tell you."

"How could you allow this?" Hu Jintao demanded. "King Abdullah is dead, the Saudi royals have been decimated, and there's nothing to take their place but chaos."

"Not chaos. Soon it will be our brothers who rule there. We need your navy to protect the new government of Islamic Arabia that will be installed tomorrow. You need not fear a true Islamic regime there. They will stabilize the situation immediately."

"And just how will they do that? You should have consulted me before you acted."

"I cannot consult on that which I do not control. These brothers are our friends, and we have long agreed with those who wanted to destroy the apostates. Now it has happened. The time for patience is over. The Americans are already talking about a UN force to restore order there. Even the Europeans want to restore the House of Saud. They fear what will come next. But we can easily convince them not to interfere. We do, however, need your help. We must be able to protect the believers who now control the two Holy Mosques. That is all that is important."

"But that is not all that is important to Beijing. We can proclaim our alliance with the new regime, but we must have guarantees that the oil will flow from Arabia to us, and that our people will be able to stay in the port to help rebuild and restore order there."

"We can do that, but only if you send a naval force to block the advance of the American navy."

"I shall have to consult with our Central Military Commission. You have acted too soon, but we shall deal with the facts on the ground."

White House Cabinet Room
12 November
1345 Hours

"Admiral, my mind is made up—even if yours isn't."

The vice chairman of the Joint Chiefs had grown accustomed to the president's glare. He'd learned through experience that icy looks couldn't kill.

"But, Madam President, we need to think this through. If we decide to invade Saudi Arabia, we'd need tens of thousands of men and millions of tons of equipment. We can't rush into something like this."

The president glared again. She had been elected as the peace candidate. Now she wanted war, and she wanted it today. The oil crisis could not go on. The United States had lost its oil supplies first from Venezuela and now from Saudi Arabia. Even the Kuwaitis were balking because they feared an Iranian invasion. And the Chinese were pressuring every other oil producer to boycott America. Only Mexico seemed hesitant. The president's poll numbers were below 40 percent approval and falling.

"Admiral, two weeks ago you said we couldn't do anything to compel Venezuela to resume its oil shipments. Now you're telling me we can't do anything about Saudi Arabia?"

"Please, ma'am. You're the policymaker. We carry out your orders. As I said two weeks ago, we can invade Venezuela and remove the Chavez regime, but we can't guarantee that the oil flow will be restored because we can't stop the Venezuelans from sabotaging their own facilities, and it's entirely possible that the Chinese there—and there are thousands of them—will get into the fight. As I also said then, we can't do that and deal with another major problem at the same time. Now you want us to go into Arabia. We can. But we can't just go in blindly. We're talking about overthrowing an Islamic regime. That means we have to simultaneously secure a huge nation and its oil fields, which are now overrun with terrorists, and replace the old regime with something, and there's nothing that comes to mind. The surviving Saudi royals are scattered all over the place. The few we've spoken with"—he glanced at the too-quiet secretary of state across the table—"don't want to come out of hiding. The British fleet is on the way, and we know—and I'm here to tell you—that Chinese ships are too. They have at least twelve surface combatants on the way, including two of their Sovremenny destroyers. They'll be off Ras Tannurah in about three days."

"Admiral, I have news for you too. If the new People's Islamic Republic of Arabia signs the treaty of commerce we've submitted, fine. No war. But I've already told them that if they don't sign, we're taking action. Now, what part of that don't you understand?"

Langley Air Force Base, Virginia
18 November
0910 Hours

"Not bad for a bus driver, sir." The colonel in the front seat made another tight turn and kicked the aircraft into "supercruise." The F-22 shrugged through the sound barrier with a purr of electromechanical satisfaction.

For Matt O'Bannon, going from a B-2 to an F-22 Raptor was like parking a pickup truck and climbing into a Porsche—every takeoff was worth a "yeeehaaah."

His headset sounded. "Colonel O'Bannon, sir. There's a message for you. The deputy said to get your ass on the ground and into his office right damn now. His words, sir." Reluctantly, O'Bannon cut his speed, turned sharply, and returned to base. In fifteen minutes, he was in his boss's office.

"O'Bannon, these are your orders for an operational deployment. Your wing is alerted to deploy to Kuwait in the next twelve hours."

"What are we up to, sir?"

"I dunno yet. You're now attached to SOCOM and you'll report to General Sutliff at Doha when you get your people on the ground in Kuwait. The Chinese have moved half their damned navy into Ras Tannurah. They're official allies of the Islamofascists running the place. The president is screwed into the ceiling, and if we can't open the port by threat and get the oil flowing again, well, we may have to do something else. Get moving, Colonel."

"Yessir. Just how bad is it?"

"All I can tell you now is that the Iranians are mobilized, the Chinese are moving troops into Arabia by the tens of thousands, and we're about bone dry on oil—and about bone dry on intel too. We're sending in a Special Forces A-team to scout around Ras Tannurah. You want any more good news?"

"No, sir. That'll do me for now."

White House Cabinet Room
21 November
1745 Hours

"Can't you people do anything right?" The president was fuming at the chairman of the Joint Chiefs. "I told you to send those soldiers in to look around—not get killed. I want a report on how badly the Saudi oil facilities are damaged. I want a report on the Chinese. I don't want reports of a catastrophe, a massacre. Have you any idea what this is going to do to us?"

The Marine four-star had his poker face on. He'd expected the president's blast. "Ma'am, we put the best people we had in there. Three of those men were Arab Americans, and the one you see on the news—the one they're torturing right now—is the son of one of my best friends. They did exactly as they were ordered to do, and their luck ran out."

"Well, General, you've managed to turn a controllable situation into a disaster. The government in Riyadh has declared war on us, Tehran has declared war on us, and China might be next. NATO isn't going to help, so you've managed to isolate us entirely from the rest of the world. Now how are you going to salvage this situation, General? I'm waiting."

Caspar the Unfriendly Ghost stirred. "Madam President, we are ready—and I'm sure the general would agree—to do whatever we need to do in order to restore a legitimate government to Saudi Arabia. We have the forces ready, and I'm sure the Chinese are only bluffing.

Regardless, they cannot project their power sufficiently to defeat us. I'm sure we can mount an operation to restore order in Arabia within a week. Don't you agree, General?"

"Sir, and ma'am, we'll do what we are ordered to do. But you cannot overestimate how hard—and bloody—this will be. The Iranians are reportedly moving troops through southern Iraq. We don't know, but they might be preparing to invade Israel. We have reports that the Iranians are arming their missiles with nuclear warheads. If we go into Arabia, they might use them against us or Israel. We could be on the brink of nuclear war, ma'am."

Beijing
Presidential Offices
26 November
1715 Hours Local

"Idiots!" shouted Hu Jintao. The Central Military Commission was full of gloomy faces. "We are allied to idiots—and you failed to stop them! Why is the American soldier tortured on television? Who allowed this to happen?"

The PLA commander stood to answer. "There is only so much control we have. We fought and captured the Americans, but when the Arabs demanded the prisoners our colonel thought it prudent to turn them over."

"It will inflame the Americans. But it's too late. Now we must prevent them from invading Arabia. Are we prepared to do so?"

"Our Sovremenny destroyers are in the Persian Gulf today. Our submarines and destroyers can keep their navy out for a time, but not forever, and the Arabs are incapable. Almost all of their pilots fled to America or Europe when the government fell. They have no naval force, only a growing army of jihadists. The Iranians are sending troops and air forces, and we are helping them move by ground and air. It will be days, perhaps weeks, before they are all there."

"I have told the American president that if they try to invade Arabia, they will be at war with us. She told me that if the Arabian oil shipments were not resumed quickly, she would be forced to act. Are we prepared for a general war with America?"

"We are better prepared than they are. We have many options. North Korea could invade the South. We can attack Taiwan or even Japan. And this president will never use nuclear weapons to stop us."

"I agree. But might they surprise us with something?"

"President Hu, they cannot fight for long without oil. No matter what they do, it will have to be soon."

White House Situation Room
26 November
0720 Hours

"Is this more guesswork, General, or are you telling me this really happened?" SWMBO was pale, her hands shaking.

"I'm not guessing, ma'am. NORAD tracked the missiles all the way. There were five of them, all fired from near Bakhtaran, in western Iran. Two were aimed at Israel. The Israelis shot one down over Iraq and missed the other. It struck north of Haifa, about twenty kilotons' worth. The other three were aimed at American and British fleets approaching the Persian Gulf in the northern Arabian Sea. Two missed by a wide margin and caused conflicting tidal waves. The other hit about three miles from one of the Brit carriers, *Prince of Wales*. It was vaporized, along with its strike group. We lost two destroyers in the tidal waves. The Brits and the Israelis aren't going to let them get away with this. Neither should we."

"You just keep our nuclear forces under lock and key, General. We're not starting any nuclear wars."

"Starting, ma'am?" At that point, the president slammed down the telephone.

Indian Ocean
Diego Garcia
16 December
0435 Hours Local

"My people are pretty beat, sir." Matt O'Bannon had been running on adrenaline and coffee for more than a week—and so had everyone else. General Sutliff tried to soften the blow.

"I know they are, O'Bannon. But at least they're not glowing in the dark. After Israel launched, the Brits hit Iran with five MIRV'd Trident missiles. Iran's a lot of sand that's been turned into glass, and the radiation cloud is already killing people in Pakistan and India. How many crews do you have operational?"

"I've got twelve B-2 squadrons and six flight crews to man them. The F-22 guys are okay, but my F-117 drivers are worn out—they need at least forty-eight hours' rest. Any intel on the Chinese?"

"No—but I can tell you that nobody's getting grounded, Colonel. R and R just ain't gonna happen. With the Strait of Malacca closed, China's choking for oil now. We've got to tighten our grip."

"We'll do what we have to, sir. You just send me the latest ATO and we'll get busy."

"It should be there by now. You hang in there, Colonel. Out here."

Matt picked up the phone. "Jerry? Is the new ATO here? Bring it in." The decoded e-mail detailed every Navy and Air Force flight assignment.

"We're back in the air. Tell the guys we're taking a B-2. Tanker people okay? They've been in the air more than anybody."

"Sir, they're even more beat than we are. And I just got off the phone with the wing commander. They confirm the loss of three KC-10s yesterday. That's gonna put a big crimp in our style."

"It's gonna be one more long freakin' day, Jerry. Call the staff in for 0615. You and I need to be in the air by 1600."

Near Xi'an, China
26 January 2014
0345 Hours Local

"Nice to see ya, boss." Romeo Wilson snapped his infrared flashlight. Cully peeled off his night-vision glasses, rubbed his eyes, and put them back on. The two trotted off.

"So where's Tai Chi Vinny?"

"Mr. Chung and the professor are inside that building. They're waiting."

Wilson and O'Bannon ran the thousand yards almost silently. No lights burned. They caught their breaths. Wilson pushed the door open and cracked a chemlite stick.

"Hiya, boss." Chung's smile was the best thing Cully had seen in months. "Welcome to Xi'an." Blackout curtains were drawn and portable lights turned on.

"Good to see ya, Vinny. And you must be the professor." The other man also smiled. Two months ago, he was teaching Asian history at Stanford. Now he was one of more than three hundred Chinese American linguists who had volunteered for some of the most dangerous tasks since the Polish Underground operated against the Nazis.

"I was a professor, but now I am a freedom fighter."

"The president approved your plan, gents," said Cully. "How far are you from getting it done?"

"Thanks to your men, we've linked with thousands of people and prompted strikes across the country. People are talking rebellion in every village, every province—reaching even into the PLA itself. A week, maybe two, and our rebels will be ready."

"Vinny, we've heard the PLA has slaughtered masses of people in some of the big cities. Nobody in Washington believes you've turned the PLA against the regime."

Three men entered suddenly, and without a word Cully pulled his 9 mm pistol, stood up, grabbed one by the back of the neck, and put his pistol to the man's temple.

Vinny shouted, "No, no, boss, it's okay." The newcomers spoke excitedly to Chung and the professor. Cully still had his Sig Sauer P-226 pistol in his hand.

"Captain O'Bannon, let me introduce you to Tai Fu. He is PLA general Wu Feng, future new leader of China."

"Well, I'll be damned."

"You said Washington didn't believe me?"

"That's why I'm here. Tell the general I'm honored—but then you tell me why you trust him."

"Boss, the general—and the officers he represents—are risking their lives, because they think there's a tipping point coming and they want to be on the right side. It all depends on if we can create the momentum."

"*If* is a word I hate, lieutenant, so lay it out for me. If your plan makes sense, the big boss promises to give you anything you need. By the way, I brought this; it's probably not as good as your mama used to make, but it's all they had at the commissary." Cully reached down into his rucksack and pulled out two large cans.

"Freakin' calamari marinara? Geez, boss."

"Don't say a word, Tai Chi. Let's just get to work. Now about this plan..."

Washington, D.C.
Halfway across Memorial Bridge into Washington
Showdown Day, 6 February
0745 Hours

The chairman of the Joint Chiefs didn't stop traffic when his car pulled over to the side of the bridge. There was almost no traffic. Civilians hadn't been able to buy gasoline at all for nearly a month. Rationing hadn't worked because there were so many people scamming the coupon plan the idiots from Homeland Security had devised.

He got out to walk and to think. He'd been rereading General Harold Moore's *We Were Soldiers Once...and Young*. He had stopped at a passage he'd remembered from long ago. In a televised address to the nation on the morning of July 28, 1965, President Johnson had described the worsening situation in South Vietnam and declared: "I have today ordered the Airmobile Division to Vietnam."

> On that day, convinced that the president's escalation without a dec-laration of emergency was an act of madness, General Harold K. Johnson, chief of staff of the U.S. Army, drove to the White House with the intention of resigning in protest. He had already taken the four silver stars off each shoulder of his summer uniform. As his car approached the White House gates, General Johnson faltered in his resolve; he convinced himself that he could do more by staying and working inside the system than by resigning in protest. The general ordered his driver to turn around and take him back to the Penta-gon. This decision haunted Johnny Johnson all the rest of his life.

White House Cabinet Room
Thirty Minutes Later

The president's face was as white as the coffee cup that sat by her right hand. "You . . . you can't do this, General."

"Yes, ma'am, I can." He unpinned the four stars from each shoulder and stood up. He walked slowly down the table to the president's seat and laid the stars on the table in front of her.

"You want me to be impeached, is that it? Is this a coup? Do I need to get the Secret Service in here to arrest you?"

"No, ma'am. It's not a coup. And all I'm saying is that I'm resigning if you go ahead with this peace treaty. I will go home, pack my bags, and start driving back to Wyoming tonight. Ma'am, I'm here to tell you we have this war won. Give us another two weeks and I'll have the Chi-nese out of Arabia along with those Islamic punks. You want stability in Arabia, we can't deliver that. But we can—if you let us—win this war. If you decide to quit now, I have no choice. I will quit too—and loudly."

"You mean to give me no choice, General."

"Respectfully, ma'am, that's right. We've probably lost more than sixty thousand men in this war. That's more than we lost in Vietnam. I'm here to tell you that we're about a week or ten days from the fall of the Beijing regime. Right now, they can't hold Taiwan because the Taiwanese are still fighting hard. South Korea is in the hands of the North Koreans, and Japan is badly damaged. We can't do anything about that if you sign the treaty. We can turn the oil back on from Arabia in another two weeks, and when we shot down his air force and two of our subs sank his whole navy in Caracas harbor, Chavez got the message. Venezuelan oil is going to come back online, too. With Iran out of the picture for a while, China can't get any oil except from the Russians. If you sign that treaty, we give it all up. This treaty offer is a bluff. Wait another week, ma'am, and we'll be able to impose peace on a new regime in Beijing. We've won, ma'am, if we have the guts to stick this out just a little longer."

"One more week, General, not a minute more. Now pin those damned stars back on."

"Yes, ma'am."

Diego Garcia
495th Wing Headquarters
12 February
0345 Hours Local

"O'Bannon? This is General Sutliff."

"Yessir. What's the ATO for the day?"

"The ATO is stand down, Colonel. Hu Jintao is dead, and there's a new bunch in charge in Beijing. We've already got a cease-fire, and the new regime is making accommodating noises. Looks to me like it's over, or will be damn soon. Go back to sleep, Matt. Well done. If all goes well, we'll get the gas turned on and get you back to training. See you at Paradise Ranch."

CHAPTER SEVEN

THE ASSASSIN'S MACE WAR

China's leaders appear to recognize the PLA's deficiencies relative to potential adversaries in the region and may have concluded that the PLA is presently unable to compete directly with other modern military powers. We assess that this conclusion might have given rise to a priority emphasis on asymmetric programs and systems to leverage China's advantages while exploiting the perceived vulnerabilities of potential opponents—the so-called Assassin's Mace (*sha shou jian*) programs.

U.S. DEPARTMENT OF DEFENSE REPORT[1]

Guangdong Province, China
Outside Foshan
Rubik's Cube Conference Room
21 September 2004
1135 Hours Local

"Comrade President, it is a great honor to welcome you. I hope it is not too late to congratulate you on your election to chair the Central Military Commission."

Hu Jintao smiled broadly. "Thank you, General. But tell me why you call this building—the most secret project of our government—'Rubik's Cube.'"

The general returned Hu's smile. "It is a small joke, Comrade President. The Rubik's Cube was a toy, once popular in the West. It was a complex puzzle. We create puzzles that will pose the same challenge to our enemies. In our operational centers I will show you how it is done."

For the next two hours, Hu Jintao followed the general, meeting the Rubik's Cube's scientists and young officers—young men and women working feverishly, constantly talking and joking, never taking their eyes off arrays of computer monitors. Hu was taken aback by the debris of empty soda cans, castaway T-shirts, and mismatched running shoes. The building smelled like a gymnasium and had the atmosphere of a kennel full of puppies.

Once he got over the mess, the program's organizational scheme impressed Hu greatly. The general's top-secret force was divided into teams, each led by a computer scientist and equipped with the most powerful computers in the world. Thanks to the American Clinton administration, which had allowed U.S. companies to sell supercomputers to China, the computers were improved every year with processor chips obtained from Taiwan. Each team also had a swarm of young PLA officers, computer scientists in their own right. Most were in their early twenties, and each had a passion. For some, it was computer espionage. Seventy-three of them worked on attacking industrial and government computers, especially in the U.S., Japan, and India. They managed almost twenty-five thousand cyber-invasions every day. They hadn't been detected except by one computer expert at a U.S. government laboratory, and his inquiry had been slammed shut by the American bureaucracy before he could prove anything. China had stonewalled the American FBI investigators, and because the Americans didn't want to make an incident of it, the matter had been dropped.[2]

Others were the architects of computer worms, trojans, and viruses, each designed to disrupt, control, or destroy the computers into which they infiltrated. And still others were the cyber-war architects, infiltrating everything from air traffic control systems to reconnaissance and communication satellites.

Hu addressed the dozens of young officers gathered around him. "Comrades, you are a unique weapon. No one—not the Americans, the British, or even the Indians—can do what you can do. And soon, very soon indeed, your country will call upon you for a great service to the Revolution. We are very proud of you. The people expect great things of you. Be sure you don't disappoint them."

The building echoed with cheers.

Ft. Meade, Maryland
National Security Agency
Conference Room SCIF[3]
8 May 2013
0710 Hours

The lady's face was as bright red as her hair. "You have no idea how hard it is for me to keep you in this job, Kath." Major General Daniel Rubia, director of the NSA, frowned at his most troublesome and most valuable lieutenant colonel. Kathleen O'Bannon Cooper was, by any measure, a genius. And, like most geniuses, she was an expert at angering the co-workers and superiors who couldn't keep up with her. She was damned lucky to have Danny Rubia for a boss, because he was just as smart and not so easily steamed.

"Look, you're doing a helluva job here. Nobody can argue with that. But you're going to brief the president of the United States in about two days, and you simply have to explain what's going on in terms she can understand."

"Boss, you know I'm being honest about Titan Rain. They are part of the most pervasive and effective cyber-war effort in the world, and we gotta not only defend against them, we need to take them the hell down. Why can't she get that into her thick skull?"

"Because, Kath, you get your Irish up every damned time you talk to someone. And you have to slow down. You have to explain every step of what the Chinese are doing in words of not more than two syllables.

You have this habit of skipping steps. And when you do, people who aren't as smart as you can't follow what you're saying. And when they don't understand, their fallback is disbelief, which results in another damn phone call to me saying you're fibbing to people when you should be giving them facts. You read me, Colonel?"

She let out a long, melodramatic sigh. "Yes, sir."

National Security Agency
10 May
1122 Hours

"Well, that went better than I'd expected it to. At least I don't have to fire you today, Kath."

General Rubia looked at Cooper, whose ears once again matched her hair color. Steaming didn't begin to describe her mood. But she was smiling as the two waved at the departing presidential helicopter. President Dorothy Clutterbuck had accepted General Rubia's invitation to the top-secret briefing after her pollster convinced her that a visit to the NSA would look presidential. The president had never been there. And Rubia didn't like going to the White House. After five years of Clutterbucking the system, the White House leaked like a sieve.

"She freakin' laughed at me, boss. She laughs when I tell her that the Chicoms can take over the White House switchboard tomorrow if they want to. What the hell is wrong with her?"

"I dunno, Kath. The FBI briefing about Chinese penetration of Boeing and Lockheed Martin got her attention, but she sure looked bored when you started."

"Sorry, boss. I screwed the pooch. We didn't get her approval to do a damned thing. Item one: create our own proprietary NSA defense net to key computer systems in government and industry. Decision? No. Item two: commence counter-strikes against Chinese computers sourcing the spy ops. Decision? Not only no, but hell no. I struck out. What the hell do we do now?"

"Personally, I'm going back to my office and pound my head against a wall. What are you gonna do?"

"Well, about the same. I think I'll head home early and start dealing with kids and homework. I only wish I could tell my brothers about this. They think I'm the biggest weapon in the O'Bannon family. But I can't even get a dumbass politician to agree to let me run a couple of computer programs."

"Calm down, Kath. You can't tell them about this, but maybe you should call Cully or Matt and blow off a little steam. I know those two, and they'll be good listeners."

"Sir, with respect, you didn't grow up as their little sister. They'll give me so much crap I'll scream. Well…maybe I'll call Matt tonight when I've calmed down a little. He's the saner of the two."

Beijing
Central Military Commission
1 June
1003 Hours Local

"Gentlemen, it is enormously distressing to hear this news from the province of Taiwan." Hu Jintao had called the meeting at short notice after his morning intelligence briefing. After more than a decade of delay, the Taiwanese felt sufficiently threatened by possible American abandonment that they had begun to rebuild their own defenses. The Legislative Yuan special committee had passed a threefold increase in the defense budget, and emissaries were on their way to Washington to beg the American president to reinstate the arms sales George W. Bush had promised ten years earlier.

The PLA commanding general stood and puffed out his chest. "Comrade President," he began, "we have many options to employ. We can do anything the Party wishes with respect to the renegade province: everything from a demonstration salvo of missiles to a seaborne invasion that can be mounted in a matter of weeks."

"Yes, yes, General. And we are all very proud of what we have built over the past two decades. But what do we gain by devastating Taiwan? Would it not be better to finally subjugate it without destroying it? Of course it would."

"But Comrade President, the Americans—even with this president—are bound to interfere if we use any sort of force. And what of the others who trade with Taiwan? What will India do, or the Europeans?"

"That is an excellent point, General. What I suggest"—Hu's eyes fell to the handwritten outline before him—"is to begin with the Europeans. We shall then proceed with tests—and only tests, mind you—on the Americans."

National Security Agency
Director's Office
3 June
0810 Hours

"Yes, Kath, what is it now?" Even Danny Rubia's patience with his favorite subordinate had its limits, which Cooper was testing—again—by barging in uninvited. The NSA director was, as usual, at his stand-up desk on the long wall of his office.

"Boss, the Chicoms have gone active with cyber-war. Look at this." She pushed a stack of papers covered in numbers in front of Rubia.

"Yeah, so what is this jumble?"

"It's the latest nav readouts from the European Union's Galileo GPS satellite systems. I got a call from a pal at NRO this morning. They'd been asked to help the Euros recalibrate their navsats. And when they did, they found the satellites were all several degrees off, and the margin of error was ranging randomly from zero to five degrees. Same kind of errors, every one of the satellites."

Rubia frowned. "So that means someone is tampering with them. And a crapload of airliners are gonna be lost in the sky because they won't even know about the error until they try to land someplace and they aren't where they thought they would be."

"Right. And I ran a whole pile of checks. I traced nine separate programs back to Guangdong province. They've placed trojans in the satellites. They can create errors and may even be able to shut them down altogether. The only issue is whether it's a test, or they're really going on the offensive."

"Hmm. Keep running tests. And don't—I repeat, Kath—don't do anything else until we get approval."

Kath looked into her boss's eyes and spoke her frown. "Yes, sir, I'll be good. For a while." She winked at him and left. It scared the hell out of him.

Near Ft. Bragg, North Carolina
People's Republic of Pineland
Guerrilla Encampment
6 June
0710 Hours

The young Green Beret officer held his rifle close to his chest. "Sorry, sir, but I'm responsible for this weapon. I can't give it to you. But if you cooperate with us, this is just like the other weapons I can get for every one of your men."

The guerrilla camp was a mess. The guerrillas—Gs in special ops speak—had no perimeter guards and what had been a huge bonfire still smoldered, producing an intermittent column of white smoke that could lead anyone there from miles away. Weapons, tents, and food were in disarray around it. So was a mob of people who needed help, and needed it badly. It was all part of the final exam at the John F. Kennedy Army Special Operations School. Residents from most of the surrounding counties had volunteered to serve as fake guerrillas. Their leaders were Spec Ops men selected to make life difficult for the trainees. The object of the exercise—called "Robin Sage" for reasons no one remembered—was for the trainee A-teams to make contact, convince the play-acting guerrillas to cooperate, and allow them to begin training the Gs in everything from tactics to first aid. This particular guerrilla chieftain was more interested in what kind of chow the trainee had in his rucksack.

"So tell me, Lieutenant, you were supposed to be here by dawn. You are two hours late. Did you get lost?" Navy SEAL captain Cully O'Bannon was having way too much fun.

"No, sir. Our GPS handsets kinda took us in the wrong direction for a while, and by the time we figured that out with a regular compass, we were a couple of miles off. And some bastard—er, excuse me, sir, someone stampeded our mules at about two in the morning when we stopped for a short break." O'Bannon smiled to himself. It had been a hoot sneaking up to the trainees and running their mules off.

"So, this American technology you brag so much about isn't worth much, is it?"

Before the young man could reply, Cully picked up the ruck and dumped it on the ground. He turned to the stone-faced black man behind him and said, "Rome, you see if what this gringo is carrying is worth anything, and then you tell me if we should just shoot him for failing to carry out America's promise."

O'Bannon stalked off to where his favorite green beanie, Colonel Burt Carstairs, was looking on in huge amusement. "Hey, Burt, what's the beef with the GPS?"

"Dunno, Cully, but you oughta come back to the HQ building with me for a while. Something's up."

Fifteen minutes later, hot coffee and cheeseburgers in hand, the two finished reading the latest briefings on the Taiwan crisis and on the strange interference in the European GPS system. The American system had shut down for only an hour, but chaos reigned in airports all over Europe.

The White House
Oval Office
Same Day
2145 Hours

"So how bad is it, Freddie?" President Clutterbuck was on the phone with the treasury secretary, who had nothing but bad news.

"Madam President, from what the Taiwanese finance minister just told me, this is a total failure of their computer systems. The Japanese say they have lost literally billions. Not as in reduced profits. They just don't know where tens of billions of dollars in stock trades went. As a result, their shares are falling like rocks in markets all over the world. I don't know what's going on, but the computer experts are telling me they can't think of any cause except a cyber-invasion. Someone has gotten into the systems and is screwing them up altogether, flooding them with false trades."

"How long will it take to fix?"

"They don't know. It could be minutes. It could be weeks."

"Well, keep me posted on this." Clutterbuck hung up, only to have her assistant buzz in the next call.

"Madam President, the secretary of defense wishes to speak with you." The president sighed and pressed another button on the big phone. "Yeah, Clarence, what's up?"

"Madam President, I just got a call from the NSA director. He thinks he knows what's haywire with the Asian stock exchanges."

"Is this another one of that arrogant colonel's exercises in paranoia? Is it?"

"Madam President, this may not be paranoia. They have traced some cyber-attacks back to Guangdong, China. This may be connected to your offer to sell arms to the Taiwanese. Don't forget, Hu Jintao told the secretary of state yesterday that we'd better not sell those submarines and anti-missile destroyer defense ships to them or we'd suffer grave consequences.

Well, the Taiwanese can't pay for them anyhow, because their money is all lost in the ether."

"Come on, Clarence. Where's the proof? What do those cowboys want to do? Declare war on China?"

Beijing
Central Military Commission
6 June
2230 Hours Local

"That is our final word on the subject, Madam President." Hu Jintao slammed the telephone down. Then he grinned and studied his papers for a good three minutes before speaking. The Politburo member sitting to his right began to speak, but Hu waved him to silence. Finally, his eyes rose from the table.

"The American president demands to know if we are behind the collapse of the Asian stock markets and the interference in the European GPS system. Of course, I denied it. She refuses to cancel the arms sales to Taiwan for any reason but she is wavering on her promise to extend them credit. She will, I am sure, back down on that within minutes. I told her that would be a further aggression against us, and she promised to reconsider. We have disrupted Taiwan and Japan successfully. Now, comrades, how should we capitalize on this victory?"

A general said, "Comrade President, we have proven that we have the ability to crush the renegades in Taiwan at our pleasure, and"—he looked around the room with a melodramatic glare—"now is the time to do it. Let us demand that Taiwan immediately agree to assimilation in our government or suffer the consequences. And if they refuse, we should use all the power our new weapons grant. Shut down their economy entirely, their air traffic control, and even their electrical power grid. Then we can send in a military relief force. They will be hard pressed to mount even a token opposition force. We can begin by firing missiles into Taiwan."

"Good. Let it proceed as our written plan states. Is there anything else?"

A Politburo member stood to be recognized. "Comrade President, should we not accelerate the next step in the plan? What if the Americans launch their missiles in response to our small demonstration attack on Taiwan?"

"No, we shall take our time, comrade. There is no reason to rush. This matter is in very capable hands."

National Security Agency
8 June
0810 Hours

"Get Colonel Cooper in here right now." Rubia hung up the phone. He and his deputy stared at each other for the two full minutes it took for Kathleen to run down the halls. As she entered his office, he pressed the button on his desk that turned on the "top secret" lights outside his door.

"Okay, Kath. I just got off the phone with the chairman of the Joint Chiefs. He wants to know how quickly we can get our proprietary defense net up and running."

"Uh, sir, it's gonna take weeks. I need cooperation from NRO, State, CIA, and—"

Rubia cut her off. "We don't have weeks, Kath. What can you do before the sun sets today?"

"Wow, sir, I can maybe get something going on the JCS system if I get lucky. But the other stuff, for the satellites and the other government nets, will take days or weeks, even if the stuff we've been working on works the first time out. The commercial stuff isn't going to be ready for at least ten days and that's if we work 24/7. What's the rush?"

"Well, the Chicoms are going active on Taiwan. Their navy is blockading the place and they're buzzing it from the air. We're sending two carrier battle groups there at top speed. Can you protect the operational forces?"

"Dunno, sir. If we're in a shooting war, this is gonna be fast and dirty. We can probably protect comms, but what if they've already invaded the command system? I've been running tests all the time, and we've detected a few ghost attacks, but nothing serious. At this point the secure sat nets are okay, but I don't know how long that will last. We've blocked most of the access, but the stuff coming out of China is being rerouted so fast through a net of dummy servers all over the world, we can't block them all, at least not yet."

"Why?"

"Because they're now routing attacks through our secure nets and several other secure nets in NATO and the UK. Damned if I can tell how they're doing it. I should be able to tell you that in a couple of hours."

"Kath, the president is determined to avoid a shooting war, but she wants to send the message to the Chicoms that we will shoot if they try to send ground forces into Taiwan. The Taiwanese are basically defenseless, and they're howling for protection. You do everything you can to get that net up now. You'll have everything you ask for."

From Cooper's scowl, Rubia knew what was coming and cut her off. "And no, Colonel, no offensive operations against the Chinese cyber-war centers. Not yet."

"What's she frigging waiting for, sir?"

"You tell me."

The White House
12 June
2230 Hours

"What the hell do you mean they *all* missed, Clarence?" The president was in no mood to hear the defense secretary say that every SM-3 interceptor missile fired by U.S. Aegis destroyers had failed to neutralize its target.

"I'm sorry to be the one to have to tell you, Madam President, but that's what happened. The Chinese missiles struck their targets in Taiwan without any of our anti-missile weapons hitting any of them. But it wasn't much of an attack. There were only ten missiles, and they all hit Taiwanese airfields. It does appear that most of the Taiwanese air force was destroyed on the ground."

"What went wrong with our missiles? Did the Bush administration lie to Congress when it said the missiles worked?"

"We don't know what went wrong. The SM-3 system had been tested thoroughly. I don't think they lied about that."

"So what the hell can we do?"

"Ma'am, we can't do much now unless we want to start shooting at the Chinese forces. We have both USS *Kitty Hawk* and USS *John C. Stennis* on station near Taiwan. The choice is, we either talk Beijing into backing off, or we have to attack in defense of Taiwan."

"And just how are you going to do that if our missiles and God knows what else doesn't work?"

"We have to try, Madam President."

Andersen Air Force Base, Guam
13 June
0950 Hours Local

"So what the hell do you mean, baby sister?" Brigadier General (select) Matt O'Bannon mused as he read the "Top Secret—Noforn" e-mail from the National Security Agency warning of possible cyber-attacks against command and control systems. The two squadrons of B-2s under his command weren't vulnerable—or at least they weren't supposed to be. But they were utterly dependent upon the five Milstar and three AHEF satellites that supposedly provided secure command and control for high-priority combat systems. Not to mention the constellation of twenty-eight secure GPS navigation satellites. O'Bannon pressed the intercom calling in his deputy commander.

"Tom, get everyone on the line, and schedule hourly tests of the sat systems and see if there's anything unusual. I want to know immediately if something is offline or not working."

"Sure thing, boss. But what about the ATO? The 325th is about an hour from targets."

"I know, Tom. They'll be over Taiwan in no time. Tell them to switch to inertial navigation and test comms. We have to risk it."

"Okay, boss. But we're gonna have four really pissed pilots. Testing comms is like ringing the Chicoms' doorbell to tell them, 'We're here!'"

The White House
Oval Office
14 June
1209 Hours

"You're telling me that all the money being transferred between banks has just disappeared?"

"Well." The treasury secretary took a deep breath. "It's *like* it disappeared, Madam President. But the flood of false transfers mixed everything up so badly, no one really knows. It's possible that hundreds of billions of dollars have just been misplaced. The chairman of the New York Stock Exchange just told me he had to close trading twenty minutes ago because the same thing was happening with stock trades."

The defense secretary piped in, "That's not the worst of it."

"What the hell could be worse?" screamed the president. "Our economy is stopped cold, millions of people will be out of work by tomorrow morning, and you're telling me we can't stop the Taiwanese from surrendering to China today. Now what, Clarence, is going to be worse? Tell me. Tell me right frigging now."

"Madam President," said the chairman of the Joint Chiefs, "if I may interject. There has been a well-organized cyber-attack on the United States, and it is going on as we speak. I just got off the phone with the director of the NSA. He confirms that the Chinese are taking us apart piece by piece. If we can't stop them, people won't just be out of work. They'll be sitting home in the dark."

"What the hell are you talking about, General?"

"Ma'am, this is *sha shou jian*: 'the assassin's mace.' They're going for the quick kill and hoping we won't see it coming. China isn't satisfied with taking Taiwan. They're in the process of doing the same thing to us. If we can't stop them, they can shut down a lot more than the stock market. They can take out air traffic control, the telephone satellite network, even the electric power grid. We think we know where this is coming from. I need your permission, right now, to launch a counter-attack."

"And what does that mean?"

"Ma'am, we need to bomb their cyber-war center in Guangdong province, or take it out some other way faster than the bombers can get there. And we'd better take out their missile launch facilities. Our recon sats confirm they are readying the launch of a whole bunch of satellites. This can only mean one thing: they're launching the rest of their satellite-killers. They can't get into some of our secure sats with their cyber-attack, so they're going to take them out the hard way. We need to hit them before they hit us. And I say again, we need to do it right damn now."

"Don't you take that tone with me, General. I'm trying to stop a war. You're trying to start a bigger one."

"I mean no disrespect, ma'am. But I have to tell you: we're already at war. The Chinese are attacking us electronically and they're defeating us to a degree no enemy ever has. If we don't act immediately, we're sunk. It's that simple."

"All right, gentlemen. I will think this over and then call you, Clarence, with my decision."

Andersen Air Force Base
15 June
0310 Hours Local

"Rolling, Jerry." Matt O'Bannon was grateful that the Andersen main runway was almost twelve thousand feet long. The B-2 was loaded with every ounce of fuel it could carry. The four B-61 Mod 7 nuclear weapons in its rotary launcher were a trivial addition weight-wise, but not other-wise. O'Bannon took a long time to lift the big ship off the runway, try-ing to save every drop of fuel. They climbed ahead of the other three bombers in the squadron, leveling off at forty-five thousand feet.

"Okay, Jerry. What are the numbers?"

"Well, it's about eighteen hundred miles to Foshan, boss. I make it three hours, fifty-five minutes to target."

"How's Milstar?"

"All okay, so far. I ran the checks three times before we rolled."

"This is the damndest operation I've ever flown. We're supposed to get a fail-safe transmission before we cross their border?"

"That's what we both read on the e-mail, boss. No call, no bombs dropped. This is like a remake of a bad movie."

National Security Agency
Ten Minutes Later

"You look like hell, Kath."

"Great to see you too, sir." Cooper and her team of three cyber-geeks and one college professor on loan from the University of Maryland had been there for more than three days without more than an occasional power snooze and protein bar. They were trying to design a cyber counter-attack against the Chinese.

"Any idea?"

"No, sir. We had all the viruses and trojans in the world designed and stored, but the attack is still a little out of reach. Six hours, maybe seven." She gestured to the man she had introduced to her boss as "the smartest sonofabitch in the world."

"Whaddya think, Dr. A?"

Dr. Ashnapuri, an Indian American with a Ph.D. from Princeton, shrugged. "I think Kath is about right, General. Another few hours. Maybe a little, tiny bit more."

Over the Western Pacific
15 June
0515 Hours Local

"About 820 miles to feet dry, skipper."

"Okay, about another ninety minutes. Anything on Milstar?"

"Nope. All still good to go. But there's nothing on the air about the tankers."

"Nothing?"

"Nope. Looks like they may be on the ground, or lost, or maybe ready to go, but I can't tell."

"Hope you got your water wings with you, Jerry. We can get to the target, but it's a long swim back if we have to ditch."

Outside Foshan, China
Rubik's Cube
15 June
0605 Hours Local

The general was clocking his second straight twenty-four-hour day. He walked the halls, watching his team in action, proud of their accomplishments. First the American stock markets and bank wires. Then they had taken down the air traffic control system. Their first strike on the American government—ordered by Hu Jintao—collapsed the Department of Homeland Security's whole computer system. Now, at this early hour, they were readying the final phase of their attack. In about fifteen minutes, Hu Jintao would arrive. And soon after he did, the American electrical power grid would shut down and the American GPS and other satellites would be attacked. The general walked to the back of his office, into the small private bathroom he had built for himself. It was a luxury he had earned. There was just enough time for a quick shower and a fresh uniform before President Hu arrived.

National Security Agency
15 June
Five Minutes Later

Kathleen Cooper's ears weren't red, but her whole head appeared ready to explode. "You're friggin' kidding me. I gotta talk to her *now?*"

"Kath, calm down. She's the commander in chief. Your boss. Just tell her what you told me." Cooper stomped across the room to the telephone Rubia held out.

"Colonel, I need to know when our counter-attack is going to be launched. Tell me, and tell me right now."

"Madam President, we're working as hard as we can. I think we can do it in another hour or two. Maybe sooner."

"Is that the best you can do, Colonel? What the hell are you waiting for?"

"The only thing I'm waiting for, *Madam* President, is for you to get the hell out of my hair and let me get back to work. Now, if you'll excuse me, I'll try to save our collective ass." She slammed down the phone, which spared her the president's screaming promise of a court-martial.

Outside Foshan, China
Rubik's Cube
15 June
0635 Hours Local

"You have done well, General. I have just talked to the American president. She threatens us with nuclear war if we do not restore America's economic power by restoring its computers. I told her I could not restore what I did not destroy, and she hung up. But it is true, what I told her. It was not I, but you and your soldiers who have brought us to the brink of this great victory. You shall proceed."

Hu and the general stood behind a row of computer consoles. Sitting at the computers were three PLA officers.

"We are ready, Comrade General," said one.

"Proceed."

National Security Agency
Same Time

"We got it, boss. We got their number now."

"So go, Kath. Don't stand on freakin' ceremony." Rubia stood behind Cooper's little team as they pounded keyboards and clicked computer mice.

"Keep your fingers crossed....What the hell?" The lights flickered for a moment, and came back on as the emergency generators started up.

"What did we lose, Kath?"

"Nothing, sir, but it'll take a minute to restore the backups. Okay, Dr. A?"

"Yes, Kath. Let's do it."

"Okay, here goes." They worked feverishly for another five minutes. "Okay, it's done. But what about the power outage?"

Approaching the Chinese Coast
Same Day
0648 Hours Local

"Almost to feet dry, skipper."

"Roger. One hour to target. Anything on the comlink?"

"Nada, boss. If we don't get the message in about two minutes, we turn back. Hope the other guys are okay." The squadron had separated an hour after takeoff, each of the four aircraft heading to different targets.

"Yeah, me too." They flew on, listening for a call that never came. At the designated point, they turned their aircraft around for the flight home.

Somewhere Underneath the Mountains of Southern Pennsylvania
Site R
Same Day
1005 Hours

"The evacuation of the White House and the Capitol were successful, Madam President. And at least some of our satellites survived the attack, so we still have some communications. Madam President?"

The commander in chief just stared in response. One day America was there, the next day it was gone. Yes, the people were unharmed—at least those who hadn't been killed or injured in the riots. But the whole country had suffered an electrical blackout that shut down banks, the stock market, the entire economy, and even the government. The military—or at least most of it—was still working, if slowly.

The good news was that no enemy was about to invade, and no missiles were raining down on American cities. But the last call from Hu Jintao had driven her into a near-hypnotic state. America would surrender its claims in the Pacific. It would agree to a Chinese trade zone in the Hawaiian Islands, and its treaties of security with Japan and other nations would be voided. There had always been an answer, a poll that could guide her. But there was none now.

It could be worse, couldn't it? Site R, they called it. The rising summer heat would dampen the wind this afternoon, and she would take a walk in the woods, no matter how many times the generals told her not to go aboveground. What did they know, anyhow? They had gotten her into this mess, hadn't they?

CHAPTER EIGHT

CHINA, THE *EU*NUCHS, AND ARMS

Resolved, that the Senate:

(1) strongly supports the United States embargo on the People's Republic of China

(2) strongly urges the European Union to continue its ban on all arms exports to the People's Republic of China

(3) requests that the president raise United States objections to the potential lifting of the European Union arms embargo against the People's Republic of China in any upcoming meetings with European officials

(4) encourages the Government of the United States to make clear in discussions with representatives of the national governments of European Union member states that a lifting of the European Union embargo on arms sales to the People's Republic of China would potentially adversely affect transatlantic defense cooperation, including future transfers of United States military technology, services, and equipment to European Union countries.

EXCERPT FROM U.S. SENATE RESOLUTION 91, CONSIDERED AND AGREED TO, MARCH 17, 2005

S O MUCH FOR SCENARIOS OF THE FUTURE. What's happening today? Can America form an alliance with its old European Cold War allies to contain China? The answer is probably not, because our "allies" aren't so allied anymore.

Europe is much more interested in lifting the Western arms embargo on China than with stopping China's military buildup. Even without lifting the embargo, Europe is providing China with goods and technology that have military applications. In March 2005, Airbus, the subsidized European aircraft conglomerate, announced that it had picked a Chinese partner to manufacture parts for its A-350 aircraft. Announcing the partnership, Airbus China president Laurence Barron commented that China will need about 1,790 commercial aircraft, amounting to a $230 billion market, in the next twenty years.[1] Such sales only whet Europe's appetite for further profits.

Since the 1989 Tiananmen Square massacre, the United States and the countries of the European Union have embargoed arms sales to China. In 2005, the EU—led by the French and German governments—was about to lift the embargo. President George W. Bush intervened to stop them. At a European summit in February 2005, he warned that such European action could alter the balance of power in the Taiwan Strait.[2] As unremarkable as that was, the reaction from key members of Congress was anything but mundane. It takes a great deal to rouse congressional anger against Europe, but the prospect of the EU lifting the arms embargo did—in spades.

California congressman Tom Lantos, a Democrat, said Congress would "take strong, strong and outraged retaliatory action" if the embargo were lifted, adding that Congress was united against "this degree of arrogant, in-your-face sale to a Communist dictatorship of advanced military equipment." Lantos told the Associated Press, "People who advocate it in Europe should go down to the American military cemeteries and remind themselves of the lives we sacrificed to liberate Europe."[3] Even the mild-tempered Senator Richard Lugar, a Republican from Indiana, came out swinging, threatening to cut off American technology-sharing with Europe if the embargo were lifted.

Even in the face of this uncharacteristically harsh barrage from Congress, the Europeans didn't give up. On March 31, then German chancellor Gerhard Schröder said he was determined to lift the European arms embargo.[4] France's foreign minister, Michel Barnier, in what can only be labeled diplomatic doubletalk, pooh-poohed American criticisms of the European plan, saying "warnings and threats" were not "useful" at a time when both sides were trying to repair transatlantic relations. Barnier said, "Our intention is at no point to multiply the sale of arms in this region. This lifting of the embargo has a political dimension."[5]

Not to mention a commercial dimension. The licensed arms sales by Europe to China grew in value from about €54 million in 2001 to at least €416 million in 2003 (which, according to the *Financial Times*, is the last year for which the full data are available).[6]

By June 2005, the EU had backed down, postponing action on the embargo for perhaps a year. But the dispute is far from settled, because the EUnuchs of Old Europe think profits are more important than allies, and arms sales more essential than the defense of freedom.

In November 2005, former French prime minister Jean-Pierre Raffarin made it clear that France would gladly sell Taiwan into slavery in exchange for arms sales to China. In a state visit to China, Raffarin "signed or finalized major business deals with Beijing valued at around €3.2 billion"[7] and endorsed China's anti-secession law targeted against Taiwan. He said, "The anti-secession law is completely compatible with the position of France."[8]

President Bush and congressional leaders have made it clear that America won't tolerate the EU lifting the arms embargo on China. It is very rare in our history—unheard of in at least a decade—for America to throw the gauntlet at Europe's feet in this manner. The president has gotten the EU's attention, and, according to Defense Department officials involved in the negotiations, has bought at least a year's delay in Europe's plan.

If Europe goes ahead regardless, it would be serious. While the Europeans are slashing their own defense budgets, European companies are manufacturing highly sophisticated weapons and electronics systems for export. China can buy most of what it wants from Russia. But Europe has crucial high-tech weapons and electronics that could rapidly transform

China's military. Consider just one system, a little-known Czech electronics system called "Vera-E."

According to a report by the Jamestown Foundation, "Beginning in late 2003, the Chinese government started negotiations with a Czech electronics firm, ERA, about the possibility of acquiring the Vera-E passive surveillance system (PSS), an advanced electronic intelligence (ELINT) platform." The report said that "Vera-E would provide the People's Liberation Army (PLA) with a quantum leap in its command, control, communications, computers, and intelligence (C4I) capabilities. The Czech-made Vera-E is a highly advanced sensor that is able to detect aircraft, ships, and ground vehicles from signals emitted by their radar, communications, and other onboard electronic systems. Vera-E is called a 'passive' radar because it emits no signals, and therefore cannot be detected by sensor platforms of opposing forces."[9]

As the Jamestown Foundation report indicates, if Beijing were able to buy Vera-E, Chinese forces would have a decisive advantage against Taiwanese air forces and an almost decisive one against American forces operating in the Taiwan Strait (or elsewhere). As retired Air Force lieutenant general and FOX News Channel senior military analyst Thomas McInerny put it, "I think it would be unconscionable if the Europeans would approve that [sale]. To me, that would help destabilize the region and would hurt our efforts at deterrence in that part of the world."

Ships and aircraft could be tracked and targeted by a sensor aircraft that itself might not be detected or identified as a foe. If Beijing has Vera-E, it could track the U.S. Air Force JSTARS battle-management aircraft easily, making both JSTARS and the forces it directs much more vulnerable to attack by aircraft or ship-borne missiles.

Europeans aren't the only ones who want to sell critical arms to China. There's also Israel. Israeli defense industries make excellent products but have limited markets, and they are completely cut out of the profitable Arab market. But Israel has for years capitalized on arms sales to China and Third World nations. The United States tolerated this, but in 2000 the Clinton administration's permissive attitude toward Israeli arms sales began to diminish.

One of the reasons American air forces dominate the skies is the E-3 Sentry aircraft, also known as "AWACS": airborne early warning and control. The E-3 is an old Boeing 707 on which a massive rotating radome is mounted. AWACS can monitor all aircraft within about two hundred miles and direct both defensive and offensive aircraft in real time. China, desiring this capability, contracted with Israel in 1997 to use its Phalcon radar to create an AWACS-like aircraft on Russian-built Ilyushin-76 Candid aircraft.

Overcoming its earlier ambivalence, the Clinton administration began objecting to the sale, and Israel cancelled the deal with China in September 2000. But that wasn't the end of the problem. At around the same time that it made the deal to sell Phalcon, Israel had apparently agreed to sell China an unknown number of its Harpy unmanned aerial vehicle. Harpies are capable of launching cruise missile–like attacks from long distances. American defense experts were also increasingly worried that the technology used in the now-cancelled U.S.–Israeli Lavi fighter had been sold to China. The dispute came into the open in 2004, when defense undersecretary Douglas Feith demanded the resignation of Israeli general Amos Yaron, who was the director general of Israel's ministry of defense.[10]

America has leverage over Israel that it lacks in Europe. Israel, a usually faithful ally, is dependent on the United States for the advanced weapons it needs to defend itself. One of the two major combat aircraft the U.S. is developing is the F-35 joint strike fighter. The F-35 is the designated replacement for several classes of U.S. fighters and fighter-bombers. Many nations, Britain and Israel included, have been eager to participate in its development with an eye toward buying F-35s. America has been eager to have their experts participate, to help build in features that will be dedicated to their particular needs and fighter tactics.

In early May 2005, the Department of Defense terminated information-sharing with Israel on the F-35, closing it out of the aircraft's development.

This action sent shockwaves through the Israeli government, which resolved to settle the problems it had with America. After months of negotiations, the Israelis signed a "memorandum of understanding" with the Defense Department that will govern future Israeli defense sales to China and other nations.

CHAPTER NINE

CONTAINMENT, ENGAGEMENT, OR DETERRENCE: WORKING TO PREVENT A SINO-AMERICAN WAR

China has made contributions to safeguarding world peace and promoting international cooperation. On the basis of the Five Principles of Peaceful Coexistence, China has developed friendly, cooperative relations with other countries and promoted peaceful coexistence and equal treatment among countries. China has always adhered to the principle of being a friendly neighbor, and has constantly developed good and cooperative relationships with surrounding countries and other Asian countries and expanded common interests with them. China has established various cooperative relationships with major powers, and unremittingly augmented mutual dialogues, exchanges, and cooperation. China has also expedited cooperation with a vast number of developing countries, to seek common development by drawing on one another's advantages within the South-South cooperation framework. Active in the settlement of serious international and regional problems, China shoulders broad international obligations, and plays a responsible and constructive role.

BEIJING STATE COUNCIL POLICY STATEMENT TITLED

"CHINA'S PEACEFUL DEVELOPMENT ROAD," DECEMBER 22, 2005[1]

"Peaceful coexistence" is a term that had a deep ideological significance to the Soviets before the fall of the Berlin Wall, and it has an equally deep ideological significance to the Chinese now. To the Communists—and China is still determinedly Communist—"peaceful coexistence" means the consolidation of the Communist Party's power at home and expansion to subject satellite states without interference from the West. In other words, it is China's label for its Cold War against the West.

The Bush administration understands that fanning the flames of freedom is better than "peaceful coexistence." On his way to Beijing, President Bush stopped in Japan to meet with Japanese prime minister Junichiro Koizumi. In Kyoto, the president held up Taiwan as an example for China's future. He said

> By advancing the cause of liberty throughout this region, we will contribute to the prosperity of all—and deliver the peace and stability that can only come with freedom.... [M]odern Taiwan is free and democratic and prosperous. By embracing freedom at all levels, Taiwan has delivered prosperity to its people and created a free and democratic Chinese society.... Other Asian societies have taken some steps toward freedom, but they have not yet completed the journey.... As China reforms its economy, its leaders are finding that once the door to freedom is opened even a crack, it can not be closed. As the people of China grow in prosperity, their demands for political freedom will grow as well. President Hu has explained to me his vision of "peaceful development," and he wants his people to be more prosperous. I have pointed out that the people of China want more freedom to express themselves, to worship without state control, to print Bibles and other sacred texts without fear of punishment. The efforts of Chinese people to improve their society should be welcomed as part of China's development. By meeting the legitimate demands of its citizens for freedom and openness, China's leaders can help their country grow into a modern, prosperous, and confident nation.[2]

The Beijing regime is unused to such lectures from America. Even so, they received President Bush warmly. They did so because they had to, because they recognize that the Bush administration understands the nervousness of China's Asian neighbors about Beijing's emergence as a regional superpower. Japan, India, Singapore, Thailand, Vietnam, Malaysia, the Philippines, and Indonesia do not want to become Chinese satellites.

JAPAN

President Bush got a huge gift from Japan on Christmas Eve 2005. Japan is not ignorant of China's military buildup. Early in December 2005, Japanese foreign minister Taro Aso said that China's buildup was a threat to Japan.[3] A Beijing spokesman said that Aso's comments were "highly irresponsible" and questioned his motives.[4] But both Washington and Tokyo weren't diverted by Beijing's bluster. On Christmas Eve, the Koizumi government made an announcement that shook the region: Chief Cabinet Secretary Shinzo Abe said Japan had decided to proceed with the United States to jointly develop missile interceptors for a ballistic missile defense of Japan.[5]

INDIA

India, the world's largest democracy, was alienated from the United States in 1998 when President Clinton imposed sanctions on it for nuclear testing. But as a democratic state with China on its northern borders, India is a natural ally of the United States. On September 22, 2001, President Bush lifted the Clinton-era sanctions[6] and India is now cooperating with the United States on regional security concerns.

The United States and India had no productive relationship during the Clinton years. But as Michael Barone of *U.S. News & World Report* wrote in July 2005, "You didn't see it in the headlines this week, but it's likely to be more important in the long run than many things that received much more notice. The 'it' in question is the New Framework for the U.S.–India Defense Relationship signed . . . by U.S. Defense Secretary

Donald Rumsfeld and Indian Defense Minister Pranab Mukherjee. This agreement provides for increased cooperation on research and development of high-tech weaponry and joint and combined training exercises."[7] This initiative is the stuff from which alliances grow. India's considerable power and influence in the region, if allied with America's, would be an enormous obstacle to Chinese aggression.

TAIWAN

President Bush and his successors must take a "tough love" approach with the Taiwanese. If the Taiwanese are unwilling to spend the necessary money to defend themselves they should be told in unmistakable terms that we will not spend blood and treasure in their defense. The Taiwanese need a big dose of reality.

SINGAPORE, THAILAND, VIETNAM, AND SOUTH KOREA

In 2005, America signed a strategic framework with Singapore. Thailand, an ally during the Vietnam War, now hosts thousands of U.S. airmen, sailors, soldiers, and Marines. Vietnam itself is now engaged in military-to-military cooperation with the United States.[8] Even the South Koreans, who have dismissed American advice on dealing with North Korea, are indicating some cooperation with U.S. initiatives because of their fear of China.

During the first Cold War, American governments spoke about "containing" the Soviet Union. American officials don't use the word "containment" now because the Beijing regime finds it offensive. But containment is what we're talking about, and the Bush administration has been more successful at countering Beijing's military, diplomatic, and economic initiatives than any administration since the Korean War.

Aside from containment, the United States has employed "constructive engagement." In 2005, President Bush and Defense Secretary Donald Rumsfeld made separate visits to China. Peter Rodman, assistant secretary of defense for international security affairs, said one lesson learned during Secretary Rumsfeld's China visit was that "you can be firm

with the Chinese and frank with the Chinese and yet have a very constructive relation with them."

But we also need deterrence. China is heavily engaged with every
major terrorist nation, from Sudan to Somalia and from Iran to North
Korea. Beijing's arms race—aimed at catching up to and surpassing the
United States—will also enable it to supply advanced arms to these nations
on the condition that they fall under China's military and political domi-
nation. China's development of purely offensive weapons—anti-satellite
weapons, cyber-war weapons, and the like—may soon give China military advantages that could prove decisive unless we develop effective
counter-measures. In 2005, Congress killed one such counter-measure
when it denied the Air Force's plan to place defensive weapons in space
to protect key satellites.

It would take another book to detail the other investments in military
technology and capital systems that will be needed to ensure America's
ability to defend its interests against Chinese aggression, but the necessary investments fall into several general categories:

- Cyber-war systems: Secure communication and computer networks
  are essential for the military and intelligence communities to be
  able to perform their tasks. The Defense Department, the NSA, the
  CIA, and every other national security–related agency are making
  protection against cyber-attack a priority. But too little is being
  done because budgets are tight. The Defense Department and the
  NSA should coordinate a two-year plan, thoroughly revised and
  updated every two years, to defend against cyber-attacks, and Congress needs to authorize the money to implement it. Congressmen
  need to put national security ahead of their usual pork-barrel
  spending. Since September 11, stock markets and other financial
  institutions have erected firewalls against cyber-attacks and have
  taken other precautions. Power grids, nuclear power plants, air
  traffic control systems, and other crucial elements of our electronic
  infrastructure need similar protection. We also need offensive

cyber-war systems and strategies so that we can strike—sometimes preemptively—or counter-strike and defeat enemies who would attack our computer networks.

- Anti-satellite weapons: China is investing heavily in weapons to destroy military and commercial satellites that provide navigational assistance, intelligence, and secure communications. There is no treaty that prevents the United States from using space-based weapons to protect American satellites—and there is no excuse for not protecting these key assets. Congress needs to authorize the funds to develop and deploy such space-based defensive weapons, and we need offensive weapons to destroy enemy satellites as a matter of deterrence. Military and commercial satellites need to make better use of stealth technology and cyber-war defenses like firewalls.

- Stealth: Stealth technology gives America a decisive advantage in land and sea warfare, but our fleets of B-2 bombers and F-117 fighter-bombers are aging, and we don't have enough of the stealthy F-22 fighters, now entering the Air Force inventory, to accomplish their mission: air supremacy in any battlespace. Congress needs to dramatically increase the purchase of F-22s and consider the next generation of bomber aircraft, which must renew the advantages the small fleet of B-2s now provides.

- Submarines: China and Russia are massively expanding their fleets of submarines. Our most advanced submarines are being purchased in very small—too small—numbers. A submarine is an expensive weapon system, but also one of the most effective. Unless we dominate the seas with submarine supremacy, we cannot hope to project power and defend our interests in the Pacific.

- Tanker aircraft: The average age of U.S. Air Force tankers—which guarantee our ability to project airpower—is over fifty years, and the acquisition of new tankers has been delayed because of a scandal involving an Air Force acquisition executive and Boeing. Unless Congress acts, it will be another decade or more before we get the tankers we need now. And we should make sure the tankers are American-made. We cannot afford to contract the job out to Airbus, the subsidized European aircraft builder that wants the contract and which would then have control of repairs and spare parts. Whichever American company is chosen as the new builder, it should be under a contract that provides significant financial penalties for delay and major bonuses for exceeding contractual performance and schedule requirements.

- People: Our most valuable military assets are the skills of our soldiers, sailors, airmen, and Marines. We need many more of them—now. And we need to do what our schools have not done. We need to make sure every recruit has or gets rudimentary knowledge of at least one foreign language and takes a military-taught survey course of the histories of our potential enemies.

America is failing badly at making the investments it needs to meet the military challenge from China. A possible future Democratic administration—with the anti-military mindset of that party—would make matters even worse. If we are to prevail in this Cold War as we did in the last, we need to invest constantly and significantly in the future capability of our military—and in our resolve to defend our interests and counter the rise of China.

China understands American politics as well as any foreign nation does. The Beijing regime recognizes that American attitudes and policies change with each administration. During the Clinton years, China enjoyed a lackadaisical tolerance from the White House that enabled it to obtain—legally and otherwise—many advanced technologies it could not otherwise have bought. After George W. Bush was inaugurated, China tested the new president's courage and resolve as the Soviets had in the European Cold War.

For decades, American reconnaissance aircraft have plied the skies over international waters near China. They are part of the normal scenery of the Pacific Cold War, just as the Chinese reconnaissance flights near

Taiwan and over the South China Sea are. The routine includes Chinese naval vessels trespassing in Taiwanese and Japanese waters. But on April 1, 2001, less than three months after George W. Bush's first inauguration, the Chinese went aggressive against an unarmed American EP-3 Navy reconnaissance aircraft flying over international waters near China. Chinese air force F-8 jets hunted the EP-3, closed with it, and one—in a very dangerous move—tried to "thump" it (pass so close to its nose that the American aircraft would feel a hard bump and be momentarily destabilized by the jet wash). Chinese pilot Wang Wei miscalculated and collided with the EP-3, forcing the damaged aircraft to make an emergency landing on Hainan Island. Wang Wei's fighter crashed, killing him.

The Chinese followed the old Soviet Cold War incident model to the letter. Having first manufactured the confrontation, they actively turned it into a crisis. Beijing demanded an American apology for the aircraft collision that killed their pilot. George W. Bush refused. The Chinese held the American crew hostage for eleven days, until the president issued a statement of regret about the Chinese pilot's death, though President Bush refused to say the American aircraft was at fault. The incident was a cold-blooded provocation intended to test the mettle of the new president. It could have escalated into war, because, as events showed, China has no fear of America. President Bush's cautious reaction avoided a war, and the incident could have been called a draw but for the fact that America refused, only a short time later, to sell the Taiwanese Aegis missile-defense destroyers.

The Aegis decision was partially reversed. The United States offered Taiwan a large arms package, including diesel-electric submarines. But four years later the Taiwanese still hadn't made up their minds about it. Meanwhile, the dead Chinese pilot, Wang Wei, was honored and revered as a "revolutionary martyr" throughout Communist China.[9] The next American president—whoever he or she is—needs to be as decisive, cool, and resolute as President George W. Bush. Otherwise, a war with China is a near certainty.

Beijing seeks to be the most unconventional adversary we have ever fought, so America will have to be more unconventional, more imaginative, and more steadfast than ever before. This we can do. But will we? And if we do, will that prevent war with China? Unless we see the Bush administration act more aggressively on ramping up the defense budget, the answer to both questions is probably no. If, however, the Bush administration makes a priority of rapidly increasing our high-tech defense capability, and if succeeding administrations continue what President Bush has begun, the Pacific region may, for some years, remain at peace. Then we might accomplish what Sun Tzu wrote about in chapter six of *The Art of War*. He wrote that an enemy can be manipulated by maneuver:

> When I wish to give battle, my enemy, even though protected by high walls and deep moats, cannot help but engage me, for I attack a position he must succor. When I wish to avoid battle I may defend myself simply by drawing a line on the ground; the enemy will be unable to attack me because I divert him from going where he wishes.[10]

Our primary objective must be deterrence, but diplomacy is vital too. We must continue to improve our cooperation with Asian nations, from Japan to South Korea, from Indochina to Thailand and Malaysia, from India to Afghanistan. China understands soft power as well as any nation. Its Shanghai Cooperation Organization (SCO) is an example of how it, with Russia's help, is spreading its influence wherever it sees an opening.

The Shanghai Cooperation Organization is a quasi-alliance between China and Russia on one hand and Kazakhstan, Kyrgystan, Tajikistan, and Uzbekistan on the other.[11] Its alleged purpose is to increase stability and disarmament in the region. These nations are the strategic key to Southwest Asia and the Caucasus. Some of them harbor terrorists and some of them—importantly for China—have rich, undeveloped oil resources. Since the organization's founding in 2001, Iran, Pakistan, and India have been granted nonmember participant status.[12] The SCO is not a modern equivalent of the Warsaw Pact, but its clear purpose is to challenge American influence in the region, cast China as the protector of Muslim states, and perhaps prevent American counter-terrorist operations in the area. But we can, if we try, use soft power as well as or better than China. The Asian states have every reason to fear China and to increase their economic and military ties to the United States.

In the 1950s, the Southeast Asian Treaty Organization (SEATO) was formed as a parallel to NATO. Its members—Australia, France, Great Britain, New Zealand, Pakistan, the Philippines, Thailand, and the United States—were drawn together to defend themselves from the Soviet Union and China. A formal mutual defense treaty such as SEATO is probably beyond our reach today. But we might be able to achieve SEATO's goals without the formality of a treaty.

To win the Pacific Cold War, we must first understand that it has begun, and that its cause is China's regional ambitions and military buildup. We do not have the luxury of finishing the War on Terror before we rise to the challenge of China. We need to win both, and there is no time to waste.

GLOSSARY

Advanced EHF (AHEF): a system of three satellites providing secure, global command, and communications functions for high-value assets such as the B-2 bomber

AFB: Air Force base

ASAT: anti-satellite weapon

B-2 Spirit: U.S. Air Force stealthy long-range strategic bomber

Chicom: military slang term for Communist Chinese

C4: command, control, communications, and computers

C4ISR: command, control, communications, computers, intelligence, surveillance, and reconnaissance

CNO: computer network operations

EMP: electromagnetic pulse. A blast of energy created by certain weapons, both nuclear and non-nuclear

EP-3 Orion: U.S. Navy long-range four-engine reconnaissance, electronic intelligence, and monitoring aircraft. Range: approximately 2,000 miles. Speed: approximately 200 mph

EU: European Union

F-8: Chinese Shenyang J-8 single-engine multi-role fighter, 1970s vintage still in operation[1]

F-11: Chinese-manufactured version of Russian SU-27

F-22 Raptor: U.S. Air Force twin-engine stealthy supersonic fighter aircraft. Range: 2,000+ miles, supersonic cruise

Galileo: planned European Union GPS satellite constellation

GPS: global positioning satellites used for navigation and communications

JSTARS: E-8 "Joint STARS" modified Boeing 707 designed for battle management, ground surveillance, command, and control

Milstar: a system of five satellites providing jam-resistant secure command and control communications worldwide, linking command with ground, sea, and air forces

MIRV: multiple independently targeted reentry vehicles. The several nuclear warheads may be carried by a ballistic missile.

Misty: a top-secret stealthy reconnaissance satellite program allegedly leaked to the press by three Democratic senators in December 2004[2]

MOAB: massive overhead air blast weapon. A non-nuclear fuel-air bomb

Noforn: a designation of classified information indicating that it may not be shared with any foreign governments

NRO: National Reconnaissance Office

NSA: National Security Agency, headquartered at Ft. Meade, Maryland

OAS: Organization of American States

PACAF: U.S. Pacific Air Forces

PACOM: U.S. Pacific Command

Patriot PAC 3: U.S.-built (Raytheon) anti-aircraft and anti-missile system. The ORD (operational requirements document for PAC 3) identifies additional performance requirements needed to counter advanced stealth technology, advanced electronic counter-measure techniques by air-breathing targets, unmanned remotely piloted vehicles, anti-radiation missiles, tactical air-to-surface missiles, and tactical ballistic missiles. The ORD requires that the PAC 3 system be rapidly deployable, robust in firepower, tactically mobile, survivable, low in force structure demands, and able to interoperate with other TMD systems.[3]

PLA: People's Liberation Army

PLAN: People's Liberation Army (Navy)

PLAAF: People's Liberation Army (Air Force)

PRC: People's Republic of China

RCS: radar cross-section. A measure of visibility to radar

ROK: Republic of Korea

SCIF: secure compartmented information facility. A room or series of rooms deemed safe for top-secret conversation

Sovremenny-class destroyers: Russian-built high-speed surface combatant ships of approximately 8,500 tons displacement, designed to defeat U.S. aircraft carriers

SU-27 Flanker: Russian-built twin-engine (and twin-tailed) Mach 2+ fighter-bomber, capable of carrying a mixture of weapons for a range of 2,000+ miles

SU-30MKK: an export version of the SU-27 with ground-attack and maritime operational capability

Tai Chi: ancient Chinese (actually Mongol) noble title borne by the son of a princess of the first or second rank

Tai Fu: "grand tutor"

trojan (also Trojan horse): In computers, a Trojan horse is a program in which malicious or harmful code is contained inside apparently harmless programming or data in such a way that it can get control and do its chosen form of damage, such as ruining the file allocation table on your hard disk. In one infamous case, a Trojan horse was a program that was supposed to find and destroy computer viruses. A Trojan horse may be widely redistributed as part of a computer virus.[4]

TU-22M Backfire: Russian twin-engine supersonic nuclear-capable bomber, combat radius approximately 2,000 miles, maximum speed Mach 2+

Virus: a program or programming code that replicates by being copied or initiating its copying to another program, computer boot sector, or document. Viruses can be transmitted as attachments to an e-mail note or in a downloaded file, or be present on a disk or CD. The immediate source of the e-mail note, downloaded file, or disk is usually unaware that it contains a virus. Some viruses wreak their effect as soon as their code is executed; other viruses lie dormant until circumstances cause their code to be executed by the computer. Some viruses are benign or playful in intent and effect ("Happy Birthday, Ludwig!") and some can be quite harmful, erasing data or causing your hard disk to require reformatting. A virus that replicates itself by resending itself as an e-mail attachment or as part of a network message is known as a worm.[5]

WMD: weapons of mass destruction

Yuan: PRC currency

APPENDIX

ANNUAL REPORT TO CONGRESS

The Military Power of the People's
Republic of China
2005

Office of the Secretary of Defense

The Military Power of the People's Republic of China

A Report to Congress
Pursuant to the National Defense Authorization Act
Fiscal Year 2000

Section 1202 of the National Defense Authorization Act for Fiscal Year 2000, Public Law 106-65, provides that the Secretary of Defense shall submit a report "on the current and future military strategy of the People's Republic of China. The report shall address the current and probable future course of military-technological development on the People's Liberation Army and the tenets and probable development of Chinese grand strategy, security strategy, and military strategy, and of the military organizations and operational concepts, through the next 20 years."

EXECUTIVE SUMMARY

The rapid rise of the People's Republic of China (PRC) as a regional political and economic power with global aspirations is one of the principal elements in the emergence of East Asia, a region that has changed greatly over the past quarter of a century. China's emergence has significant implications for the region and the world. The United States welcomes the rise of a peaceful and prosperous China, one that becomes integrated as a constructive member of the international community. But, we see a China facing a strategic crossroads. Questions remain about the basic choices China's leaders will make as China's power and influence grow, particularly its military power.

The Chinese People's Liberation Army (PLA) is modernizing its forces, emphasizing preparations to fight and win short-duration, high-intensity conflicts along China's periphery. PLA modernization has accelerated since the mid-to-late 1990s in response to central leadership demands to develop military options for Taiwan scenarios.

In the short term, the PRC appears focused on preventing Taiwan independence or trying to compel Taiwan to negotiate a settlement on Beijing's terms. A second set of objectives includes building counters to third-party, including potential U.S., intervention in cross-Strait crises. PLA preparations, including an expanding force of ballistic missiles (long-range and short-range), cruise missiles, submarines, advanced aircraft, and other modern systems, come against the background of a policy toward Taiwan that espouses "peaceful reunification." China has not renounced the use of force, however. Over the long term, if current trends persist, PLA capabilities could pose a credible threat to other modern militaries operating in the region.

The PLA is working toward these goals by acquiring new foreign and domestic weapon systems and military technologies, promulgating new doctrine for modern warfare, reforming military institutions, personnel development and professionalization, and improving exercise and training standards. We assess that China's ability to project conventional military power beyond its periphery remains limited.

This report outlines what we know of China's national and military strategies, progress and trends in its military modernization, and their implications for regional security and stability. But, secrecy envelops most aspects of Chinese security affairs. The outside world has little knowledge of Chinese motivations and decision-making and of key capabilities supporting PLA modernization. Hence, the findings and conclusions are based on incomplete data. These gaps are, of necessity, bridged by informed judgment.

The PLA's routine publication of a biannual Defense White Paper demonstrates some improvement in transparency. However, China's leaders continue to guard closely basic information on the quantity and quality of the Chinese armed forces. For example, the U.S. Department of Defense still does not know the full size and composition of Chinese government expenditure on national defense. Estimates put it at two to three times the officially published figures.

CHAPTER ONE
KEY DEVELOPMENTS

Several significant developments in China's national strategies and military capabilities in the last two years relate to the questions posed by the Congress in Section 1202 of the National Defense Authorization Act for Fiscal Year 2000 (P.L. 106-65). These developments include:

Grand Strategy, Security Strategy, and Military Strategy

- In December 2004, Beijing released *China's National Defense in 2004* (hereinafter, Defense White Paper), the fourth such paper since 1998. The paper explains China's public views on security and provides information on military-related policies, organization, and regulations. Although a modest improvement over previous years, this newest Defense White Paper provides only limited transparency in military affairs.

- China continued its strategic focus on building "comprehensive national power," with an emphasis on economic development. This year, China will complete its 10th Five Year Plan and finalize preparations for the 11th Five Year Plan (2006-2010).

- State President and Chinese Communist Party (CCP) General Secretary Hu Jintao replaced Jiang Zemin as Chairman of the Central Military Commission (CMC) in September 2004. This transition is unlikely to produce significant change in China's strategy for military modernization, or in its approach to the United States, or Taiwan.

- The CMC expanded from eight to eleven members and added the commanders of the PLA Air Force, Navy, and the Second Artillery (or Strategic Rocket Forces). Air Force and Navy officers were also appointed Deputy Chiefs of the General Staff, reflecting China's emphasis on joint capabilities and inter-service coordination.

- In 2004, China began to express increased concern over a perceived technology gap between modern Western forces and its own. The 2004 Defense White Paper identifies the "technological gap resulting from the Revolution in Military Affairs" as a development that will have a "major impact on China's security." China's increased emphasis on asymmetric, non-linear, and "leap ahead" technologies through the 1990s – and for the foreseeable future – will, in our judgment, help it to close or mitigate this gap.

- Domestic protests, mainly directed at local policies and officials, have grown violent over the past year, posing increasing challenges to China's internal security forces. The number of these incidents in 2004 reached an all-time high of at least 58,000, according to official Chinese estimates. The rising number of protests reflects growing popular dissatisfaction with official behavior related to property rights and forced relocations, labor rights, pensions, corruption, and political reforms.

Trends in China's Strategy in the Asia-Pacific and Other Regions of the World

In 2004, China became more active in the global arena, deploying its growing political and economic weight to increase its influence not only regionally but globally. China's decision to deploy peacekeepers to Haiti and its growing engagement in Latin America are emblematic of this effort. In the Asia-Pacific region, some of its diplomacy was geared to regional institutions that would exclude the United States. Globally, competition with Taiwan and constraining Taiwan's international profile are important elements of China's foreign and diplomatic strategy, particularly among developing countries.

- China introduced "peaceful rise," a new term to describe China's emergence. Although China's leaders themselves spoke of "peaceful rise" when it first appeared, they quickly withdrew the term – apparently reflecting unresolved internal debate over whether or not the term itself was too unsettling to the region or, for some, too soft. Elements of that debate continue to appear in the Chinese press and professional journals. Nevertheless, China's leaders continue to highlight peaceful themes to describe its rise.

- China became the world's second largest consumer and third largest importer of oil in 2003. As China's energy and resource needs grow, Beijing has concluded that access to these resources requires special economic or foreign policy relationships in the Middle East, Africa, and Latin America, bringing China closer to problem countries such as Iran, Sudan, and Venezuela. Resource concerns, among others, played a role in increased Sino-Japanese tensions over the disputed East China Sea.

- Beijing continued to play its role as the chief organizer of the Six-Party Talks aimed at resolving the North Korea nuclear issue. China continues to call publicly for a "nuclear-free Korean Peninsula." China has unique potential, due to its historic ties and geography, to convince North Korea to give up its nuclear ambitions.

- China expanded upon the successful conclusion in 2003 of the China-ASEAN Joint Declaration of a Strategic Partnership for Peace and Prosperity – the first such agreement China has ever concluded with a regional organization – and China's 2003 accession to the ASEAN Treaty of Amity and Cooperation – the first non-ASEAN country to do so – by signing in 2004 a memorandum of understanding with ASEAN on Cooperation in the Field of Non-Traditional Security Issues and endorsing the ASEAN Code of Conduct for the South China Sea. Meanwhile, China maintains active diplomacy, including military relations, with most ASEAN member states to promote positive views of China's rise, gain access to resources, and isolate Taiwan.

- China continued to make progress on resolving its border dispute with India. In Beijing, improved ties with New Delhi serve as a way to stabilize its periphery and balance perceived improvements in U.S.-India relations. At the same time, Beijing is encouraging New Delhi and Islamabad to reduce tensions while preserving China's historical strategic partnership with Pakistan.

- The PLA conducted joint maritime search and rescue drills for the first time with British, Indian, and French naval forces in 2004. China and Russia announced plans to hold a combined exercise in China sometime in 2005.

The Security Situation in the Taiwan Strait

- The 2004 Defense White Paper characterized the cross-Strait situation as "grim," and elevated Taiwan and sovereignty concerns to top priority for China's armed forces – an intensification of rhetoric from the previous Defense White Paper (2002).

- China's National People's Congress passed an "anti-secession law" in March 2005 as a means to pressure the Taiwan leadership, build a legal foundation to justify a use of force, and form a rhetorical counter to the U.S. Taiwan Relations Act.

- China held two large-scale amphibious exercises in 2004 (division to group-army level in size), one of which explicitly dealt with a Taiwan scenario, bringing the total number of amphibious exercises to ten over the past five years.

Chinese Strategy Regarding Taiwan

- China used diplomatic pressures and verbal warnings to try (unsuccessfully) to derail Taiwan President Chen Shui-bian's re-election in March 2004. Beijing sought to preempt Chen's May 20 inaugural address by issuing a statement on May 17 warning of the consequences of Taiwan's "pursuit of a separatist agenda."

- China continued to adhere to its policy of peaceful unification under the "one country, two systems" framework that offers Taiwan limited autonomy in exchange for Taiwan's integration with the mainland.

- Kuomintang Chairman Lien Chan and the People's First Party Chairman James Soong visited the mainland in the Spring of 2005. China did not change its policy of no direct negotiations with the leadership of Taiwan's democratically-elected government.

- Beijing continues to see the threat and possible use of force as integral to its policy of dissuading Taiwan from pursuing independence and moving Taiwan ultimately to unite with the mainland.

The Size, Location, and Capabilities of Chinese Forces facing Taiwan

China continued to deploy its most advanced systems to the military regions directly opposite Taiwan. These new weapon systems represent significant improvements from the older, less capable hardware that remains the bulk of China's inventory. To realize the potential in the technologically advanced equipment, China's armed forces are attempting to integrate the systems into the force structure, develop modern doctrine and tactics, and improve training and exercises.

- Ballistic Missiles. China has deployed some 650-730 mobile CSS-6 and CSS-7 short-range ballistic missiles (SRBMs) to garrisons opposite Taiwan. Deployment of these systems is increasing at a rate of about 100 missiles per year. Newer versions of these missiles feature improved range and accuracy.

- China is exploring the use of ballistic missiles for anti-access/sea-denial missions.

- China is modernizing its longer-range ballistic missile force by replacing older systems with newer, more survivable missiles. Over the next several years China will begin to bring into service a new road-mobile, solid-propellant, intercontinental-range ballistic missile (ICBM), the DF-31, an extended range DF-31A, and a new submarine-launched ballistic missile, the JL-2.

- Air Power. China has more than 700 aircraft within un-refueled operational range of Taiwan. Many of these are obsolescent or upgrades of older-generation aircraft. However, China's air forces continue to acquire advanced fighter aircraft from Russia, including the Su-30MKK multirole and Su-30MK2 maritime strike aircraft. New acquisitions augment previous deliveries of Su-27 fighter aircraft. China is also producing its own version of the Su-27SK, the F-11, under a licensed co-production agreement with Moscow. Last year, Beijing sought to renegotiate its agreement and produce the multirole Su-27SMK for the remainder of the production run. These later generations of aircraft make up a growing percentage of the PLA Air Force inventory.

- China's indigenous 4th generation fighter, the F-10, completed development in 2004 and will begin fielding this year. Improvements to the FB-7 fighter program will enable this older aircraft to perform nighttime maritime strike operations. China has several programs underway to deploy new standoff escort jammers on bombers, transports, tactical aircraft, and unmanned aerial vehicle platforms.

- China is acquiring from abroad or developing advanced precision strike munitions, including cruise missiles and air-to-air, air-to-surface, and anti-radiation munitions.

- The PLA appears interested in converting retired fighter aircraft into unmanned combat aerial vehicles (UCAVs). China has hundreds of older fighters in its inventory that could be converted for this purpose.

- Naval Power. China's naval forces include 64 major surface combatants, some 55 attack submarines, more than 40 medium and heavy amphibious lift vessels, and approximately 50 coastal missile patrol craft. Two-thirds of these assets are located in the East and South Sea fleets.

- China deployed its first two Russian-made SOVREMENNYY-class guided missile destroyers (DDG) to the East Sea Fleet. An additional two SOVREMENNYY DDGs are under contract for delivery. The SOVREMENNYY DDGs are fitted with advanced anti-ship cruise missiles (ASCM) and ship-borne air defense systems.

- China's SONG-class diesel electric submarine has entered serial production. The SONG is designed to carry the YJ-82, an encapsulated ASCM capable of submerged launch. Last year, China launched a new diesel submarine, the YUAN-class, improving the capabilities of its submarine force. China's next generation nuclear attack submarine, the Type 093, is expected to enter service in 2005.

- China is acquiring eight additional KILO-class diesel electric submarines from Russia to augment the four previously purchased units. The new KILOs will include the advanced SS-N-27 ASCM, and wire-guided and wake-homing torpedoes.

- Air Defense. In August 2004, China received the final shipment from Russia of four S-300PMU-1/SA-20 surface-to-air missile (SAM) battalions. China has also agreed to purchase follow-on S-300PMU-2, the first battalion of which is expected to arrive in 2006. With an advertised intercept range of 200 km, the S-300PMU-2 provides increased lethality against tactical ballistic missiles and more effective electronic counter-counter measures.

- The PLA fielded a new self-propelled tactical SAM to its air defense brigades, the FM-90 (CSA-7). The CSA-7 is an improved copy of the French Crotale system. With a 15km range, the CSA-7 more than doubles the range of the man-portable air defense SAMs the PLA previously relied upon.

- Ground Forces. China has 375,000 ground forces personnel deployed to the three military regions opposite Taiwan. China has been upgrading these units with amphibious armor and other vehicles, such as tanks and armored personnel carriers.

- The PLA is expected to complete another round of downsizing, by some 200,000, by the end of 2005, bringing the size of the PLA to about 2.3 million, according to official statistics. The inclusion of paramilitary People's Armed Police and reserves increases that figure to over 3.2 million. The 2004 Defense White Paper claims that China can also draw upon more than 10 million organized militia members.

- China acquired more Mi-17/171 medium-lift helicopters from Russia in 2004 and is developing its own attack helicopter, the Z-10, which may enter service in 2014.

Developments in Chinese Military Doctrine

- China's latest Defense White Paper deployed authoritatively a new doctrinal term to describe future wars the PLA must be prepared to fight: "local wars under conditions of informationalization." This term acknowledges the PLA's emphasis on information technology as a force multiplier and reflects the PLA's understanding of the implications of the revolution in military affairs on the modern battlefield.

- The PLA continues to improve its potential for joint operations by developing a modern, integrated command, control, communications, computers, intelligence, surveillance, and reconnaissance (C4ISR) network and institutional changes.

- During 2004, the PLA began to integrate military and civilian suppliers in the procurement system and outsourced a number of previously military jobs to civilian industry. The PLA is placing greater emphasis on the mobilization of the economy, both in peacetime and in war, to support national defense.

- The PLA fielded its first experimental "joint logistical unit" in July 2004.

- China is digesting lessons learned from coalition military operations in Afghanistan and Iraq. China can be expected to incorporate these lessons into updated doctrine, planning, and acquisition programs.

Technology Transfers and Acquisitions to Enhance Military Capability

- China will continue to press the European Union (EU) to lift its embargo on the sale of arms to China, established in response to the Tiananmen crackdown in 1989. A decision by the EU to lift the embargo would allow China access to advanced technologies that could add new weapons systems to its inventory and increase the quality of, and production capabilities for, its current and future systems.

- In addition to deliveries and standing orders for the Su-30MKK and Su-30MK2 multirole fighters, SOVREMENNYY-class DDGs, KILO-class submarines, associated weapons, and advanced SAMs from Russia cited above, China may acquire additional IL-76 transport planes and the IL-78/MIDAS air refueling aircraft from Russia in 2005.

Assessment of Challenges to Taiwan's Deterrent Forces

- The cross-Strait military balance appears to be shifting toward Beijing as a result of China's sustained economic growth, growing diplomatic leverage, and improvements in the PLA's military capabilities.

- Taiwan defense spending has steadily declined in real terms over the past decade, even as Chinese air, naval, and missile force modernization has increased the need for countermeasures that would enable Taiwan to avoid being quickly overwhelmed.

- A $15.3 billion Special Budget for the purchase of Patriot PAC-III air defense systems, P-3C Orion anti-submarine aircraft, and diesel attack submarines, approved by the United States for sale to Taiwan in 2001, is now before the Taiwan Legislative Yuan.

CHAPTER TWO
UNDERSTANDING CHINA'S STRATEGY

"Observe calmly; secure our position; cope with affairs calmly;
hide our capacities and bide our time; be good at maintaining a low profile;
never claim leadership."
-- Deng Xiaoping[1]

Cooperative, Candid, and Constructive U.S.-China Relations

The EP-3 incident in April 2001 damaged U.S.-China relations. Thereafter, the United States developed a cooperative and constructive relationship with China in which the United States has stressed the values of candor and transparency.

- The United States and China have worked together to pursue the common objective of a nuclear weapons-free Korean Peninsula, to establish the Six-Party Talks process, and to cooperate on counter-terrorism – including China's joining the U.S. Container Security Initiative.

- Through the Joint Commission on Commerce and Trade and the Joint Economic Committee, senior economic policy officials are trying to manage bilateral trade, advance the goals established when China joined the World Trade Organization (WTO), and deal with such issues as China's compliance with Intellectual Property Rights standards.

- The United States and China have agreed to a new, periodic senior dialogue on global issues of mutual concern that will begin this summer.

- In our military-to-military relationship, we have expanded exchanges, including high-level visits and contacts between our military academies.

Nonetheless, questions remain about China's future and the choices Chinese Communist Party (CCP) leaders will make as China becomes a more powerful and influential regional and global actor. These choices will have significant implications – not merely for the United States, but for China, the Asia-Pacific region, and the world.

Images of China's Future

China is developing on the world stage as a regional power, but its emergence also has global implications. China faces a strategic crossroads. It can choose a pathway of peaceful integration and benign competition. China can also choose, or find itself upon, a pathway along which China would emerge to exert dominant influence in an expanding sphere. Or, China could emerge less confident and focused inward on challenges to

---

[1] As cited in "Deng Puts Forward New 12-Character Guiding Principle for Internal and Foreign Policies," Ching Pao (Hong Kong), No. 172, pp. 84-86, 5 November 1991. FBIS HK0611100091.

national unity and the Chinese Communist Party's claim to legitimacy. The future of a rising China is not yet set immutably on one course or another.

United States policy welcomes the rise of a peaceful and prosperous China. However, there are forces – some beyond the control of China's military and national security planners – that could divert China from a peaceful pathway. These include:

- nationalistic fervor bred by expanding economic power and political influence;

- structural economic weaknesses and inefficiencies that could undermine economic growth;

- an inability to accommodate the forces of an open, transparent market economy;

- a government that is still adapting to great power roles; and,

- an expanding military-industrial complex that proliferates advanced arms.

The interactions of these forces are difficult to predict, as are the implications of these interactions on China's strategic behavior and future strategic direction. Regarding the possible courses set out below, we have not attempted to give weight to any one over another, nor do we assert that any one is more likely than the others:

- *More Assertive Foreign and Security Policies.* Continued strong economic performance, combined with rising nationalism and confidence, could lead China to translate its economic gains into fielding an increasingly capable military. It could use its economic weight, backed by military power, to attempt to dictate the terms of foreign security and economic interactions with its trading partners and neighbors.

- *Economic Stagnation.* Economic stagnation – which could aggravate domestic political problems for Communist Party leaders – could lead Beijing to reduce military spending, or alternatively, to shift investments to the military in a bid to sustain domestic support through nationalistic assertions abroad.

- *Economic Downturn.* An economic downturn might occur at some time in the future, possibly as a result of the following factors: financial institutions are vulnerable, the transition to a market economy is incomplete, demographic change is placing stress on the social welfare system, and poor environmental practices have set the conditions for regional ecological disasters. A major economic downturn could have broad effects across regional economies, produce internal unrest, and generate refugee flows that could challenge central government control.

- *Internal Unrest.* Party leaders have relaxed their grip on the economic sphere and now allow greater public discourse on some issues, but continue to repress any challenges to their monopoly on political power. As documented in the latest U.S. Department of State report on human rights, independent trade and labor unions are suppressed, ethnic-Tibetan and Uighur minorities are repressed, and religious groups continue to face harassment. Since 1999, as many as 2,000 adherents of the spiritual movement Falun Gong have died in prison from torture, abuse, or neglect. By suppressing the sort of civil society that can provide stability in crises, the Party has become less susceptible to small impacts but remains vulnerable to larger perturbations.

- **Territorial Disputes.** China has made progress in recent years toward settling long-standing territorial disputes with Russia, Vietnam, India, and Central Asia, but continues to have overlapping territorial claims with Japan, Vietnam, the Philippines, Malaysia, Brunei, and India. China fought small wars and skirmishes with several of these countries in the past. Conflicts to enforce China's claims could erupt in the future with wide regional repercussions, especially if tensions flare over exploration or exploitation of resources.

Direct Insights into China's Strategy are Few

Direct insights into China's national strategies are difficult to acquire. To assess China's intent, analysis of official Chinese strategy documents and White Papers must be augmented by examination of what China has accomplished in recent years and is attempting to accomplish in the future.

Chinese military strategists define grand strategy as "the overall strategy of a nation or alliance of nations in which they use overall national strength" to achieve political goals, especially those related to national security and development. Put another way, Chinese strategy, as they define it, is one of maintaining balance among competing priorities for national economic development and maintaining the type of security environment within which such development can occur.

Two concepts central to understanding how China would achieve this balance are "comprehensive national power" (CNP) and the "strategic configuration of power," or "*shi.*" CNP is the concept by which China's strategic planners evaluate and measure China's national standing in relation to other nations. It includes qualitative and quantitative measures of territory, natural resources, economic power, diplomatic influence, domestic government, military capability, and cultural influence.
The "strategic configuration of power," or "*shi,*" is roughly equivalent to an "alignment of forces," although there is not a direct western equivalent. Chinese linguists also suggest that "*shi*" refers to the "propensity of things," or the "potential born of disposition," that only a skilled strategist can exploit. Conversely, only a sophisticated assessment by an adversary can recognize how "*shi*" can or will be exploited.

Resource Demands as a Driver of Strategy

As China's economy grows, its desire for markets and natural resources (e.g., metals and fossil fuels) will influence China's strategic behavior. The combined total of these imports accounted for just under 60 percent of all imports in 2003.

China still relies on coal for some two-thirds of its energy. The demand for coal – mostly from domestic sources – will increase as China's economy expands. China's demand for oil and gas is increasing rapidly. In 2003, China became the world's second largest consumer and third largest importer of oil. China currently imports over 40 percent of its oil. By 2025, this figure could rise to 80 percent (9.5 – 15 million barrels per day). Nuclear power and natural gas account for smaller, but growing, portions of energy consumption. China plans to increase natural gas utilization from 3 percent to 8 percent of total consumption by 2010. Similarly, China plans to build some 30 1,000 megawatt nuclear power reactors by 2020.

Chinese Premier Wen Jiabao, recognizing the rapid growth in Chinese oil and gas consumption, recently stated that the "shortage of oil and gas resources has become a restricting factor in our country's economic and social development," and called upon China to "implement a strategy for sustainable development of our oil and natural gas resources."

China began the process of constructing a strategic petroleum reserve (SPR) in 2004. By 2015, Beijing plans to build the SPR to the International Energy Agency standard of 90 days' supply. Poor logistics and transportation networks suggest this may still prove inadequate. For the foreseeable future, China will rely on overseas sources for oil and other strategic resources, meaning China will remain reliant upon maritime transportation to meet its energy demands.

This dependence on overseas resources and energy supplies, especially oil and natural gas, is playing a role in shaping China's strategy and policy. Such concerns factor heavily in Beijing's relations with Angola, Central Asia, Indonesia, the Middle East (including Iran), Russia, Sudan, and Venezuela – to pursue long-term supply agreements – as well as its relations with countries that sit astride key geostrategic chokepoints – to secure passage. Beijing's belief that it requires such special relationships in order to assure its energy access could shape its defense strategy and force planning in the future. Indicators of such a shift would include increased investment in a blue-water capable fleet and, potentially, a more activist military presence abroad.

Figure 1. China's Energy Consumption.

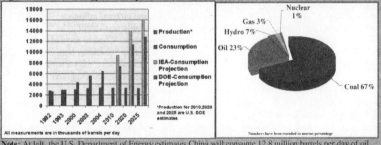

Note: At left, the U.S. Department of Energy estimates China will consume 12.8 million barrels per day of oil by 2025. Some industry projections place this figure between 16-20 million barrels per day. Production figures are estimates. At right, based on 2003 data, China relied on coal for approximately two-thirds of its energy

Since the early 1980s, as former paramount leader Deng Xiaoping pressed forward with China's "reform and opening up," Chinese leaders have described their national development strategy as a quest to increase China's CNP. As China's leaders pursue national development, they must constantly assess the broader security environment, or "strategic configuration of power," for potential challenges and threats – as well as opportunities – that might prompt an adjustment in national strategy.

The "24 Character" Strategy

In the early 1990s, former paramount leader Deng Xiaoping (d. 1997) gave guidance to China's foreign and security policy apparatus that, collectively, has come to be known as the "24 character" strategy: *"observe calmly; secure our position; cope with affairs calmly; hide our capacities and bide our time; be good at maintaining a low profile; and never claim leadership."* Later, the phrase, "make some contributions (*you suo zuo wei*)" was added.

This strategy is often quoted by senior Chinese national security officials, especially as it relates to China's diplomacy. Although certain aspects of this strategy have been debated in recent years within China's security establishment – namely the relative emphasis placed upon "never claim leadership" or "make some contributions" – taken as a whole, the strategy suggests both a short-term desire to downplay China's ambitions and a long-term strategy to build up China's power to maximize options for the future.

The prospect of large-scale conflict, such as a war between China and Taiwan that included direct U.S. involvement, would likely prompt China's leaders to place the reestablishment of a favorable "strategic configuration of power" ahead of national development. Both Deng Xiaoping and Jiang Zemin indicated that in these circumstances, one of China's war aims would be to terminate the conflict on favorable terms as quickly as possible to refocus national resources on developing CNP. There is no evidence that China's new leaders' views on this point are any different.

In peacetime, we can expect China to pursue economic progress as part of its strategy to build comprehensive national power. It has established a goal of doubling by 2010 the size of its economy in 2000 and raising GDP per capita ($1,250 in 2004) to the levels of an "intermediate developed country" (roughly $3,400) by 2049. Chinese leaders value such progress for its own sake, as well as for the enhancements to military forces and national power this progress will allow. Moreover, in contrast to a "development first model," evidence suggests they seek to integrate the two to obviate, or at least minimize, traditional "guns vs. butter" trade-offs.

In May 2003, President Hu Jintao stated that: "it is necessary . . . to establish a mechanism of *mutual promotion and coordinated development* between national defense building and economic development." China's modernization indicates a buildup of armaments that reinforces this notion of coordinated, integrated civilian and military development.

Military Modernization . . . Beyond Taiwan

The Chinese military forms an important, and growing, part of Beijing's overall national strategy. China's leaders believe that control and use of the armed forces and other instruments of power are essential to ensure that the Party remains dominant, and that China can secure its borders, defend its territorial claims, and shape its security environment in a way that allows its continued economic growth and development. As China's economy expands, so too will its interests and the perceived need to build an armed force capable of protecting them. In its latest Defense White Paper, China notes that, "[t]he military factor plays a greater role in . . . national security," and, "[t]he role played by military power in safeguarding national security is assuming greater prominence."

Consequently, although the principal focus of China's military modernization in the near term appears to be preparing for potential conflict in the Taiwan Strait, some of China's military planners are surveying the strategic landscape beyond Taiwan. Some Chinese military analysts have expressed the view that control of Taiwan would enable the PLA Navy to move its maritime defensive perimeter further seaward and improve Beijing's ability to influence regional sea lines of communication. Conversely, some of these analysts believe, the political status quo with Taiwan constrains China's ability to project power. General Wen Zongren, Political Commissar of the elite PLA Academy of Military Science, stated in a recent interview that resolving the Taiwan issue is of "far reaching significance to breaking international forces' blockade against China's maritime security. . . . Only when we break this blockade shall we be able to talk about China's rise. . . . [T]o rise suddenly, China must pass through oceans and go out of the oceans in its future development."

Analysis of Chinese military acquisitions also suggests the PLA is generating military capabilities that go beyond a Taiwan scenario. All of China's SRBMs, although garrisoned opposite Taiwan, are mobile and can deploy throughout the country to take up firing positions in support of a variety of regional contingencies. China is also developing new medium-range systems that will improve its regional targeting capability. There are corresponding improvements in intercontinental-range missiles capable of striking targets across the globe, including in the United States.

Similarly, China's air and naval force improvements – both complete and in the pipeline – are scoped for operations beyond the geography around Taiwan. Airborne early warning and control and aerial refueling programs for the PLA Air Force will extend the operational range for its fighter and strike aircraft, permitting extended operations into the South China Sea, for example. Naval acquisitions, such as advanced destroyers and submarines, reflect Beijing's pursuit of an "active offshore defense," to protect and advance its maritime interests, including territorial claims, economic interests, and critical sea lines of communication. Over the long-term, improvements in China's command, control, communication, computers, intelligence, surveillance, and reconnaissance (C4ISR) capability, including space-based and over-the-horizon platforms, could enable Beijing to identify, target, and track foreign military activities deep into the western Pacific and provide, potentially, hemispheric coverage.

Figure 2. Short, Medium and Intermediate Range Ballistic Missiles

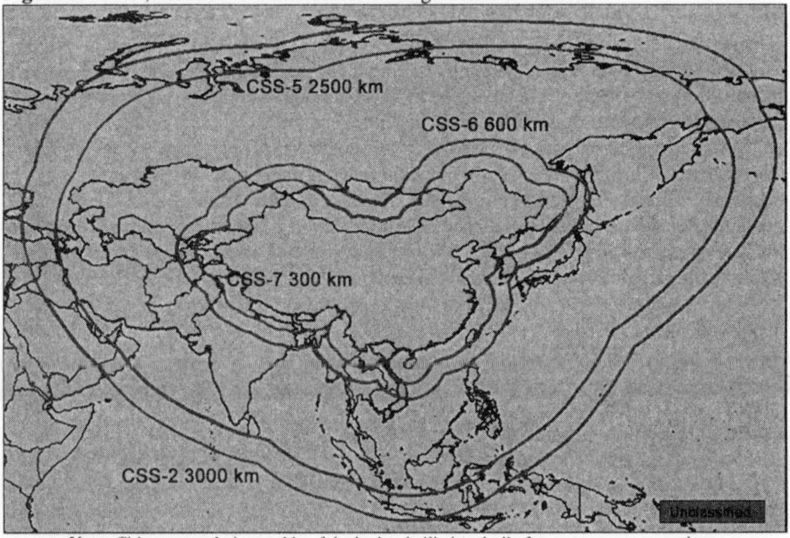

Note: China currently is capable of deploying ballistic missile forces to support a variety of regional contingencies.

Chinese forces have increased operations beyond China's borders and home waters, most notably the highly publicized intrusion of a HAN-class nuclear submarine last year in Japanese territorial waters during operations far into the western Pacific Ocean. After completing its first around-the-world cruise in July 2002, China continues to send its fleet abroad to show the flag and gain familiarity with open-ocean operations. Finally, China has increased participation in global peace operations. China now has some 1,000 peacekeepers abroad, including 500 attached to the UN Observer Mission in Liberia (UNOMIL), 230 with the UN Observer Mission in the Democratic Republic of the Congo (MONUC), and 125 as part of the UN Mission for Stabilization in Haiti (MINUSTAH).

China does not now face a direct threat from another nation. Yet, it continues to invest heavily in its military, particularly in programs designed to improve power projection. The pace and scope of China's military build-up are, already, such as to put regional military balances at risk. Current trends in China's military modernization could provide China with a force capable of prosecuting a range of military operations in Asia – well beyond Taiwan – potentially posing a credible threat to modern militaries operating in the region. China could accelerate its military development by using more of its civil production capacity for military hardware (industrial facilities for China's commercial ship-building – which now occupy about 10% of the global market in terms of dead weight ton production – are co-located with military shipyards, for example) or by increasing purchases of advanced military hardware and technology from abroad.

Beijing has described its long-term political goals of developing comprehensive national power and of ensuring a favorable strategic configuration of power in peaceful terms. Themes include an emphasis on peace and development, the non-use of force in settling disputes, non-intervention in the internal affairs of other countries, the defensive nature of China's military strategy, a policy of no first use of nuclear weapons, and support for nuclear weapons-free zones.

Nevertheless, China's military modernization remains ambitious. In the recent past, moreover, military responses in support of Chinese claims to disputed territory or resource rights have produced crises and conflicts with China's neighbors, including India, Japan, the Philippines, the then-Soviet Union, and Vietnam. In the future, as China's military power grows, China's leaders may be tempted to resort to force or coercion more quickly to press diplomatic advantage, advance security interests, or resolve disputes.

CHAPTER THREE
CHINA'S MILITARY STRATEGY AND DOCTRINE

"You fight your way and I fight my way."
                                                      -- Mao Zedong

It is clear that China's leaders view the military instrument as playing a central role in support of national goals and objectives. China's strategy for the employment of the military to support these goals, or the conditions under which China's leaders would select military over non-military methods in problem-solving, however, are less clear.

China does not have a public document directly equivalent to the U.S. *National Military Strategy*. Outside observers, therefore, have few direct insights into central leadership thinking on the use of force. Based on analysis of authoritative documents, speeches, and writings, we can discern that China uses the term "active defense" to describe its national military strategy. "Active defense" posits a defensive military strategy and asserts that China does not initiate wars or fight wars of aggression, but engages in war only to defend national sovereignty and territorial integrity and attacks only after being attacked.

Beijing's definition of an attack against its territory, or what constitutes an initial attack, is left vague, however. In instances where Beijing's use of force involves core interests, such as Taiwan, it could claim, as it has in the past, that preemptive uses of force are strategically "defensive" in nature, such as the 1979 "counter-attack in self defense" against Vietnam. Consequently, the term "active defense" indicates little about when or how China would initiate hostilities. Once Beijing determines that hostilities have begun, evidence suggests the characteristics of "active defense" are distinctly offensive. The PLA text, *The Study of Campaigns* (*Zhanyi Xue*), published in 2000, explains:

> While strategically the guideline is active defense, in military campaigns, though, the emphasis is placed on taking the initiative in active offense. Only in this way, the strategic objective of active defense can be realized.

"Active defense" calls for forces to be postured to defend against perceived security threats. China's forces also seek to shape their security environment and prevent adversaries from engaging in actions contrary to China's national interests. Returning to the 1979 conflict with Vietnam, Beijing launched that invasion as a punitive measure to "teach Hanoi a lesson" following its incursion into Cambodia. China used military coercion short of war when it launched missiles into closure areas off Taiwan in 1995 and 1996 to pressure Taipei.

Assessments indicate that Beijing's capability for limited and relatively precise uses of force is growing. Since the 1990s, PLA strategists have discussed in professional journals the efficiency of limited applications of force to accomplish limited political goals. Advances in military technology provide Beijing with an expanded set of limited force options. Chinese operational-level military doctrine defines these options as "non-war" uses of force – an extension of political coercion and not an act of war.

Deception in Military Strategy

Over the past several decades, there has been a resurgence in the study of ancient Chinese statecraft within the PLA. Whole departments of military academies teach the precepts of *moulue*, or strategic deception, derived from Chinese experience through the millennia, particularly military aspects surrounding the dynastic cycle. Modern China also has a track record of successfully deceiving opponents. Through effective use of deception from the strategic to the tactical levels, China's intervention in the Korean War caught the United States by surprise. Similarly, India, the Soviet Union, and Vietnam, as well as many outside observers, did not anticipate Chinese incursions into the territories of those countries.

One might expect some secrecy in technological and weapon system development and tactical deception about the location of units. China's practice encompasses this and more. In recent years, for example, China rolled out several new weapon systems whose development was not previously known in the West.

Strategic Direction of PLA Modernization

PLA reform and reorganization started in the early 1980s, accelerated in the latter half of the 1990s, and will continue for the foreseeable future. The PLA is transforming from a mass army designed to fight a protracted war of attrition within its territory to a smaller, modern, professional force capable of fighting high-intensity, local wars of short duration against high-tech adversaries. PLA theorists and planners believe future campaigns will be conducted simultaneously on land, at sea, in the air, in space, and within the electronic sphere. The PLA characterizes these conflicts as "local wars under conditions of informationalization."

Local Wars Under the Conditions of Informationalization

In its December 2004 Defense White Paper, China authoritatively used a new term to describe the type of war the PLA must be prepared to fight and win: "local wars under the conditions of informationalization." By introducing this new term, the PLA effectively discarded "local wars under high-tech conditions," the concept that guided force structure developments for the better part of the last decade.

This new concept sums up China's experiences and assessments of the implications of the revolution in military affairs – primarily the impact of information technology and knowledge-based warfare on the battlefield. While appearing to reinforce many of the trends in China's force modernization that prevailed under "local wars under high-tech conditions," the implications of this new concept are not yet known.

The PLA desires to project joint conventional military power rapidly into its geographic frontier to meet the enemy at or beyond Chinese territory. It is modernizing in all services and at all levels to build a force capable of meeting the requirements of future war, primarily through the improvement of the PLA's joint operational capabilities.

The PLA's ambition to conduct joint operations can be traced to lessons learned from U.S. and allied operations since the Persian Gulf War. Although the PLA has devoted considerable effort to develop joint capabilities, it faces a persistent lack of inter-service cooperation and a lack of actual experience in joint operations. The PLA hopes eventually to fuse service-level capabilities with an integrated C4ISR network, a new command structure, and a joint logistics system. The inclusion of service commanders on the Central Military Commission last year is an example of how China is strengthening inter-service cooperation to develop joint capabilities. The lack of experience in joint operations is a subset of the overall lack of operational experience in the Chinese force.

The PLA's future joint force has been influenced by U.S. capabilities and concepts and by Soviet/Marxist-derived characteristics of warfare, but will unlikely mirror either. For example, it appears that the PLA's concept of joint operations provides for coordination at or above the operational level of war. Since 2000, it has conducted some 14 multiservice exercises with "joint" characteristics and/or "joint" command and control, improving PLA experience levels, and yielding some insights into its future direction. These insights will become clearer as more advanced weapons, sensors, and platforms enter the inventory and training begins to reflect true multiservice operations. For a combination of technical and doctrinal reasons, the PLA has not demonstrated a capability to conduct U.S.-style joint operations, nor is it likely to do so in the near future.

Perceptions of Modern Warfare and U.S. Defense Transformation

China observes closely foreign military campaigns and defense modernization initiatives. The United States factors heavily in these observations as a model of how a modern military engages in modern warfare. China draws from U.S. military operations by adopting or emulating lessons in some areas, and in others, by identifying exploitable vulnerabilities in potential high-tech adversaries. In addition, U.S. defense transformation, as demonstrated by recent U.S. operations, has highlighted to China the expanding technological gap between modern military forces and those of developing countries. The 2004 Defense White Paper identifies the "technological gap resulting from the revolution in military affairs" as having a "major impact on China's security." These concerns have prompted China's leaders, including President Hu Jintao, to order the PLA to pursue "leap ahead" technologies and "informationalized" capabilities to increase the mobility, firepower, and precision of PLA weapons and equipment.

Operation DESERT STORM (1991) was a primary motivator behind China's efforts to prepare for future warfare. The PLA noted that the rapid defeat of Iraqi forces revealed how vulnerable China would be in a modern war. The Gulf War drove the PLA to update doctrine for joint and combined operations to reflect modern warfare and to accelerate reform and modernization. The Gulf War also spurred PLA debates on the implications of the revolution in military affairs, and led China to seek modern C4ISR and to develop new information warfare, air defense, precision strike, and logistics capabilities.

Operation ALLIED FORCE (1999) had a similar impact on PLA thinking, although more as a validation of earlier assessments of the requirements of modern warfare than as a catalyst for change. NATO's air operations over Serbia provided the PLA insights into how a technologically inferior force could defend against a superior opponent. PLA observers noted how low-tech counter-reconnaissance and tactical deception measures, such as camouflage, decoys, dispersion, and frequent movement of forces could deny an adversary situational awareness and precision-strike capabilities. The air campaign reinforced the PLA's focus on passive defense measures such as hardening or burying high-value targets, shifting to fiber-optic communications, and concealing supply depots.

The PLA applied the most significant lessons from Operation ALLIED FORCE in a revised air defense training regime referred to as "Three Attacks, Three Defenses" (attack stealth aircraft, cruise missiles, and helicopters; defend against precision strikes, electronic warfare, and enemy reconnaissance). PLA theorists also began to conclude that airpower and long-range strike diminished the role of ground forces. These observations led to discussion of the value of precision air and missile strikes against leadership and command and control targets to isolate and "decapitate" the enemy, and thereby force a rapid capitulation with a minimum commitment of ground forces. These observations most likely led to accelerated development and deployment of more capable ballistic and cruise missiles and to acquisition of newer multi-role fighter aircraft to support an evolving doctrine for independent, strategic air operations.

The PLA is digesting coalition operations in Afghanistan and Iraq to gain a better understanding of the implications of modern war. At a minimum, it appears to have drawn new lessons on the application of UAVs for reconnaissance and strike operations, special forces for precision targeting, and the integration of psychological operations with air and ground operations to target leadership and communication nodes. PLA observers were impressed with weapon system integration and interoperability, and flexible logistic support to mobile operations.

In contrast to conclusions drawn from previous conflicts, Operation IRAQI FREEDOM appears to have prompted the PLA to rethink the notion that airpower and precision-strike technology alone are sufficient to prevail in a conflict. In June 2003, for example, Jiang Zemin noted: "the Iraq war has once again proven that under high-tech conditions, the factor determining the outcome of war is still human quality."

Observations of Operation IRAQI FREEDOM

In May 2003, PLA Deputy Chief of the General Staff Xiong Guangkai authored an article assessing the broad implications of Operation IRAQI FREEDOM for Chinese assessments of modern war. Some of his more salient observations follow:

-- **On gleaning lessons from coalition operations:** ". . . the trend of new military changes is developing rapidly in the world, and the recent Iraq war has reflected this trend. *We should not only profoundly research and analyze this trend but also actively push forward military changes with Chinese characteristics* according to our country's actual conditions."

-- **On precision strike:** ". . . the Iraq war reflected the tendency toward the development of informationalized weapons and equipment . . . more precision-guided munitions were used . . . military aerospace strength played an ever more important role [and there were] new developments in guided missiles. U.S. troops used as many as 90 military satellites, which provided continuous intelligence information and played a most important role in directing the war, especially in launching accurate attacks."

-- **On mobility:** "Either driving straight in along the south route or adopting air-mobility tactics along the north route reflected the fact that through more than 10 years of readjusting their establishment and system, the U.S. armed forces are ever smaller in number but ever more highly trained, are of a lighter type, and have an ever higher mobility."

-- **On integrated operations:** "The U.S. and British allied forces gave full expression to the joint warfare theory [and] *had all their arms and services to do everything possible to coordinate their actions in all directions and at all times to achieve rapid dominance on the battlefield,* and their actions included air strikes, ground attacks, sea-based missile launches, satellites and information warfare."

-- **On non-contact warfare:** "Under the conditions in which high-tech weapons and equipment have been continuously developing, the effect and importance of non-contact fighting have become increasingly clear, *but contact fighting is not to be ignored.*"

-- **On implications for the PLA:** "While studying this war, we should . . . pay attention to viewing issues from an overall view of development; we should note the general trend of new military changes in the world with information technology as the leading factor and not negate the role played by people only because the role of high-tech weapons is becoming increasingly conspicuous."

-- **Conclusion:** "We should push forward the military reform with Chinese characteristics, which means that *we should study and draw on the experiences and lessons of various countries in making military changes, including all the local wars fought under high-tech conditions, [but] we should not mechanically copy other countries' pattern of military changes.*"

CHAPTER FOUR
RESOURCES FOR FORCE MODERNIZATION

*"The PLA learns from and draws on the valuable experience of foreign
armed forces, and introduces, on a selective basis, technologically
advanced equipment and better management expertise from abroad to
advance the modernization of the Chinese armed forces."*
                                                    -- China's National Defense in 2004

Continued economic growth and reform are essential to PLA modernization. In absolute
terms, this translates into increased funding available for defense. Broad-based growth
and modernization also expands China's economic capacities in industry, technology, and
human resources, enabling its leaders to accelerate military modernization in relative
terms, as well. If China is able to sustain past growth rates – a challenge due to projected
demographic changes, maturation of the industrial and technology base, and persistent
financial inefficiencies – its economy could expand to almost $6.4 trillion by 2025. For
comparison purposes, in 2025 Russia's GDP is projected to be $1.5 trillion, Japan's $6.3
trillion, and the U.S., $22.3 trillion. Based on past patterns, China's defense sector will
probably benefit from continued overall economic performance.

Figure 3. China's Projected GDP Through 2025 (Constant 2005 Prices)

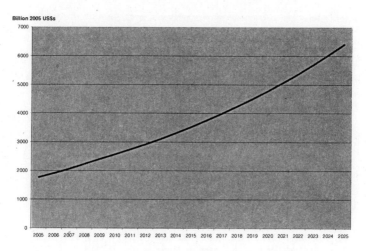

Billion 2005 US$s

Source: Economist Intelligence Unit (EIU) and Global Insight.
Note: Projections, in constant 2005 dollars, place China's GDP at $2.6 trillion
in 2010, $3.5 trillion in 2015, $4.8 trillion in 2020, and $6.4 trillion in 2025.

Defense Budget Trends

Tracking defense budgets is critical to understanding trends in China's military modernization as the budget reflects China's capability to generate military power from its economic base. Since the early 1990s, China has steadily increased resources for the defense sector. On March 4, 2005, a spokesperson for China's National People's Congress announced that China would increase its publicly disclosed defense budget in 2005 by 12.6 percent, to approximately $29.9 billion – double the figure for 2000. This year's increases continue trends that have prevailed for the past fifteen years of double-digit annual increases in China's published figures. When adjusted for inflation, the nominal increases have produced double-digit actual increases in China's official defense budget every year since the mid-1990s. However, the officially published figures substantially underreport actual expenditures for national defense.

The opacity of the PLA budgeting system precludes significant outside analysis. A further complication in the analysis of China's defense spending trends is the wide variation in methodologies (e.g., calculations based on market exchange rates, purchasing power parity, or a mixture of the two, and in varying proportions).

Figure 4. China's Projected Defense Expenditures to 2025

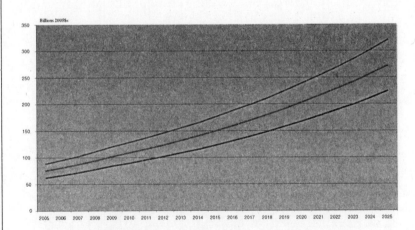

Source: Defense Intelligence Agency.
Note: Projections, in constant 2005 dollars, show low, medium, and high-end estimates of China's future defense spending.

According to some estimates, the official budget does not include foreign weapons procurement (up to $3.0 billion annually from Russia alone), expenses for the paramilitary People's Armed Police, funding to support nuclear weapon stockpiles and the Second Artillery, subsidies to defense industries, some defense-related research and development, and local, provincial, or regional contributions to the armed forces. Combined, these additional monies could increase actual defense expenditures by two to three times the publicly available figure, suggesting the defense sector in China could receive up to $90.0 billion in 2005, making China the third largest defense spender in the world after the United States and Russia, and the largest in Asia.

Projecting out defense spending over a long period is problematic for the reasons cited above. Assuming that China's defense burden (proportion of defense expenditure as a percentage of GDP) remains constant, China's defense budget could rise three-fold or greater by 2025.

Defense Industry Trends

According to intelligence community estimates, China's defense industries are inefficient and dependent on foreign suppliers for key technologies. Exceptions are few, such as ballistic missile research, development, and production. China is reorganizing defense industry, modernizing industrial facilities, and acquiring foreign technology to develop and produce advanced weapons systems to support PLA modernization.

Civil-Military Integration

An important aspect of China's overall modernization strategy is civil-military integration. According to a recent RAND report, "China's leaders remain convinced that the integration of civilian and military production is the key to developing an advanced military. Although in the early 1980s the primary hope was that China's defense manufacturers would be able to use their technological capabilities to generate profits on civilian markets, today the principal hope seems to be that, through participation in commercial production, China's defense manufacturers will acquire dual-use technological capabilities." Civil-military integration, as noted in the 2004 Defense White Paper, "will adhere to the strategic guideline of combining military needs with civilian needs, reserving military potential within civilian capability...." Civil-military integration will exploit civil technological development for military application and maintain a pool of resources (people, material, facilities) to support modernization in peacetime and necessity in wartime.

Reorganization and Modernization. China is changing industrial organizations and business practices to encourage cooperation and collaboration among companies. These changes have implications across the domestic industrial base, but, significantly, indications are that they have enabled it to modernize and expand its defense industry across all sectors since the late 1990s to increase production capacity, develop and produce new or upgraded weapons, and modernize production processes. These infrastructure improvements could enable China to produce higher-quality equipment more rapidly and efficiently.

China's space launch vehicle industry is expanding to support the national emphasis on satellite launch capability and the manned space program. Aircraft manufacturing plants and naval shipyards have increased production floor space to support new military programs and accommodate additional work from commercial contracts and joint ventures. China continues to expand its research, development and testing capabilities, particularly at universities and research institutes.

China is also modernizing key basic industries, such as strategic metals, by building new facilities and equipping them with advanced manufacturing technologies, often purchased for civil purposes. This has enabled Chinese firms to produce specialty metals and alloys used in a variety of defense and commercial industries. Joint ventures in China now manufacture semiconductors and integrated circuits used in military computers, missile guidance systems, communications and electronic warfare equipment, and radar systems.

Acquisition Guidance

Beijing's approach to technology acquisition is called the "Three-Ways Policy": 1) foreign import, 2) joint development (China plus a foreign entity), and 3) domestic development. Beijing would prefer to produce systems indigenously, but is not yet capable and must rely heavily on foreign sources. Priorities for technology acquisition – microelectronics, nanotechnology, space systems, innovative materials, propulsion systems, missile systems, computer-aided manufacturing and design, and information technologies – mirror those identified in the outline documents for China's current five-year plan (2001-2005).

Importing Solutions from Russia and the West. Over the past decade, Russia and Israel have been China's primary foreign sources of weapon systems and military technology. Russia has supplied over 85% of all of China's arms imports since the early 1990s and has been a significant enabler of China's military modernization. According to the Defense Intelligence Agency, Russian conventional weapon technology transfers, including better aircraft, quieter submarines, and more advanced munitions, have advanced the lethality of every major category of weapon system under development in China.

As China's defense industries continue to mature, Beijing is purchasing from abroad systems to meet near-term requirements. For example, China received deliveries of Su-30MK2 multi-role FLANKER aircraft in 2004 to fill a gap until the F-10 or a license-produced multi-role FLANKER could be deployed. China is also purchasing the Russian AL-31FN aero-engine for the F-10 fighter, while working on an indigenously produced turbofan engine. China received advanced Russian SA-10 and SA-20 SAM systems as interim air defense solutions while it develops its own. The purchase of KILO-class diesel electric submarines and SOVREMENNYY-class destroyers from Russia helped equip the PLA Navy with modern systems while China produces its own SONG-class diesel electric submarine and LUYANG-class destroyers. China will likely acquire additional Su-30MK2, IL-76 transport planes, and IL-78 MIDAS air refueling aircraft from Russia during 2005.

China also cooperates with Russia on licensed production and technical advice. To acquire a modern, fourth generation fighter, China contracted with Russia to license-produce the Su-27SK/F-11 FLANKER. In 2004, China requested to renegotiate the last half of this contract to build a multi-role version of the FLANKER, the Su-27SMK. Russia and China reportedly are cooperating on the seeker, rudder control actuation system design, and inertial navigation system for the PL-12 air-to-air missile, which continued testing in 2004. In 2004, China launched a new class of submarine, which appears to incorporate Russian design characteristics, including possible air independent propulsion, greatly increasing submerged endurance. China received help from Russia on a turret for a new infantry fighting vehicle. Russian design features also appear in a new multiple launch rocket system, the A-100.

Although Israel began the process of canceling the PHALCON program with China in 2000, Beijing continues to pursue an AWACs variant built on an IL-76 airframe. The Israelis transferred HARPY UAVs to China in 2001 and conducted maintenance on HARPY parts during 2003-2004.

China receives assistance from other nations too. For example, in 2001, China bought British Spey Mk202 engines to install on the FB-7 fighter-bomber until a license-produced version could be manufactured. Italy and France may be assisting China with a new medium-lift helicopter. Over the last thirty years, China also has benefited from the sale of munitions and dual-use use technologies from France, Germany, Italy, and the United States.

Strengths and Weaknesses: China has invested in its human resources. Improved technical education – including Western education – is providing positive feedback to China's defense industrial sector. On the other hand, quality and innovation remain weaknesses. Chinese industry is still learning the importance of reliability and repeatability. China has not yet demonstrated the ability or innovation to go through a research, development, and acquisition process for a sophisticated weapon system without foreign assistance. Also, many of the new and upgraded facilities are hampered by inadequate electrical power generation and distribution systems. Raw materials are backlogged by inadequate road, rail, and port services. Finally, China's strategic metals industry relies on imported raw materials and foreign mining and production facilities.

Implications of Lifting the EU Arms Embargo

The effort by the European Union in 2004 to lift its arms embargo on China – in place since the 1989 Tiananmen Square crackdown – followed intense lobbying by China to remove the ban, which it refers to as a "relic of the Cold War." The consequences of an EU arms embargo lift would be serious and numerous. Although the EU stated that any lifting of the embargo would produce no qualitative or quantitative increases in China's military capabilities, the EU's tools to enforce such a commitment remain inadequate. Lifting the embargo could allow China access to military and dual-use technologies that would help China to improve current weapon systems and to improve indigenous industrial capabilities for production of future advanced weapons systems. Ending the embargo could also remove implicit limits on Chinese military interaction with European militaries, giving China's armed forces broad access to critical military "software" such as modern military management practices, operational doctrine and training, and logistics expertise.

If the embargo is lifted, China's strategy will likely center on establishing joint ventures with EU companies as a means to acquire access to expertise and technology. China can be expected to move slowly to avoid undermining its position that the embargo was merely symbolic. Even if China were to move quickly, its defense industries would require time to integrate new technologies, processes, and know-how into weapons manufacturing or retro-fits. In the medium to long term, however, the acquisition of European defense technology would significantly improve PLA capabilities. China is most likely interested in acquiring advanced space technology, radar systems, early-warning aircraft, submarine technology, and advanced electronic components for precision-guided weapons systems.

Lifting the EU embargo would also lead to greater foreign competition to sell arms to the PLA, giving Beijing leverage over Russia, Israel, and other foreign suppliers to relax limits on military sales to China. Potential competition from EU countries already may have prompted Russia to expand the range of systems it is willing to market to China. In 2004, Russia provided a new version of the FLANKER, the Su-30MK2, to China and signed a contract to sell S-300PMU2 SAM systems. The Su-30 aircraft features an enhanced radar system and is equipped with long-range R-77 and R-27 missiles, enhancing the capability of China's air forces to conduct over-the-horizon and beyond-visual-range attacks. Russia is also discussing the sale of advanced conventional submarine co-production rights to China in anticipation of competition from the EU.

Such an acceleration of China's military modernization would have direct implications for stability in the Taiwan Strait and the safety of U.S. personnel; it would also accelerate a shift in the regional balance of power, affecting the security of many countries.

Finally, Beijing's track record in transfers of conventional arms and military technologies suggests EU or other third-party sales to China could lead to improvements in the systems that Chinese companies market abroad, including to countries of concern, such as Iran. Of note, some of China's major recipients of military assistance – Burma, Sudan, and Zimbabwe – all are subject to EU arms embargoes.

CHAPTER FIVE
FORCE MODERNIZATION GOALS AND TRENDS

"We should draw on the experiences in new military changes of the world and seize the opportunities to achieve leapfrog development in national defense and army modernization."

-- President Hu Jintao, May 2003.

"We should achieve developments by leaps and bounds in the modernization of weaponry in our armed forces."

-- Gen Li Jinai, then-Director, PLA General Armaments Department, August 2004.

Overview

China has stated its intentions and allocated resources to pursue force-wide professionalization, improve training, conduct more robust, realistic joint exercises, and accelerate acquisition of modern weapons. The U.S. Intelligence Community estimates that China will require until the end of this decade or later for its military modernization program to produce a modern force, capable of defeating a moderate-size adversary.

Meanwhile, China's leaders appear to recognize the PLA's deficiencies relative to potential adversaries in the region and may have concluded that the PLA is presently unable to compete directly with other modern military powers. We assess that this conclusion might have given rise to a priority emphasis on asymmetric programs and systems to leverage China's advantages while exploiting the perceived vulnerabilities of potential opponents – so-called Assassin's Mace (*sha shou jian*) programs.

Consequently, as PLA modernization progresses, there are twin misperceptions that may lead to miscalculation or crisis. First, other countries may underestimate the extent to which Chinese forces have improved. Second, China's leaders may overestimate the proficiency of their forces by assuming that new systems are fully operational, adeptly operated, adequately supplied and maintained, and well integrated with existing or other new capabilities.

The following sections explore advances in Chinese military modernization in the areas of: nuclear deterrence, precision strike, expeditionary operations, air defense, anti-access, lines of communication protection, joint logistics, space and counter-space, and computer network operations.

China's Armed Forces at a Glance

China has the largest military in the world. China's military comprises four services: ground forces (PLA), naval forces (PLAN, includes marines and aviation components), air forces (PLAAF, includes airborne forces), and strategic missile forces (Second Artillery). Following downsizing this year, the active force will total some 2.3 million personnel. A fifth element consists of the paramilitary People's Armed Police (PAP) and reserves. The combined total, distributed across seven military regions, exceeds 3.2 million. China also has some 10 million organized militia members throughout the country.

Figure 5. China's Military Regions

Nuclear Deterrence

China is qualitatively and quantitatively improving its strategic missile force. This could provide a credible, survivable nuclear deterrent and counterstrike capability. It is fielding more survivable missiles capable of targeting India, Russia, virtually all of the United States, and the Asia-Pacific theater as far south as Australia and New Zealand. Beijing maintains a small strategic arsenal. Its stated nuclear weapons doctrine remains one of "no first use."

Figure 6. Medium and Intercontinental Range Ballistic Missiles

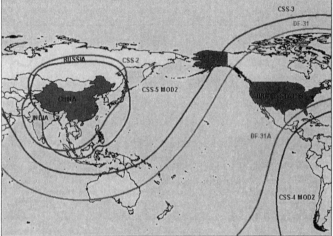

Note: China currently is capable of targeting its nuclear forces throughout the region and most of the world, including the continental United States. Newer systems, such as the DF-31 and DF-31A, will give China a more survivable nuclear force.

China's future strategic force will likely comprise enhanced silo-based CSS-4 ICBMs (currently deployed), solid-fueled, road-mobile DF-31 (initial operational capability 2005-06) and DF-31A ICBMs (IOC 2007-09), and sea-based JL-2 SLBMs (IOC 2008-10). China will also maintain a force of nuclear-armed CSS-5 MRBMs for regional contingencies.

China currently deploys approximately twenty silo-based, liquid-propellant CSS-4 ICBMs, which constitute its primary nuclear deterrent. The Second Artillery also maintains approximately twenty liquid-fueled, more limited-range CSS-3 ICBMs to sustain its regional nuclear deterrent. The Second Artillery will likely keep this older missile in service until it is replaced by the more survivable, road-mobile DF-31. China supplements the aged CSS-2s with solid-propellant, road-mobile CSS-5 MRBMs.

The introduction of the road-mobile DF-31-series ICBMs will supplement China's silo-based strategic force. The mobility of the new DF-31-class missiles will enable these systems to operate over a larger area, making them more difficult to locate and neutralize. The introduction of a new generation of SLBMs on China's new ballistic-missile submarine will provide an additional survivable nuclear option. Finally, replacement of the older, silo-based CSS-4 Mod 1 with the longer range CSS-4 Mod 2, coupled with the ongoing migration to mobile, solid-fueled systems will enhance the operational capabilities and survivability of China's strategic missile force.

Precision Strike

The PLA envisions the use of precision strike to hold at risk such targets as Western Pacific airbases, ports, surface combatants, land-based C4ISR and integrated air defense systems, and command facilities. Most of the PLA units associated with precision strike are rapid reaction units and/or those that would likely lead any contingency operation around the mainland periphery.

- *Short-Range Ballistic Missiles (SRBMs) (conventionally armed).* China's SRBM force constitutes the bulk of its precision strike capability. Its first-generation SRBMs do not possess true "precision strike" capability, but later generations have greater ranges and improved accuracy. According to DIA estimates, China's SRBM force totals some 650-730 missiles, increasing at a rate of 75 to 120 missiles per year.

- *Land-Attack Cruise Missiles (LACMs) (conventionally armed).* China is developing LACMs to achieve greater precision than historically available from ballistic missiles for hard target strikes, and increased standoff. A first- and second-generation LACM remain under development. There are no technological bars to placing on these systems a nuclear payload, once developed.

- *Air-to-Surface Missiles (ASMs).* China is believed to have a small number of tactical ASMs. China is pursuing foreign and domestic acquisitions to improve airborne anti-ship capabilities.

- *Anti-Ship Cruise Missiles (ASCMs).* The PLA Navy and Naval Air Force have or are acquiring nearly a dozen varieties of ASCMs, from the 1950s-era CSS-N-2/STYX to the modern Russian-made SS-N-22/SUNBURN and SS-N-27/SIZZLER. The pace of indigenous ASCM research, development, and production – and of foreign procurement – has accelerated over the past decade. Objectives for current and future ASCMs include improving closure speed (e.g., ramjet propulsion, such as with the SS-N-22), standoff distance (e.g., longer-range assets, such as the C-802), and stealthier launch platforms (e.g., submarines). SS-N-22 missiles may be fitted on smaller platforms in the future (e.g., the Russian Molniya patrol boat, which originated as a joint effort with China, or on the new stealth fast attack patrol boat).

Figure 7. Maximum Ranges for China's Conventional SRBM Force

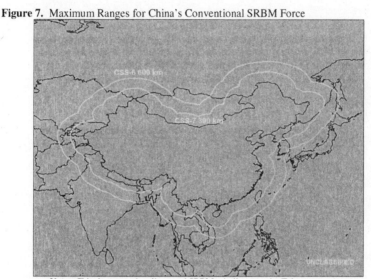

Note: China's conventionally armed SRBM missiles opposite Taiwan are
mobile and can be redeployed to support a variety of regional conflict scenarios.

- *Anti-Radiation Weapons (ARMs).* The size and scope of China's anti-radiation
  weapons inventory remains unknown. The PLA has imported both the Israeli-made
  HARPY UAV and Russian-made anti-radiation missiles. China's doctrine calls for
  seizing "electromagnetic superiority" early in a conflict. Acquiring anti-radiation
  weapons – designed to acquire targets based on the targets' own radar emissions –
  supports this doctrine and is consistent with Chinese theories on "informationalized"
  warfare.

Expeditionary Operations

PLA expeditionary forces include three airborne divisions, two amphibious infantry
divisions, two marine brigades, about seven special operations groups, and one
regimental-size reconnaissance element in the Second Artillery.

The PLA is focusing modernization for these units on procuring more equipment,
improving unit-level tactics, and coordination of joint operations. PLA ground forces in
the Nanjing and Guangzhou Military Regions have received upgraded amphibious armor
and other vehicles, such as tanks and APCs, and may add armored assault vehicles and
air-cushioned troop vehicles to improve lethality and speed for seaborne assaults.
Airborne forces will likely acquire more modern transport aircraft like the Russian
IL-76/CANDID and modern airmobile light weight vehicles. The PLA recently
increased amphibious ship production to address its lift deficiencies – although the

intelligence community believes these increases will be inadequate to meet requirements – and is organizing its civilian merchant fleet and militia, which, given adequate notification, could augment the PLA's organic lift in amphibious operations.

Notional missions for these forces include: special operations forces to facilitate amphibious operations and to disrupt critical communication nodes, air defense capabilities, and critical lines of communication; airborne to seize airfields to facilitate the flow of follow-on infantry forces; and, Second Artillery reconnaissance elements to provide targeting information and battle damage assessments.

Combined training for all these units is seldom conducted in a major amphibious assault exercise. Units tend to train for their missions in garrisons, local areas and regional training facilities. China's ability to integrate individual unit actions – or simulate integration – to assess accurately operational capability, is not known.

Trends in Ground Forces Modernization

Following planned force reductions and reorganizations, mechanized infantry, armored, and army aviation units will make up a much larger percentage of the ground force. China is also increasing the capabilities of reserve and militia units, and exploring ways to outsource some combat service support functions and use civilian assets, such as ships and aircraft, to support military operations. The fielding of new equipment for the ground forces has been limited, compared to the other services which are more technology intensive. Even with downsizing and the consolidation of ground forces into fewer units, the army remains too large to effect rapid modernization throughout its force structure.

Air Defense

The PLA has shifted from point defense of key military, industrial, and political targets to a new Joint Anti-Air Raid Campaign doctrine based on a modern, integrated air defense system capable of effective offensive counter-air (OCA) and defensive counter-air (DCA). Under this doctrine, the PLA will use aircraft, surface-to-surface missiles, long-range artillery, special operations forces, naval forces, and guerrilla units to destroy an enemy's ability to conduct offensive air operations and provide comprehensive defense of Chinese airspace.

Beijing has been acquiring foreign and domestic fourth generation tactical aircraft (e.g., Su-27 and Su-30 FLANKER variants, and the PLA's indigenous F-10, which will begin to enter service in 2005). The PLA has also acquired advanced air-to-surface missiles that will allow its air forces to attack surface targets, afloat and ashore, from greater distance and with more precision. Newer aircraft are also being equipped with advanced air-to-air missiles and electronic warfare technology that give these aircraft technological parity with or superiority over most potential adversaries.

Trends in Air Force Modernization

The PLA Air Force is replacing older fighters with 3rd and 4th generation aircraft outfitted with long-range, precision strike weapons for land attack and anti-ship missions and, in some of these aircraft, in-flight refueling capabilities, which when fully operational, will extend operating limits. Acquisition and production of AWACS aircraft and the purchase of additional refueling aircraft will significantly extend the ranges of the modern air fleet.

China is still developing the FB-7, an all-weather, supersonic, medium-range fighter-bomber to have an anti-ship mission. Improvements to the FB-7 most likely will include a better radar, night-attack avionics, and advanced weapons. China is improving the capabilities of its special-mission aircraft, with a focus on electronic warfare, C4ISR, and aerial refueling. China reportedly modified several of its larger aircraft for jamming missions, and likely has several programs for new standoff and escort jammers using bombers, transports, tactical aircraft, and UAVs. In addition, China is pursuing domestic upgrades to its F-8II fighters, and has nearly completed development and testing of an upgraded FBC-1 long-range fighter/attack aircraft.

The type and number of modern SAMs in Beijing's inventory is increasing with the acquisition of Russian-made strategic SA-10 and SA-20 systems. China is reverse-engineering its own version of the SA-10, the HQ-9, which has yet to enter the inventory. China will likely acquire the extended range S-300PMU2 system in 2006. Acquisition and deployment of the S-300PMU2 would allow China's air defenses to engage aircraft over Taiwan.

Figure 8. Surface-to-Air Missile Coverage Over the Taiwan Strait

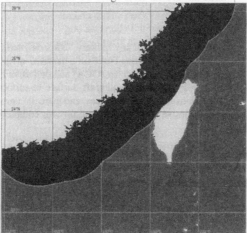

Note: This map depicts notional coverage provided by China's SA-10, SA-20 SAM systems, as well as the soon-to-be acquired S-300PMU2. Actual coverage would be non-contiguous and dependent upon precise deployment sites.

Anti-Access

Preventing foreign military intervention, particularly along China's coast, has been a goal for Beijing throughout history, reinforcing the geostrategic value of Taiwan for China's security planners. As the Soviet threat ebbed in the late 1980s, China's concern about its 9,000 mile coastline rose. China's concept of sea denial in the Western Pacific subsequently broadened beyond the independent use of naval assets to multi-dimensional defense using air, surface, and subsurface elements. Reflecting the emphasis China appears to be placing on anti-access strategies, most of the capabilities believed to fall under the Assassin's Mace program are designed to blunt adversaries' military advantages or deny entry into the theater of operations.

China is developing capabilities to achieve local sea denial, including naval mines, submarines, cruise missiles, and special operations forces. Beijing is in serial production of the domestic SONG-class submarine, acquiring more Russian KILO-class submarines, developing a new YUAN-class conventional submarine, and developing the Type-093 nuclear attack submarine for missions requiring greater at-sea endurance. China is also researching the possibility of using ballistic missiles and special operations forces to strike ships or their ashore support infrastructure. Finally, China is developing or improving counter-reconnaissance and counterspace capabilities using a range of solutions from low-tech denial and deception based on camouflage, cover and concealment, to high-tech lasers and space-tracking devices.

China does not appear to have broadened its concept of operations for anti-access and sea denial to encompass sea control in waters beyond Taiwan and its immediate periphery. If China were to shift to a broader "sea control" strategy, the primary indicators would include: development of an aircraft carrier, development of robust anti-submarine warfare capabilities, development of a true area anti-air warfare capability, acquisition of large numbers of nuclear attack submarines, development of effective maritime C4ISR, and increased open water training.

Protecting Vital Lines of Communication

China's expanding international presence reflects a growing interest in export markets and imports of key resources, especially energy. As China's economy grows, it will become increasingly concerned with securing resource flows along key lines of communication. For example, 80 percent of China's oil imports pass through the Strait of Malacca. In late 2003, President Hu referred to China's need to secure its lines of communication as the "Malacca Dilemma."

With its present force structure, according to the Intelligence Community, Chinese surface combatants would have difficulty projecting power into the Strait of Malacca, especially if it were conducting simultaneous blockade or invasion operations elsewhere. Similarly, although the PLA Navy occasionally patrols as far as the Spratly Islands, its limited organic air defense capability leaves surface ships vulnerable to attack from hostile air and naval forces. The PLA Navy Air Force and PLA Air Force currently lack the operational range to support PLA Navy operations. In recent years, however, the PLA Navy's South Sea Fleet, which has operational responsibility over the South China Sea, has been assigned more capable surface combatants and submarines, including two destroyers (one LUDA IV class and one LUHAI class) that provide it with its first short-range area air-defense capability, the HHQ-7C surface-to-air missile systems.

Figure 9. China's Critical Sea Lines of Communication

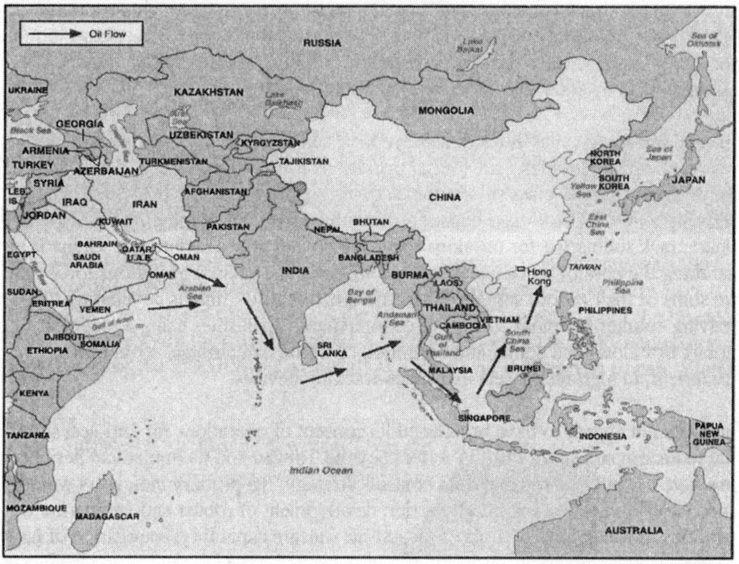

Note: In 2004, over 80 percent of Chinese crude oil imports transited the Straits of Malacca, with less than 2 percent transiting the Straits of Lombok.

Joint Logistics

China's logistics reform features the integration of the civil sector with the military procurement system as a modern adaptation of "people's war." Under this concept, the PLA will acquire common and dual-use items on the market. Increasing numbers of logistics functions will be outsourced, especially when civilian industry can perform similar functions at lower costs. In addition, the PLA is placing greater emphasis on the mobilization of the civilian economy, both in peacetime and in war, to support national defense in industry, agriculture, communication and transport, science and technology, medical care and health, urban construction, commerce and trade, and finance.

Since 2000, China has improved the structure, material coordination, and efficiency of its joint logistics system. However, the command system is still not compatible with the support system, and organization and planning is incompatible with supply management. The first experimental joint logistics unit was created only in July 2004.

Space and Counterspace

Beijing has focused on building the infrastructure to develop advanced space-based C4ISR and targeting capabilities. Building a modern ISR architecture is likely one of the primary drivers behind Beijing's space endeavors and a critical component of its overall C4ISR modernization efforts. Beijing's ongoing space-based programs with potential military applications include:

- China launched its first manned spacecraft into Earth orbit on October 15, 2003. Chinese press reports indicate that it will send up a two-person crew on a five-day mission in September 2005.

- China has two remote-sensing satellite programs known as Ziyuan-1 (ZY-1), also known as the China-Brazil Earth Resources Satellite, and ZY-2. China launched the ZY-1B in October 2003. A third ZY-2 satellite was launched in October 2004. ZY-2 payloads probably are digital imagery reconnaissance satellites and have worldwide coverage. Beijing also tested new film-based imagery satellites and small digital imagery satellites in 2003 and 2004.

- China is interested in electronic intelligence (ELINT) or signals intelligence (SIGINT) reconnaissance satellites. Although these digital data systems probably will be able to transmit directly to ground sites, China may be developing a system of data relay satellites to support global coverage. Furthermore, Beijing has acquired mobile data reception equipment that could support more rapid data transmission to deployed military forces and units.

- China is studying and seeking foreign assistance on small satellites. It has launched a number of them, including an oceanographic research satellite, Haiyang (HY)-1, in 2002 with at least two more satellites in this series, HY-2 and -3, expected. Beijing launched four small satellites during 2004; two of these probably have imagery missions and the other two possibly are conducting space environmental research. Other missions for satellites of this class include Earth observation, communications, and navigation.

- China is developing microsatellites – weighing less than 100 kilograms – for remote sensing and networks of electro-optical and radar satellites. In April 2004 Beijing launched a microsatellite with a probable imagery mission.

- A joint venture between China's Tsinghua University and the UK's University of Surrey is building a constellation of seven minisatellites – a class of satellites weighing between 101 and 500 kilograms – with 50-meter-resolution remote-sensing payloads. Later satellites in the series probably will have improved resolution.

Trends in Space Modernization

China seeks to become a world leader in space development and maintain a leading role in space launch activity. Beijing's goal is to place a satellite into orbit "within hours upon request." The Long March series of rockets can support that requirement as long as adequate satellites remain in reserve. With ever-better satellites, China is becoming a peer in quality to the world's leading producers. In manned space, after the two-person mission scheduled for this fall, China hopes to conduct space walks and docking missions with a space lab by 2010, followed by a full space station by 2020.

In 2004, China placed 10 satellites into orbit, the most of any year, and has a similar schedule through 2006. It hopes to have more than 100 satellites in orbit by 2010, and launch an additional 100 satellites by 2020. In the next decade, Beijing most likely will field radar, ocean surveillance, and improved film-based photo-reconnaissance satellites. China will eventually deploy advanced imagery, reconnaissance, and Earth resource systems with military applications. In the interim, China probably will supplement existing coverage with commercial SPOT, LANDSAT, RADARSAT, Ikonos, and Russian satellite imagery systems.

Anti-Satellite Weapons (ASATs). China is working on, and plans to field, ASAT systems. Beijing has and will continue to enhance its satellite tracking and identification network – the first step in establishing a credible ASAT capability. China can currently destroy or disable satellites only by launching a ballistic missile or space-launch vehicle armed with a nuclear weapon. However, there are many risks associated with this method, and consequences from use of nuclear weapons. China is also conducting research to develop ground-based laser ASAT weapons. Based on the level of Chinese interest in this field, the Defense Intelligence Agency believes Beijing eventually could develop a laser weapon capable of damaging or destroying satellites. At lower power thresholds, Chinese researchers may believe that low-energy lasers can "blind" sensors on low-Earth-orbiting satellites; whether Beijing has tested such a capability is unclear.

Computer Network Operations

China's computer network operations (CNO) include computer network attack, computer network defense, and computer network exploitation. The PLA sees CNO as critical to seize the initiative and "electromagnetic dominance" early in a conflict, and as a force multiplier. Although there is no evidence of a formal Chinese CNO doctrine, Chinese theorists have coined the term "Integrated Network Electronic Warfare" to describe the Chinese approach. This concept outlines the integrated use of electronic warfare, CNO, and limited kinetic strikes against key C4 nodes to disrupt the enemy's battlefield network information systems. The PLA has likely established information warfare units to develop viruses to attack enemy computer systems and networks, and tactics to protect friendly computer systems and networks. The PLA has increased the role of CNO in its military exercises. Although initial training efforts focused on increasing the PLA's proficiency in defensive measures, recent exercises have incorporated offensive operations, primarily as first strikes against enemy networks.

CHAPTER SIX
PRC FORCE MODERNIZATION AND SECURITY IN THE TAIWAN STRAIT

"Should the Taiwan authorities go so far as to make a reckless attempt that constitutes a major incident of 'Taiwan independence,' the Chinese people and armed forces will resolutely and thoroughly crush it at any cost."

-- China's National Defense in 2004

The cross-Strait balance of power is shifting toward Beijing as a result of China's economic growth, growing diplomatic leverage, and improvements in the PLA's military capabilities, including those that provide Beijing options short of full-scale invasion. Chinese air, naval, and missile force modernization is increasing demands on Taiwan to develop countermeasures that would enable it to avoid being quickly overwhelmed.

In contrast, Taiwan defense spending has steadily declined in real terms over the past decade. Taiwan has traditionally acquired capabilities, some asymmetric, to deter an attack by making it too costly, while buying time for international intervention. Taipei is continuing to acquire such capabilities, but the growth of PLA capabilities is outpacing these acquisitions.

The U.S. Government has made clear that it supports negotiation of a peaceful resolution and opposes unilateral changes to the status quo. Yet, Beijing's sustained military build-up in the area of the Taiwan Strait affects the status quo. As a result, consistent with the provisions of the Taiwan Relations Act (P.L. 96-8 (1979)), President Bush in April 2001 approved the sale of key systems to correct growing imbalances in critical areas such as missile and air defense and anti-submarine warfare. A $15.3 billion Special Budget for the purchase of Patriot PAC-III air defense systems, P-3C Orion anti-submarine aircraft, and diesel attack submarines is now before the Taiwan Legislative Yuan.

China's Strategy in the Taiwan Strait

Beijing views unification as a long-term goal. Its immediate strategy is focused on deterring Taiwan from moving toward *de jure* "independence." Its approach to preventing Taiwan independence is multi-faceted, integrating political, economic, cultural, and military instruments to coerce and shape Taiwan's behavior. Beijing insists that Taipei accept the "one-China" principle, i.e., that there is but one China and Taiwan is a part of it, as a precondition to any cross-Strait dialogue.

Anti-Secession Law

On March 14, 2005, China's legislature, the National People's Congress, passed the "anti-secession law." The law's passage followed months of speculation by outside observers over its contents and a simultaneous lobbying effort on the part of Chinese officials to cast the law in benign terms, while closely guarding the draft of the text. The law itself is broken into ten articles that codify, or render as legal instruments, policies and statements applied by the Chinese government to the Taiwan question. Key elements are described below.

Article One establishes that the law was formulated for the purpose of "opposing and checking Taiwan's secession from China."

Article Two restates Beijing's "One China" definition – Taiwan is part of China – and that China "shall never allow" Taiwan to secede from China "under any name or by any means."

Article Three asserts that the Taiwan matter is part of China's internal affairs and is subject to "no interference by outside forces."

Article Four states that China's reunification is the "sacred duty" of "all Chinese people," including "Taiwan compatriots."

Article Five reiterates China's position that acceptance of "One China" is a necessary precondition for peaceful resolution. It does not refer to the "one country, two systems" model, but claims Taiwan would "practice systems different from those on the mainland."

Article Six enumerates the steps Beijing is willing to take to realize peaceful unification, such as expanding cross-Strait exchanges, including cultural, economic, educational, science and technology, health, and sports exchanges. It also refers to "other activities" conducive to peace and stability, but does not offer details.

Article Seven specifies the range of issues that would be subject to negotiation during cross-Strait consultations. The article states such negotiations would be on an "equal footing."

Article Eight states the State Council and CMC "shall decide on and execute" non-peaceful means to "protect China's sovereignty and territorial integrity" if "secessionist forces . . . cause the fact of Taiwan's secession from China," if "major incidents entailing Taiwan's secession" occur, or if "possibilities for peaceful reunification" are exhausted.

Article Nine provides that during conflict, China will "exert its utmost" to protect lives, property, and rights of Taiwan civilians and foreign nationals on Taiwan, and the rights of Taiwan citizens in other parts of China.

Article Ten specifies that the law comes into force on the day of its proclamation.

China continues to declare a policy of peaceful resolution under the "one country, two systems" framework that offers Taiwan limited autonomy in exchange for Taiwan's integration with the mainland. China sees the potential use of force as an integral part of its policy of dissuading Taiwan from pursuing independence and encouraging it to unite ultimately with the mainland. Beijing has not renounced the use of force against Taiwan. The threat of force against Taiwan is now codified in the "anti-secession law," enacted by the National People's Congress in March 2005.

The circumstances in which Beijing has historically claimed it would use force against the island include: a formal declaration of independence by Taipei, foreign intervention in Taiwan's internal affairs, indefinite delays in the resumption of cross-Strait dialogue, Taiwan's acquisition of nuclear weapons, and internal unrest on Taiwan. These circumstances are not fixed and have evolved over the last decade in response to Taiwan actions and changes in China's own military capabilities. They are, moreover, deliberately general, allowing Beijing to determine the timing and form of its response.

Beijing's Courses of Action against Taiwan

Although the costs of the use of force against Taiwan would be high, Beijing leaders might use force if they believed they had no other way to prevent Taiwan independence or, as implied in its "anti-secession law," to guarantee reunification over the long term. The Chinese Communist Party came to power on its credentials as a defender of Chinese sovereignty; its leaders appear to see progress – or perhaps, the absence of failure – on the Taiwan issue as affecting the legitimacy of their rule.

Beijing is developing military capabilities that will enable it to pursue several courses of action against Taiwan, allowing Chinese leaders more flexibility to apply pressure against the island and minimize the risks of a military confrontation with the United States. The PLA is simultaneously developing the capability to deter and/or slow a potential U.S., or U.S.-led, response to defend Taiwan.

Persuasion and Coercion. China's current approach to preventing Taiwan independence combines diplomatic, economic, legal, psychological, and military instruments to convince Taipei that the price of declaring independence is too high. This strategy combines the credible threat to use military force with the economic and cultural tools that China has at its disposal. China uses its growing economic links with Taiwan to influence political behavior on the island. Beijing seeks to attract more Taiwan investment in China, while emphasizing that peace in the Strait will bring prosperity. Beijing is increasing its pressure on Taiwan businessmen operating in China to refrain from supporting "pro-independence" parties or individuals on Taiwan. Beijing emphasizes historic, ethnic, and cultural links between Taiwan and the mainland, and unofficial diplomacy with "Taiwan compatriots" to generate domestic propaganda in Taiwan in favor of reunification.

Beijing has also intensified its competition with Taiwan in the developing world for diplomatic recognition. This effort has focused on eroding Taiwan's diplomatic support among the 26 remaining countries that recognize Taipei. Simultaneously, using diplomatic and commercial levers, China has increased pressure on other states to limit their relationships with and to restrain Taiwan.

Portraying a military threat to Taiwan backstops the overall campaign to isolate Taiwan diplomatically and pressure Taiwan leaders. Exercises, deployments, and press operations all contribute to Beijing's policy of pressure.

Limited Force Options. Beijing could use limited strikes, employing information operations, special operations forces on Taiwan, and SRBM or air strikes at key military or political sites, to try to break the will of Taiwan's leadership and population. Although Beijing might view these as a complement to non-military coercion and as less than a full use of force, others may view such actions differently. Such a Chinese miscalculation could lead to a full-fledged conflict.

Nuclear Weapon/High-Altitude EMP Option.

Some PLA theorists are aware of the electromagnetic effects of using a high-altitude nuclear burst to generate high-altitude electromagnetic pulse (HEMP), and might consider using HEMP as an unconventional attack, believing the United States and other nations would not interpret it as a use of force and as crossing the nuclear threshold. This capability would most likely be used as part of a larger campaign to intimidate, if not decapitate, the Taiwan leadership. HEMP causes a substantial change in the ionization of the upper atmosphere, including the ionosphere and magnetosphere. These effects likely would result in the degradation of important war fighting capabilities, such as key communication links, radar transmissions, and the full spectrum of electro-optic sensors. Additional effects could include severe disruptions to civil electric/power and transportation. These effects cannot easily be localized to Taiwan and would likely affect the mainland, Japan, the Philippines, and commercial shipping and air routes in the region.

Such a campaign could include computer network attacks against Taiwan's political, military, and economic infrastructure to undermine the Taiwan population's confidence in its leadership. Simultaneously, PLA special operations forces infiltrated into Taiwan could conduct acts of economic, political, and military sabotage.

The PLA could also use limited, coordinated SRBM, special operations forces, and air strikes against air fields, radars, and communications facilities on Taiwan. Beijing could use the shock of rapid, accurate, and coordinated strikes and their effects on Taiwan's key C4ISR nodes to try to push the Taiwan leadership towards accommodation. At the same time, an information operations campaign on multiple levels could be launched to gain legitimacy for Beijing's claims on Taiwan and to reinforce the theme that military operations were limited to key military infrastructure, not the Taiwan people.

Air and Missile Campaign. Surprise SRBM attacks and precision air strikes could support a campaign designed to degrade Taiwan defenses, decapitate its military and political leadership, and break its will to fight rapidly before the United States and other nations could intervene. To attempt these effects, China could employ SRBMs to saturate Taiwan's air defense system, including air bases, radar sites, missiles, and communications facilities.

Third-Party Intervention

Beijing sees Washington and, increasingly, Tokyo as the principal hurdles to any attempt to use military force to coerce or capture Taiwan. Beijing might coerce or target other critical countries to deny or delay their willingness to provide support, basing, overflight rights, or transit authority to U.S. forces operating in the theater. Deterring, defeating, or delaying foreign intervention ahead of Taiwan's capitulation is integral to Beijing's strategy. To that end, Beijing will pursue political and diplomatic efforts to keep the United States and Japan from taking action to support Taiwan. The U.S. Intelligence Community also believes China will consider a sea-denial strategy to attempt to hold at risk U.S. naval forces, including aircraft carriers and logistic forces, approaching the Taiwan Strait.

Blockade. Beijing could threaten or deploy a naval blockade either as a "non-war" pressure tactic in the pre-hostility phase or as a transition to active conflict. On one end of the spectrum, Beijing could declare that ships en route to Taiwan ports must stop in mainland ports for inspections prior to transiting on to Taiwan. Alternatively, China could attempt the equivalent of a blockade of Taiwan ports by declaring exercise or missile closure areas in approaches and roadsteads to ports to divert merchant traffic. Chinese doctrine also includes activities such as an air blockade, missile attacks, and mining or otherwise obstructing harbors and approaches.

More traditional methods of blockade would increase the impact on Taiwan, but also would tax PLA Navy capabilities and raise the potential for direct military confrontation, particularly with U.S. naval assets. Although sea lanes closer to China (i.e., the South and East China Seas) could be interdicted, any attempt at a close-in blockade or operations on the east side of Taiwan would strain the PLA Navy, which lacks significant replenishment and open ocean surveillance capabilities. More restrictive blockades increase the likelihood of international intervention. Although any blockade would have an immediate economic impact, it would take time to realize decisive political results. It would also increase the opportunity for countervailing U.S. and international pressure and could lead to the protracted campaign Beijing seeks to avoid.

Amphibious Invasion. An invasion of Taiwan would be a complex and difficult operation relying upon timing and pre-conditions set by many subordinate campaigns. Publicly available Chinese writings on amphibious campaigns offer different strategies for an amphibious invasion of Taiwan. The most prominent of these is the Joint Island Landing Campaign. The objective of this campaign is to break through or circumvent the shore defense, establish and build a beachhead, and then launch an attack to split, seize and occupy the entire island or important targets on the island. To achieve the final objective of the Joint Island Landing Campaign, a series of sub-campaigns, such as electronic warfare, naval, and air campaigns, must be executed, including the underlying logistics support.

Amphibious operations are logistics-intensive and rely for success upon the rapid build-up of supplies and sustainment ashore and an uninterrupted flow of support thereafter. This particular amphibious operation would tax the lift capacities of China's armed forces needed to provide sustainment for this campaign. Add to these strains the combat attrition of China's forces, and an amphibious invasion of Taiwan would be a significant political and military risk for China's civilian and military leaders.

The PLA's prospects in an invasion of Taiwan would hinge on: availability of amphibious and air lift, attrition rates, interoperability of PLA forces, the ability of China's logistic system to support the necessarily high tempo of operations, Taiwan's will to resist, and the speed and scale of third-party intervention.

Factors of Deterrence

China is deterred from taking military action against Taiwan on two levels. It does not yet possess the military capability to accomplish with confidence its political objectives on the island, particularly when confronted with outside intervention. Beijing is also deterred by the potential repercussions of any use of force against Taiwan. According to the Defense Intelligence Agency, China's leaders recognize that a war could severely retard economic development. Taiwan is China's single largest source of foreign direct investment. An extended campaign would wreck Taiwan's economic infrastructure, leading to high reconstruction costs. International sanctions against Beijing, either by individual states or by groups of states, could severely damage Beijing's economic development.

Conflict with Taiwan could also lead to instability on the mainland. Maintaining internal security in wartime appears to be an important consideration in PLA planning – reflecting leadership concerns about political stability. Failure would almost certainly result in severe repercussions for those in the leadership who had advocated such a course of action. A conflict also would severely hurt the image China has sought to project regionally and globally in recent years. If Beijing chose to use force against Taiwan prior to the 2008 Olympics, China would almost certainly face a boycott or loss of the games. Finally, Beijing must calculate the probability of U.S. intervention in any conflict in the Taiwan Strait. It views the United States as having advantages over China in many scenarios involving the use of military force. China's leaders also calculate a conflict over Taiwan involving the United States would give rise to a long-term hostile relationship between the two nations – a result that would not be in China's interests.

APPENDIX
CHINA AND TAIWAN
FORCES DATA

Figure 10

Taiwan Strait Military Balance, Ground Forces			
	China		Taiwan
	Total	Taiwan Strait Area	Total
Personnel (Active)	1.6 million	375,000	200,000
Group Armies	18	9	
Infantry Divisions/Brigades (including airborne)	20/20	9/11	0/25
Armor Divisions/Brigades	10/10	4/4	0/5
Mech Infantry Divisions/Brigades	5/5	3/1	0/3
Artillery Divisions/Brigades	5/15	3/5	0/0
Marine Divisions/Brigades	0/2	0/2	1/3
Tanks	6,500	2,500	1,900
Artillery Pieces	11,000	5,500	4,400

Note: The PLA active ground forces are organized into Group Armies. Infantry, armor, and artillery units are organized into a combination of divisions and brigades deployed throughout the PLA's seven Military Regions (MRs). A significant portion of these assets are deployed in the Taiwan Strait area, specifically the Nanjing, Guangzhou, and Jinan military regions. In a major Taiwan conflict, personnel, units, and equipment from other military regions would augment existing combat power in the Taiwan Strait area. In 2004, Taiwan began transforming motorized rifle and armored infantry brigades to mechanized infantry.

Figure 11

Taiwan Strait Military Balance, Air Forces			
China			Taiwan
Aircraft	Total	Within range of Taiwan	Total
Fighters	1,500	425	420
Bombers	780	280	0
Transport	500	50	40

Note: The PLAAF and PLANAF have a total of around 2,600 combat aircraft: air defense and multi-role fighters, ground attack aircraft, fighter-bombers, and bombers. An additional 470 older fighters and bombers are assigned to PLA flight academies or R&D. The two air arms have over 90 surveillance and reconnaissance aircraft with photographic, surface search, and airborne early warning sensors. The PLAAF and PLANAF have 500 transports. The majority of PLAAF and PLANAF aircraft are based in the eastern part of the country. Currently, more than 700 aircraft could conduct combat operations against Taiwan without refueling. Taiwan has some 400 fighters of various types.

Figure 12

Taiwan Strait Military Balance, Naval Forces			
China			Taiwan
	Total	East and South Sea Fleets	Total
Personnel	290,000	140,000	60,000
Destroyers	21	13	6
Frigates	43	34	21
Tank Landing Ships	20	20	12
Medium Landing Ships	23	15	4
Diesel Submarines	51	29	4
Nuclear Submarines	6	0	0
Coastal Patrol (Missile)	51	34	50

Note: The PLA Navy has a large fleet that includes 64 major surface combatants, approximately 55 attack submarines, more than 40 medium and heavy amphibious lift ships, and some 50 coastal missile patrol craft. Two-thirds of those assets are located in the East and South Sea Fleets. In the event of a major Taiwan conflict, both fleets would be expected to participate in direct action against the Taiwan Navy. The North Sea Fleet would be responsible primarily for protecting Beijing and the northern coasts, but could provide mission critical assets to support the other fleets.

Figure 13

China's Missile Forces		
China's Missile Inventory Total	Launchers/ Missiles	Estimated Range
CSS-4 ICBM	20/20	8,460+ km
CSS-3 ICBM	10-14/20-24	5,470+ km
CSS-2 IRBM	6-10/14-18	2,790+ km
CSS-5 MRBM Mod 1/2	34-38/19-23	1,770+ km
JL-1 SLBM	10-14/10-14	1,770+ km
CSS-6 SRBM	70-80/230-270	600 km
CSS-7 SRBM	100-120/420-460	300 km
DF-31 ICBM	DEVELOPMENTAL	7,250+ km
DF-31A ICBM	DEVELOPMENTAL	11,270+ km

Note: China's SRBM force has grown significantly in the past few years. China's Second Artillery now has at least five operational SRBM brigades; another brigade is deployed with the PLA ground forces. All of these units are deployed to locations near Taiwan.

ACKNOWLEDGMENTS

THE AUTHORS wish to thank all of the friends and sources who contributed to this work. Your expertise is shown in every chapter. *Showdown* could never have been written without the support of our wives, Sharon Babbin and Cathryn Timperlake, whose patience knows no bounds. We also wish to acknowledge the wonderful work, advice, and help of the Regnery team, especially Harry Crocker and Paula Decker, the best editors in the business.

NOTES

Chapter One: The Next War

1. *Wall Street Journal*, July 15, 2005. General Chenghu's statements are amazing in their ferocity. The *Journal* quotes him as saying, "If the Americans draw their missiles and precision-guided ammunition into the target zone on China's territory, I think we will have to respond with nuclear weapons. . . . If the Americans are determined to interfere . . . we will be determined to respond, and we Chinese will prepare ourselves for the destruction of all cities east of Xi'an," the ancient city in central China. "Of course," he added, "the Americans will have to be prepared that hundreds of, or even two hundreds of [or] even more [American] cities will be destroyed by the Chinese."

2. *Economist*, November 19, 2005, 23.

3. Tkacik, Fewsmith, and Kivlehan, "Who's Hu?" http://www.heritage.org/Research/AsiaandthePacific/HL739.cfm.

4. Defense Department report, "The Military Power of the People's Republic of China, 2005," 10.

5. Ibid.

6. Though many will argue that its long history of Soviet propagandizing makes its name an exercise in black humor, the newspaper's name is the Russian word for "truth."

7. "The People's Republic of China III," http://www-chaos.umd.edu/history/prc3.html.

8. Ibid.

9. *CIA World Factbook*, August 2005.

10. *2004 Index of Economic Freedom* (Washington, D.C.: Heritage, 2004), 139.

11. *Columbia Encyclopedia*, sixth edition.

12. Zhang Liang, *The Tiananmen Papers* (New York: PublicAffairs, 2001), 233.

13. Ibid., 331–32, excerpt from June 1, 1989, report by the "Beijing Municipal Party" to the Politburo.

14. Ibid., 338–48.

15. Ibid., 361.

16. Ibid., xxi–xl.

17. *Times of London*, June 5, 1989, quoted in *Webster's New World Dictionary of Quotations* (Edinburgh: Chambers Harrap, Ltd., 2005), 261.

18. *Tiananmen Papers*, xxvii.

19. Tkacik, Fewsmith and Kivlehan, "Who's Hu?"

20. Ibid.

21. *Washington Post*, August 10, 2005.

22. Ibid.

23. http://news.ft.com/cms/s/b3d20cce-2f4d-11da-8b51-00000e2511c8.html.

24. http://newsvote.bbc.co.uk/mpapps/pagetools/print/news.bbc.co.uk/2/hi/asia-pacific/4491026.stm.

25. Ibid.

26. *International Herald-Tribune*, September 14, 2005.

27. Ibid.

28. http://archive.parade.com/2005/0213/0213_dictator.html.

29. Ibid.

30. http://www.state.gov/s/ct/c14151.htm.

31. http://www.access.gpo.gov/congress/house/hr105851/.

32. Bill Gertz, "Four arrests linked to Chinese spy ring; Major U.S. arms compromised, probers say," *Washington Times*, November 5, 2005.

33. Defense Department report, 16.

34. Qiao Liang and Wang Xiangsui, *Unrestricted Warfare* (1999, republished in English by Pan American Publishing, 2002), 53.

35. Ibid., 19.

36. Ibid., 16.

37. Defense Department analysts believe that "conditions of informationalization"— a concept they are still trying to decipher—includes not only jointness and

net-centric warfare but also propaganda, both international and domestic, cyber-war, and several other concepts.

38. *Air Force Magazine*, September 2005, 14.
39. http://www.defenselink.mil/speeches/2005/sp20050604-secdef1561.html.
40. See July 27, 2005, testimony of Richard Fisher, below.
41. http://www.worldtribune.com/worldtribune/05/front2453629.1305555557.html.
42. Ibid., 22.
43. Defense Department report, 36.
44. Liang and Xiangsui, 123.
45. Ibid. "C4" is a military abbreviation for command, control, communications, and computers.
46. Defense Department report, executive summary.
47. Defense Department report, 44.
48. http://mil.jschina.com.cn/huitong/luhai_luhu_luda.htm.
49. Ibid.
50. Testimony of Richard Fisher, vice president of the International Assessment and Strategy Center, to the House Armed Services Committee, July 27, 2005.
51. Defense Department report, 4.
52. http://www.afa.org/magazine/sept2004/0904fighter.asp.
53. http://www.fas.org/nuke/guide/russia/bomber/tu-22m.htm.
54. Jed Babbin, "New Fuel for Scandal," *American Spectator*, March 2005, 18.
55. Ibid.
56. Testimony of Richard Fisher.
57. Defense Department report, 4.
58. Ibid.
59. Ibid., 5.
60. According to one Defense Department analyst, China is upgrading its reserve forces—comprised of several millions, and previously made up of "grunts" who were not very well trained, to include experts in computer operations and other "skilled" positions.
61. Ibid., 43.
62. Testimony of Richard Fisher, 4.
63. It is unclear if Chinese and Russian special forces exercised together in this war game. China is concentrating on the development of more agile and effective special forces, and Russia may be its mentor.
64. *Financial Times*, August 2, 2005.

65. Cully and Matt O'Bannon, as well as several other characters, are also featured in the novel *Legacy of Valor* by Jed Babbin (Durham, UK: Pentland Press, 2000).

Chapter Two: The War of National Unity

1. http://www.beijingportal.com.cn/7838/2005/03/14/1820@2549662.htm.

2. Ibid. The text reads, in part, "In the event that the 'Taiwan independence' secessionist forces should act under any name or by any means to cause the fact of Taiwan's secession from China, or that major incidents entailing Taiwan's secession from China should occur, or that possibilities for a peaceful reunification should be completely exhausted, the state shall employ nonpeaceful means and other necessary measures to protect China's sovereignty and territorial integrity."

Chapter Three: The Second Korean War

1. http://news.bbc.co.uk/2/hi/asia-pacific/2644593.stm.

Chapter Four: The First Oil War

1. http://english.aljazeera.net/NR/exeres/331BCCFD-3564-4635-A72A-F9ECC14EA4D5.htm.

2. http://transcripts.cnn.com/TRANSCRIPTS/0510/17/i_ins.01.html.

Chapter Five: The Sino-Japanese War

1. The historic Dorothy Clutterbuck (1880–1951) was alleged to have been the high priestess of a coven of witches.

2. The member countries of the Association of Southeast Asian Nations (ASEAN) are Indonesia, Malaysia, the Philippines, Singapore, Thailand, Brunei Darussalam, Vietnam, Laos, Cambodia, and Myanmar.

Chapter Six: World War Oil

1. David Zweig and Bi Jianhai, "China's Global Hunt for Energy," *Foreign Affairs*, September/October 2005.

Chapter Seven: The Assassin's Mace War

1. Defense Department report, 26.

2. A huge Chinese cyber-espionage ring code-named "Titan Rain" was discovered by Sandia Laboratory employee A. Shawn Carpenter in 2003. It was, according to the *Time* magazine report on it, directed at U.S. military secrets and was penetrating both government and industry computer networks to get them. Carpenter traced the espionage ring to computer routers in the Chinese province of Guangdong. According to the *Time* report, the Titan Rain spies managed at least twenty-three thousand operations a day from about thirty computers in China. Carpenter was cooperating with FBI investigators when he was suddenly ordered to stop and later fired from Sandia. See Nathan Thornburgh, "The invasion of the Chinese cyberspies and the man who tried to stop them," *Time*, August 29, 2005.

3. Secure compartmented information facility.

Chapter Eight: China, the EUnuchs, and Arms

1. Xinhua News Service, March 17, 2005.

2. http://news.bbc.co.uk/1/hi/world/europe/4288067.stm.

3. Associated Press, February 24, 2005.

4. Financial Times.com, March 31, 2005.

5. Financial Times.com, April 6, 2005.

6. Ibid.

7. *Deutsche Welle*, November 21, 2005.

8. Ibid.

9. http://www.jamestown.org/publications_details.php?volume_id=408&issue_id=3519&article_id=2370442.

10. http://www.sinodefence.com/news/2004/news041225.asp.

Chapter Nine: Containment, Engagement, or Deterrence: Working to Prevent a Sino-American War

1. http://english.people.com.cn/200512/22/print20051222_230059.html.

2. President George W. Bush speaking in Kyoto, Japan, on November 16, 2005, on his way to Beijing.

3. http://www.japantimes.co.jp/cgi-bin/getarticle.pl5?nn20051223a1.htm.

4. Ibid.

5. http://www.foxnews.com/story/0,2933,179660,00.html. This confirmed a report two days earlier, in the *Asia Times*, which said that the missile defense

would be deployed on Aegis phased-array radar-equipped destroyers. See
Asia Times, December 22, 2005.

6. http://www.psr.org/home.cfm?id=pressroom12.

7. http://www.usnews.com/usnews/opinion/baroneweb/mb_050701.htm.

8. http://www.washtimes.com/world/20050623-120117-9105r.htm.

9. http://archives.cnn.com/2001/WORLD/asiapcf/east/04/15/china.pilot/.

10. Sun Tzu, *The Art of War* (Mineola, NY: Dover, 2003), 97.

11. http://www.globalsecurity.org/military/world/int/sco.htm.

12. http://en.wikipedia.org/wiki/Shanghai_Cooperation_Organization.

Glossary

1. http://www.janes.com/aerospace/military/news/jawa/jawa010402_1_n.shtml.

2. http://www.globalsecurity.org/space/systems/afp-731.htm.

3. http://www.fas.org/spp/starwars/program/dote99/99patriot.htm.

4. http://whatis.techtarget.com/definition/0,289893,sid9_gci213221,00.html.

5. http://searchsecurity.techtarget.com/sDefinition/0,,sid14_gci213306,00.html.?

INDEX

A

Abdullah, 104, 106

Abe, Shinzo, 149

Afghanistan, 20

Africa, 2, 10–11, 53, 54

Ahmadinejad, Mahmoud, 101, 104–5, 108–9

Air Force, U.S. (USAF), 20

al Jazeera, 28, 29, 34, 35, 66, 70

al Qaeda, 29, 33

Andersen Air Force Base, Guam, 37, 38, 39, 133, 135

Angola, 5, 10–11

anti-satellite weapons, 47–49, 83, 152

Anti-Secession Law (2005), 25, 35, 143

The Art of War (Sun Tzu), 155

ASEAN. *See* Association of South East Asian Nations

Ashnapuri, Dr., 136, 139

Asia, 5

Aso, Taro, 149

Assassin's Mace War, 121–40; CMC and, 125, 129; Europe and, 130; Hu Jintao and, 121–23, 125–26, 129, 129–30, 137, 138–39; nuclear weapons and, 138; PLA and, 121; Taiwan and, 129–33, 134–35; United States and, 122–40

Associated Press, 142

Association of South East Asian Nations (ASEAN), 79

Atkins, Colonel, 93–94

Australia, 16, 53, 88, 156

B

Barnier, Michel, 143

Barone, Michael, 149

Barron, Laurence, 142

BBC. *See* British Broadcasting
    Corporation
Berlin Wall, 7, 148
Bi Jianhai, 99
Blenheim, Caspar, 102–3, 112–13
Boeing, 124
Bolivar, Simon, 70
Bolivia, 10
Bonaparte, Napoleon, 1, 23
Boris Gudunov, 26, 42
Britain, 16, 145, 156
British Broadcasting Corporation
    (BBC), 43, 65, 70
Brown, Ludwig, 38, 39
Brownshirts, 6
Bush, George W., 81, 125, 142, 143,
    148–50, 153–55

C

capital punishment, 4, 9
Carstairs, Burt, 128
Castro, Fidel, 57–58, 70
cell phones, 7, 9, 77, 100
Central Intelligence Agency (CIA),
    6, 85, 86–87, 151; Assassin's
    Mace War and, 131; Chinese war
    against Taiwan and, 29, 33;
    Korean War, Second and, 44
Central Military Commission, Chi-
    nese (CMC): Assassin's Mace War
    and, 125, 129; Chinese war
    against Taiwan and, 25–26; Oil
    War, First and, 63; Oil War,
    World and, 99, 109, 113; Sino-

Japanese War and, 77–78, 80,
    83, 89, 91
Chavez, Hugo: Oil War, First
    and, 57–58, 60–61, 63–64, 65,
    69–73; Oil War, World and,
    101, 102, 110, 119
Chen Shui-bian, 27–28
Chen Yonglin, 15
China. *See* People's Republic of
    China (PRC)
"China's Global Hunt for Energy"
    (Zweig and Bi Jianhai), 99
"China's Peaceful Development
    Road," 147
Chinese Communist Party (Chicoms):
    Chinese nationalism and, 4; Chi-
    nese war against Taiwan and,
    41–42; corruption in, 78; credibil-
    ity of, 77–78; economic liberaliza-
    tion and, 3–4. *See also* People's
    Republic of China (PRC)
Chung, Vinny, 106–8, 116–17
CIA. *See* Central Intelligence
    Agency
Clancy, Tom, 20
Clinton administration, 122, 145,
    149, 153
Clutterbuck, Dorothy: Assassin's
    Mace War and, 123, 124–25,
    129–30, 132–33, 134–35, 138,
    140; Oil War, World and, 102,
    103, 109–13, 118–19; Sino-Japan-
    ese War and, 75–77, 79–80,
    81–82, 84–85, 87–89, 90–92,
    94–96

CMC. *See* Central Military Commission, Chinese

Cold War, European, 1, 153–54

Cold War, Pacific, 1–3, 153–56

Communist Chinese. *See* Chinese Communist Party

constructive engagement, 150–51

containment, 3, 141

Cooper, Kathleen O'Bannon, 123–25, 126–27, 131–32, 136, 138, 139

Cox, Chris, 11

Cuba, 10; Oil War, First and, 57–61, 64, 65, 70–73

Cultural Revolution of 1966–76, 5, 6, 8

D

death penalty, 4, 9

Defense Department, U.S., 18, 151; arms sales and, 145–46; Chinese military buildup and, 15; Chinese navy and, 19; PLA and, 22

democracy, 5, 8

Deng Xiaoping, 6, 7–8

deterrence, 3, 151, 155

Diaoyu Islands, 89

Diego Garcia, 60, 98, 115, 119

diplomacy, 3

E

Economist, 4

environment, 6

EU. *See* European Union

EUnuchs, 143–44

Europe: arms embargo on China and, 141–44; Assassin's Mace War and, 126, 130; Chinese military buildup and, 12

European Union (EU), 126; arms embargo on China and, 141–44

F

FBI. *See* Federal Bureau of Investigation

Federal Bureau of Investigation (FBI), 124

Feith, Douglas, 145

Financial Times, 8, 143

Five Principles of Peaceful Coexistence, 147

FOX News Channel, 144

Fox, Vicente, 65

France, 31, 61, 156

freedom of speech, 6–7

Ft. Bragg, North Carolina, 127

Ft. Meade, Maryland, 123

G

Germany, Nazi, 2

Greater East Asia Co-Prosperity Sphere, 15–16

Greater Neighboring Region, 15

Guam, 21, 36, 37, 60, 133, 135

guang gun ("bare branches"), 9

H

Hawaii, 21, 54
Heritage Foundation, 6
Hitler, Adolf, 6
Homeland Security Department,
U.S., 137
Hu Jintao: Assassin's Mace War and,
121–23, 125–26, 129–30, 137–39;
Chinese war against Taiwan and,
25–26, 28, 31–33, 40–41; eco-
nomic reform and, 6; Korean
War, Second and, 45–46, 52; Oil
War, World and, 99–100, 101,
103–4, 108–9, 113–14, 119;
peaceful intent and, 2, 4, 148;
Second Great Leap Forward and,
77; Sino-Japanese War and,
77–78, 80, 83–84, 88, 89–90,
92–93; Tiananmen Square Mas-
sacre (1989) and, 8
Hussein, Saddam, 14
Hu Yaobang, 7

I

India, 16, 115, 149, 149–50, 156
Indochina, 15
Indonesia, 5, 15, 19, 77, 149
informationalization. *See* network-
centric warfare
Integrated Network Electronic War-
fare, 18
Internet, 4, 6–7, 10, 77, 100
Iran, 5, 10, 44, 151, 156; Oil War,
World and, 101, 104–5, 110, 113

Iraq, 14, 50, 53, 66
Israel, 12, 21, 88, 115; arms
embargo on China and, 144–46;
Chinese military buildup and, 12

J

Jamestown Foundation, 144
Japan, 135–36, 149; Chinese military
buildup and, 149; Chinese spy
trials and, 83, 87–88; defense
spending and, 88; Imperial,
15–16; Korean War, Second and,
53; Oil War, World and, 119;
Sino-Japanese War and, 16,
75–98
Jerry, 38, 93–94, 97, 115, 137,
139–40
Jiang Zemin, 8
John F. Kennedy Army Special
Operations School, 127–28
Johnson, Harold K., 118
Johnson, Lyndon B., 118
jointness, 13–14, 22
JSTARS (Joint Surveillance Target
Attack Radar System), 13, 144
Jumper, John, 21

K

Kennedy, John F., 84
Kim Jong-nam, 45, 52
Kim Jung Il, 44, 45, 48, 50, 90, 91,
93
kleptocracy, 11

Koizumi, Junichiro, 148, 149
Korea, 15
Korean Central News Agency, 43
Korean War, Second: anti-satellite
    weapons and, 47–49; China and,
    43–55; Hu Jintao and, 45–46;
    Kim Jung Il and, 44, 45, 48, 50;
    nuclear weapons and, 43, 44; oil
    and, 54; United States and,
    43–45, 46–55

media: Chinese, 4, 10; Chinese eco-
    nomic liberalization and, 4;
    Tiananmen Square Massacre
    (1989) and, 7
Mexico, 65, 110
Middle East, 2, 5, 21, 54, 102
Monteverde, General, 72
Moore, Harold, 117
Mugabe, Robert, 11
Mukherjee, Pranab, 150
mutually assured destruction, 1

L

Langley Air Force Base, Virginia, 66
Lantos, Tom, 142
Latin America, 10
Lebanon, 53
Lenin, Vladimir, 101
Lhasa, Tibet, 8
Li Peng, 7, 52, 53, 77, 80
Little Red Book (Mao Tse-tung). *See
    Quotations from Chairman Mao*
    (Little Red Book)
Lockheed Martin, 59, 124
Lugar, Richard, 142

N

National Defense University, China,
    2
National People's Congress, Chi-
    nese, 28, 33
National Security Agency, U.S.
    (NSA), 123, 124, 126, 131, 136,
    151
National Security Council, U.S., 25,
    33, 41, 90
nationalism, Chinese, 4, 77
NATO. *See* North Atlantic Treaty
    Organization
Nazi Germany, 2
Nellis Air Force Base, Nevada, 59,
    102
network-centric warfare, 13–14,
    17–18, 22
New Framework for the U.S.–India
    Defense Relationship, 149–50
New York Times, 4, 34–36, 65, 89
New Zealand, 156

M

Malaya Peninsula, 19
Malaysia, 15, 77, 149
Manchuria, 15
Mao Tse-tung, 4, 6, 8, 77
McCain, John, 76
McInerny, Thomas, 144
McPherson, Henry, 31–32

Nigeria, 101

North Atlantic Treaty Organization (NATO), 21, 112, 132, 156

North Korea, 10, 151; China and, 45–46; Korean War, Second and, 43–55; nuclear weapons and, 3, 43, 44; Oil War, World and, 119

Nowak, Manfred, 9

NPT. *See* Nuclear Non-Proliferation Treaty

NRO, 44, 126, 131

NSA. *See* National Security Agency, U.S.

Nuclear Non-Proliferation Treaty (NPT), 43

nuclear weapons: Assassin's Mace War and, 138; Chinese espionage and, 11; Chinese use of, 2; North Korea and, 3, 43, 44; Oil War, World and, 101, 113; Sino-Japanese War and, 88, 91, 94–98

O

O'Bannon, Cully, 125, 128; Chinese war against Taiwan and, 30–31; Korean War, Second and, 43–45, 46–47; Oil War, First and, 62; Oil War, World and, 105–8; Sino-Japanese War and, 86–87, 96–97

O'Bannon, Matt, 50–51, 125; Assassin's Mace War and, 133–34, 135–36, 137, 139–40; Chinese war against Taiwan and, 38; Oil

War, First and, 59–60, 61–62, 64, 66–67, 67–68; Oil War, World and, 102–3, 111–12, 115, 117, 119; Sino-Japanese War and, 82–83, 93–94, 97–98

OECD. *See* Organisation for Economic Cooperation and Development

oil: China and, 9, 16, 19; Cold War, Pacific and, 2; Korean War, Second and, 54; Oil War, First, 57–73; Oil War, World, 99–119; U.S. economy and, 3; as weapon, 65

Oil War, First: Chavez, Hugo and, 57–58, 60–61, 63–64, 65, 69–73; China and, 57–73; Cuba and, 57–61, 64, 65, 70–73; France and, 61; Russia and, 61; UN and, 59, 61, 64, 65; United States and, 59–60, 61–62, 64–69; Venezuela and, 57–73

Oil War, World, 99–119; CMC and, 99, 109, 113; Hu Jintao and, 99–100, 101, 103–4, 108–9, 113–14, 119; Iran and, 101, 104–5, 110, 113; nuclear weapons and, 101, 113; Russia and, 119; Saudi Arabia and, 101–3, 105–6, 110, 112–13; United States and, 101, 102–3, 105–8, 109–13, 114–19; Venezuela and, 110, 119

OPEC. *See* Organization of Petroleum Exporting Countries

Operation Iraqi Freedom, 14

Organisation for Economic Cooperation and Development (OECD), 8

Organization of Petroleum Exporting Countries (OPEC), 72

P

Pace, Peter, 14–15

Pakistan, 115, 156

Parade magazine, 9

Paradise Ranch, Nevada, 59, 119

Parker, Al, 86

Patterson, Duke, 31, 39, 40

Peace Mission 2005, 23

peaceful coexistence, 148

peaceful intent, 2, 4, 9, 14–15

Pentagon, 13

People's Armed Police, 9

People's Islamic Republic of Arabia, 111

People's Liberation Army (PLA), 9, 14; Assassin's Mace War and, 121; Chinese ground forces and, 22; Chinese navy and, 19; Chinese war against Taiwan and, 25, 26, 33; Oil War, World and, 116–17; Sino-Japanese War and, 84; size of, 22

People's Liberation Navy, 26, 27

People's Republic of China (PRC): arms embargo against, 12, 141–46; Assassin's Mace War and, 121–40; defense spending of, 16–23; economy of, 3–4, 6, 8–11; environment and, 6, 9; espionage campaign of, 11–12; internal crises in, 4, 6, 7; Korean War, Second and, 43–55; military buildup of, 2, 11–16, 23–24; nationalism in, 4, 77; oil and, 4–5, 9, 16, 19; Oil War, First and, 57–73; Oil War, World and, 99–119; Olympic Games in, 79; one-child policy of, 9; population of, 5, 9; Sino-Japanese War and, 16, 75–98; as superpower, 1, 4, 149; Taiwan, war against and, 2, 3, 12, 16, 25–42; terrorism, state sponsor of, and, 10, 11; as totalitarian state, 5, 9; as U.S. adversary, 1–2, 10, 23; U.S. defense against, 147–56; as U.S. partner, 3–5; as U.S. trading partner, 2, 9, 79–80

Peripheral Nations, 77, 78

Philippines, 15, 149, 156

Politburo, Chinese, 7, 25, 26

PRC. *See* People's Republic of China

propaganda, 2

Q

Qiao Liang, 13, 17–18

Quincannon, Dale, 86–87, 96

Quotations from Chairman Mao (Little Red Book), 4, 8, 77

R

Raffarin, Jean-Pierre, 143

Rangoon, 46

Rape of Nanking, 84

Red Guard, Chinese, 6, 8

Rich, Ben, 59

Rodman, Peter, 150–51

Roosevelt, Franklin D., 95

Rubia, Daniel, 48–49, 123–25, 126–27, 131–32, 139

Rumsfeld, Donald, 15, 150, 150–51

Russia, 5, 155; Chinese air and missile forces and, 20–21; Chinese ground forces and, 23; Chinese navy and, 19; Chinese war against Taiwan and, 26, 27, 31, 42; defense spending of, 16; Oil War, First and, 61, 70; Oil War, World and, 119; Sino-Japanese War and, 76, 82. *See also* Soviet Union

Ryukyu Islands, 91

S

Saudi Arabia, 72; Oil War, World and, 101–3, 105–6, 110, 112–13

Schaeffer, Stan, 47

Schröder, Gerhard, 142–43

SCO. *See* Shanghai Cooperation Organization

SEATO. *See* Southeast Asian Treaty Organization

Second Artillery, Chinese, 22

Second Great Leap Forward, 77

Senkaku Islands, 76, 82–83, 84, 85, 90

September 11, 21, 151

Shanghai Cooperation Organization (SCO), 155–56

Singapore, 15, 19, 35, 77, 149, 150

Sino-Japanese War, 75–98; CMC and, 77–78, 80, 83, 89, 91; cyberwar and, 83, 92; Hu Jintao and, 77–78, 80, 83–84, 88, 89–90, 92–93; Japanese prime minister and, 76, 80–82, 87–89, 90–92; Kim Jung Il and, 90, 91, 93; nuclear weapons and, 88, 91, 94–98; Russia and, 76, 82; Senkaku Islands and, 76, 82–83, 84, 85, 90; Taiwan and, 90; UN and, 91, 92; United States and, 75–77, 78–83, 84–98; Yakusuni Shrine and, 80, 81, 87–88, 92

Skrzypczak, General (COB), 44, 53

"Skunk Works," 59

smart bombs, 16

Socialist Education Movement, 6

Somalia, 151

South Korea, 150; Korean War, Second and, 43–55; Oil War, World and, 119

South Pacific Islands, 21

Southeast Asian Treaty Organization (SEATO), 156

Soviet Union, 7; Cold War, European and, 1; economic growth of, 5; as superpower, 1. *See also* Russia

Spain, 21

speech, freedom of, 6–7

Spirit of San Diego, 50

Spratly Islands, 83, 85, 86

Stahl, Eric, 26–28, 29, 31, 33

Stalin, Joseph, 12

State Department, U.S., 48, 131

Strait of Malacca, 19, 77, 115

Sudan, 5, 10, 11, 101, 151

Sun Tzu, 155

Sutliff, General, 111

Syria, 10, 53, 102

T

Taiwan, 148, 150; Assassin's Mace
    War and, 129–33, 134–35; Chi-
    nese conflict with, 2, 3, 12, 16;
    Chinese ground forces and,
    22–23; Chinese war against,
    25–42; Cold War, Pacific and, 2;
    Japan and, 15; Korean War, Sec-
    ond and, 53, 54; Oil War, World
    and, 119; Sino-Japanese War
    and, 90; U.S. defense of, 12

Tarawa Island, 39, 40, 48

Telesur, 35, 66, 70

terrorism: China and state sponsors
    of, 10, 11. *See also* War on Terror

Thailand, 149, 150, 156

Tiananmen Papers, 3

Tiananmen Square Massacre (1989),
    4, 5, 7–8, 9, 12, 142

Tibet, 4, 8

Titan Rain, 123

torture, 9

Turkey, 102

2004 Index of Economic Freedom, 6

U

UN. *See* United Nations

United Nations (UN), 9; Chinese
    war against Taiwan and, 31, 32;
    diplomatic battles at, 2; Oil War,
    First and, 59, 61, 64, 65; Sino-
    Japanese War and, 92

United Nations Security Council, 33,
    35, 61, 64, 91

United States: arms embargo
    against China and, 12, 141–46;
    Assassin's Mace War and,
    122–40; China as adversary of,
    1–2, 23; China as partner of, 2,
    3–5, 9, 79–80; Chinese economic
    liberalization and, 3–4; Chinese
    espionage campaign against,
    11–12; Chinese nuclear weapons
    and, 2; Chinese war against Tai-
    wan and, 26–28, 29–42; defense
    spending of, 16; hegemony of, 4;
    Imperial Japan and, 16; Korean
    War, Second and, 43–45, 46–55;
    Oil War, First and, 59–60, 61–62,
    64–69; Oil War, World and, 101,
    102–3, 105–8, 109–13, 114–19;
    Sino-Japanese War and, 75–77,
    78–83, 84–98; as superpower, 1;
    Tiananmen Square Massacre
    (1989) and, 7

Unrestricted Warfare (Qiao Liang
    and Wang Xiangsui), 17–18
USAF. *See* Air Force, U.S.
U.S. News & World Report, 149
USS *Harry S. Truman*, 106–8
USS *John C. Stennis*, 27, 29, 32, 36,
    133
USS *Kitty Hawk*, 32, 40, 133
USS *Nimitz*, 32, 36, 40
USS *Ohio*, 43, 46

V

Venezuela, 5, 10, 21; Chinese war
    against Taiwan and, 35; Oil War,
    First and, 57–73; Oil War, World
    and, 100, 101, 110, 119
Vietnam, 149, 150
Vietnam War, 118, 150
Voice of America, 7
von Braun, Werner, 38

W

Wang Wei, 154
Wang Xiangsui, 13, 17–18
War on Terror, 3, 33, 156
warfare: cyber-, 83, 92, 121–40,
    151–52; jointness and, 13–14, 22;
    network-centric, 13–14, 22
Warsaw Pact, 156

Washington Post, 8
Washington Times, 11
*We Were Soldiers Once...and
    Young* (Moore), 117
Wen Jiabao, 6
Whiteman Air Force Base, Missouri,
    38, 60, 61, 64
Wilson, Romeo, 30–31, 44, 46–47,
    106–7, 116
World War II, 1, 16, 81
Wu Feng, 117

X

Xi Yuanqing, 27
Xin, General, 58, 60, 63–64, 65
Xinhua, 23
Xiong Guangkai, 14

Y

Yakusuni Shrine, 80, 81, 87–88, 92
Yaron, Amos, 145
Yokota Air Base, Japan, 82, 93

Z

Zhou Yongkang, 8
Zhu Chenghu, 2
Zimbabwe, 11
Zweig, David, 99

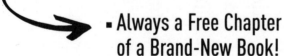